THE ASSESSMENT OF DOCTORAL EDUCATION

THE ASSESSMENT OF

DOCTORAL EDUCATION

Emerging Criteria and New Models
for Improving Outcomes

Edited by

Peggy L. Maki and *Nancy A. Borkowski*

Foreword by
Daniel D. Denecke

STERLING, VIRGINIA

COPYRIGHT © 2006 BY STYLUS PUBLISHING, LLC.

Published by Stylus Publishing, LLC
22883 Quicksilver Drive
Sterling, Virginia 20166-2102

Library of Congress Cataloging-in-Publication Data
The assessment of doctoral education : emerging criteria
and new models for improving outcomes / edited by Peggy
L. Maki and Nancy A. Borkowski ; foreword by Jody
Nyquist.
      p.   cm.
    ISBN-13: 978-1-57922-178-2 (hardcover : alk. paper)
    ISBN-13: 978-1-57922-179-9 (pbk. : alk. paper)
    1. Doctor of philosophy degree—Evaluation. I. Maki,
Peggy. II. Borkowski, Nancy A., 1958–
    LB2386.A76 2006
    378.2—dc22
                                                    2006016351

ISBN: 1-57922-178-5 (cloth) / 13-digit ISBN: 978-1-57922-178-2
ISBN: 1-57922-179-3 (paper) / 13-digit ISBN: 978-1-57922-179-9

Printed in the United States of America

All first editions printed on acid free paper
that meets the American National Standards Institute
Z39-48 Standard.

Bulk Purchases

Quantity discounts are available for use in workshops
and for staff development.
Call 1-800-232-0223

First Edition, 2006

10   9   8   7   6   5   4   3   2   1

For their support, patience, and inspiration, Nancy dedicates this book to Fritz and Louise and family; Ron, Katie, and Trish; and especially Andrea, Margie, Joey, and Michelle.

Peggy dedicates this book to Mr. Blu for his companionship and devotion.

CONTENTS

ACKNOWLEDGMENTS

The willingness to share experiences and findings that often challenge long-standing practices takes courage. Thanks to the authors of this collection for their willingness to share their research, work, experiences, insights, and self-reflections in the interest of improving educational practices, as well as providing a foundation for the development of new practices for our doctoral students. We applaud contributors to this book, including authors who focused on graduate students' perspectives and experiences, for opening new doors into doctoral education and inviting others to enter.

Peggy L. Maki

Two questions loom large in current doctoral assessment discussions. First, how well are doctoral programs doing to ensure that talented and able students successfully complete their Ph.D.s? And second, how well are they preparing those students to succeed in their subsequent careers as scholars and researchers in both academic and nonacademic settings?

From a national vantage point, the answer to both questions in the United States at present is that we don't really know. The paucity of national data on completion rates and time to degree, as well as on attrition patterns and time to withdrawal is disconcerting. Several contributors to this volume have made major contributions to our understanding of these topics, but we still do not have anything resembling national data sets that would equip us to answer either question with confidence. The wide variety of definitions afloat, of institutional capacities to collect these data, and of missions and demographic composition among different universities make benchmarking with such data a daunting task. The Council of Graduate Schools' Ph.D. Completion Project and the revised doctoral assessment being conducted by the National Research Council will advance our knowledge of how to ensure that our doctoral programs are doing all they can to create conditions for student success by enhancing all aspects of the doctoral experience, especially for students from underrepresented groups (such as minorities in all fields and women in the sciences, who have traditionally completed at lower rates than majority students and men, respectively).

Just as we know very little about why those who finish and why those who leave do so, we also know surprisingly little about where students go after they earn their degrees. More importantly, we therefore have little information about how effective doctoral programs are in preparing doctorates for short- and long-term career success. Our ignorance on these matters and the lack of comprehensive national data is particularly surprising because there is so much interest on the part of the those who fund doctoral education (especially the federal agencies), as well as employers, universities, and students. Here again, contributors to this volume have paved the way with groundbreaking research that is likely to make a more comprehensive national understanding of these issues possible.

While degree completion/attrition and career outcomes data are only a few of the objective indicators that may be used in the assessment of doctoral programs, the growing importance of these indicators in the graduate community reflects a broader trend toward rethinking what we mean when we speak of research productivity. Traditional measures of research productivity were largely faculty-centric, referring to such things as publications, citations, and research grants. While such measures still play an important role in ratings, rankings, and program review, doctoral program assessment tends to focus more on what might be called student-focused measures of research productivity: "on what *students* know and can do as a result of their graduate education and/or on what programs do to help students develop these competencies."[1]

Objective indicators such as completion rates, attrition patterns, and career outcomes are among the best overarching measures of doctoral education quality, for they reflect or refract virtually everything else that a program does to select, retain, and ensure the success of its students. Such data may be used to assess aspects of the selection and admissions process, mentoring and advising practices, curricular processes and procedures, the overall program environment and levels of socio-academic integration, the adequacy and structure of financial support, the degree of transparency about faculty expectations, and the efficacy and timing of professional development experiences and programs.

Regional accreditors of graduate programs and even some state legislatures in the United States are beginning to accord greater weight to such measures in the assessment of doctoral programs, as the wave of "accountability" that has already hit the shores of primary and secondary education is just now reaching the shores of doctoral education. Beyond compliance with minimal threshold criteria, however, there are immediate benefits to a doctoral program of using measures such as these in formative assessment. These benefits include (1) ensuring that the program is meeting faculty expectations and institutional goals and (2) enhancing the competitiveness of

---

[1] Council of Graduate Schools (2005), *Assessment and review of graduate programs.* Washington, DC: Council of Graduate Schools, p.23 (my emphasis).

doctoral programs and their responsiveness to students, employers, and the public. This book serves as both a practical and a conceptual toolkit for those faculty, researchers, and administrative leaders responsible for making doctoral programs more responsive and therefore more competitive in the current global environment.

As evidenced by this volume's assembly of national experts on the topic, the strength of a university's doctoral assessment strategies correlates strongly with the extent of its awareness of and participation in one or more of the major graduate reform initiatives that have enhanced doctoral education over the past two decades: the Woodrow Wilson National Fellowship Foundation's Responsive Ph.D. initiative; the Re-envisioning the Ph.D. project; and the Carnegie Initiative on the Doctorate (sponsored by the Carnegie Foundation for the Advancement of Teaching), as well as the Mellon Foundation's Graduate Education Initiative; the Preparing Future Faculty (PFF) Program (cosponsored by the Council of Graduate Schools and the Association of American Colleges and Universities); and, most recently, the Ph.D. Completion Project, not to mention the many recent innovations in private and federal fellowship and traineeship programs. Many of the experts represented in this volume have been prominent leaders in these graduate reform initiatives. These authors and the editors of this volume are to be commended for raising the visibility of concerns about student success, for articulating ways to research that success (including the identification of potential obstacles and lingering inequities), and for recommending strategies to improve a doctoral education system that is already the jewel in the crown of U.S. education.

Daniel D. Denecke
Director, Best Practices
Council of Graduate Schools

INTRODUCTION

Peggy L. Maki

Those who venture outside the parameters of conventions and norms simultaneously experience both exhilaration and trepidation. Exhilaration emerges from the prospects of discovery and renewal; trepidation emerges from uncertainty about how discovery and renewal will challenge conventions and norms and those individuals who are comfortable with and accustomed to supporting those conventions and norms. Authors of the chapters in *The Assessment of Doctoral Education: Emerging Criteria and New Models for Improving Outcomes* share the results of their journeys to explore new approaches to or perspectives on assessing doctoral programs, thereby demonstrating that it is possible to build on, challenge, and even transcend conventions, norms, and educational practices that have traditionally served as evidence of the quality and effectiveness of doctoral programs. Through the avenues of research, the development of internally established program- and student-level assessment criteria, and the use of multiple assessment methods, this book lays groundwork for faculty, administrators, and institutional leaders to build and advance a robust internal collaborative process of assessing the quality and effectiveness of doctoral programs.

In her landmark *Change* article at the beginning of this century, "The Ph.D.: A Tapestry of Change for the 21st Century" (November/December, 2002, pp. 13–20), Jody Nyquist characterizes the current national focus on doctoral education as distinctly different from previous times of rethinking or reinvisioning the Ph.D.—times that typically resulted in affirmation of the success of doctoral education. Graduate students' expression of their views on their education; employers' expression of dissatisfaction in the kinds of preparation they experience in their hires; enhanced multiple efforts across foundations, disciplinary societies, and government agencies prompting reassessment of doctoral programs, practices, and structures; national organizations and regional accrediting agencies seeking evidence of student learning; and changing societal needs altogether have created a context for inquiry that differs from previous times. Not that the Ph.D. was "done wrong," Nyquist asserts, "In fact, it has been done magnificently. But changes in society create new requirements, and we need to honestly assess the efficacy of the Ph.D. now to ensure that its recipients continue to make the kinds of contributions in the public and private spheres that the nation needs to remain strong" (p. 14). Identifying the range of national projects focused on examining doctoral education, she optimistically concludes her description of them with these sobering words: "As always, what matters most is what happens next" (p. 20).

A significant part of "what has happened" since Nyquist's 2002 article is reflected in the focus of this book—developments in criteria for assessment and models to assess (1) doctoral program norms, structures, practices, values, and traditions, and to assess (2) doctoral student achievement through the representative kinds of work graduate students produce along the continuum of their studies. The collective voices represented in this book, consisting of faculty, administrators, leaders in national organizations, researchers, and doctoral students themselves recognize that there is, indeed, more to assessing doctoral education than is represented in externally developed evaluation criteria that have historically been used to rank doctoral programs, such as the research productivity of faculty. Rather, doctoral programs consist of a variety of other factors, such as curricular design and sequencing, pedagogy, sets of educational experiences, educational practices, and rites of passage that form the fabric of students' learning. Integrated into this fabric are also mentoring and advising processes that support and guide students as they progress through their studies, engage in and produce representative work in their field of study, and become acculturated and socialized to doctoral program expectations as well as to the expectations of their field or profession. Also, how graduate students experience their doctoral journey and how they view its relevance once they make the transition into a career are valuable sources of evidence about the efficacy of doctoral educational practices.

This collection also comes at a time when external stakeholders, such as accreditors and national organizations, are increasingly seeking evidence of doctoral program quality and effectiveness that includes documentation of student achievement—beyond graduation and placement rates. Stakeholders are focused more and more on ascertaining how well doctoral programs use the results of their inquiry into program quality and effectiveness to improve doctoral program outcomes, including student learning. Benefiting from the emerging commitment to assessing student learning at the undergraduate level, doctoral programs are now exploring, developing, sharing, adapting, innovating, and implementing relevant assessment models and practices to engage faculty and administrators in a collaborative examination of representative student work or performances, such as dissertations or capstone projects. This examination occurs within the context of collaboratively agreed-upon performance expectations that emerge from the curricular design, pedagogy, and structures that faculty and other contributors to student learning believe promote or foster student achievement.

In this volume, assessment refers to the collaborative process of gathering, analyzing, interpreting, and using interpretations of various kinds of evidence to answer internally raised questions about the quality and effectiveness of doctoral programs. The results of this process verify strengths in a program as well as identify areas, structures, or educational practices that warrant improvement to enhance doctoral student learning. Focusing on internal collaboratively established criteria, rather than solely on externally established criteria, chapters describe or propose different avenues through which to develop a comprehensive assessment of doctoral programs. Collectively, these chapters expand the kinds of questions faculty and administrators have raised about their doctoral programs, the channels of inquiry they have routinely used to gather evidence about their programs, and the sources of evidence they have examined to engage in collaborative critical self-examination of and self-reflection on overall program quality and effectiveness. This book positions faculty and academic leaders of doctoral programs to promote inquiry into the educational practices that define their programs and contribute to doctoral students' learning. Specifically, it provides representative examples of program- and student-level assessment practices that prepare faculty and academic leaders to

1. formulate new questions and employ new lenses to inquire into the quality and efficacy of educational practices, structures, norms, values, and program-level expectations for student learning.

2. collaboratively articulate doctoral program goals, student learning outcome statements, and performance expectations to (a) orient and guide students through their journey toward becoming experts in their field, discipline, or profession and to (b) ground internally driven program-level and student-level assessment.

3. expand program review to include collaborative assessment of student learning—that is, students' representation of their knowledge, abilities, habits of mind, ways of knowing, ways of problem solving, and dispositions—through direct and indirect assessment methods that verify or challenge the efficacy of educational practices. These methods provide both faculty and students with ongoing evidence of patterns of students' strengths and weaknesses against the design and sequencing of doctoral curricula and educational practices.

4. engage in ongoing assessment of doctoral programs as opposed to periodic assessment to initiate changes in practices that directly benefit students during their educational journey.

5. listen to and respond to doctoral students as they progress through their studies as well as after they graduate when they reflect on the relevance of their studies within the context of their careers, including careers outside of the academy in business, government, and industry.

6. examine ways in which faculty-student mentoring and advising socialize and acculturate students to their doctoral program, field of study, and performance expectations for their doctoral level work, such as the dissertation or other key performance pieces.

Organization and Progression of the Book

All together these chapters represent new perspectives on and practices in assessing doctoral education that deepen the academy's knowledge about the relevance and efficacy of educational norms and practices and thereby contribute to improving program- and student-level outcomes. Part 1, Emerging Criteria and New Models for Assessing Doctoral Programs, consists of four chapters that focus on developing internally designed criteria and models to assess graduate programs. Part 2, Emerging Criteria and New Models for Assessing Student Learning Outcomes, focuses on the rationale for including assessment of student learning in program review and identifies representative ways to assess student achievement—a valuable source of evidence about how well students achieve against the fabric of the curriculum, instruction, educational experiences, norms, and traditions.

Part 1: Emerging Criteria and New Models for Assessing Doctoral Programs

In chapter 1, "Changing Our Thinking about Assessment at the Doctoral Level," Borkowski takes a two-part approach to providing a context for the representative chapters that follow. The first part of her chapter traces historical developments in and outside of the academy that have led to the current focus on examining doctoral programs. In the second part of her chapter she summarizes internal and external factors shaping the assessment of doctoral education, such as a focus on best practices in graduate education, and maps out key doctoral-level assessment efforts that have catapulted a change in the thinking about what constitutes success in doctoral education, including Re-envisioning the Ph.D. Project, led by Jody Nyquist at the University of Washington; the Responsive Ph.D. Initiative, organized by the Woodrow Wilson Fellowship Foundation; and the Carnegie Initiative on the Doctorate (discussed more fully in chapter 2). This chapter ends with a list of projects and studies focused on assessment at the doctoral level as well as a list of resources.

Beginning with a survey of traditional approaches to assessing doctoral programs, such as national rankings and external program reviews, in chapter 2, "The Challenges of Doctoral Program Assessment: Lessons from the Carnegie Initiative on the Doctorate," authors Golde, Jones, Bueschel, and Walker identify the kinds of hurdles, as well as successes, they and departmental representatives from six disciplines—chemistry, education, English, history, mathematics, and neuroscience—encountered in a national project focused on assessing doctoral program quality. Among the successes of the Carnegie Initiative on the Doctorate, including documented examples of program-level changes, has been the development of a public online tool kit, KEEP, that now serves as a means to encourage openness among doctoral programs through the sharing of changes doctoral programs have made and the strategies they have used to design and implement these changes.

In chapter 3, "Using an Alignment Model as a Framework in the Assessment of Doctoral Programs," Wulff and Nerad present a framework for formative (ongoing) program-level assessment that involves a process of aligning program components—activities, students, faculty, staff, desired program outcomes, and internal and external contextual factors, such as the cultural context of a discipline. Results of this approach to program review focus faculty and administrators on broad issues of what is or is not working for students, faculty, and staff who are direct beneficiaries of this kind of inquiry. Examples of sample questions, data sources, and procedures for improvement-based study of the intersections of some program components provide direction for this multidimensional, cyclical approach.

In chapter 4, "Paths and Perceptions: Assessing Doctoral Education Using Career Path Analysis," Aanerud, Homer, Nerad, and Cerny illustrate the importance of incorporating students' self-descriptive data in the assessment of doctoral programs. Focusing on graduate students' survey responses in two disciplines—mathematics and English—in the 1999 national study Ph.D.s Ten Years Later, authors illustrate the value of incorporating students' views about their education in light of their actual career paths, including those in business, government, and industry. Integrating students' responses about their doctoral education into program review prompts dialogue about the relevance of curricular content and design for contemporary societal needs and employment.

Part 2: Emerging Criteria and New Models for Assessing Student Learning Outcomes

Part 2 consists of five chapters that describe and provide examples of developments in actual assessment of student work as evidence of student learning. In chapter 5, "Using the Assessment Process to Improve Doctoral Programs," which provides a context for chapters 6 through 9, Funk and Klomparens make the case for the importance of developing an assessment plan to examine student work along the chronology of their studies as a new component of program assessment. Specifically, this chapter describes the collaborative assessment process and identifies a range of direct and indirect methods to assess how well doctoral students integrate, transfer, and apply their learning.

The dissertation, still the major, final, written requirement and means of assessment that characterizes doctoral program achievement, is the subject of chapter 6, "Making the Implicit Explicit: Faculty's Performance Expectations for the Dissertation." In this chapter Lovitts presents the results of a study in which 276 high-producing Ph.D. faculty from 74 departments across 10 disciplines at 9 doctoral/research extensive universities made explicit their implicit standards or criteria for evaluating dissertations and their components. She reviews the small extant literature on dissertation evaluation, briefly discusses the methodology for her study, and presents the result of her work with Ph.D. faculty. This chapter also includes auxiliary information provided by focus group faculty on their views on issues such as the differences among students who achieve at different levels, reasons why students may or may not live up to their capabilities, and ways in which faculty do or do not help students achieve to their fullest. The chapter concludes with recommendations for how faculty can develop similar performance expectations for dissertations at their own universities and departments with strong caveats about how performance expectations should and should not be used. Miller's case study at the end of chapter 6 provides an administrator's perspectives on how the University of Colorado at Boulder's participation in the Lovitts study has shaped administrative and faculty educational practices related to the dissertation. Allowing the university to observe and investigate the dissertation process from the perspectives of high-producing Ph.D. faculty in 10 disciplines, this project made clear the importance of orienting and supporting doctoral students through the writing of their dissertations. Miller lists the kinds of current changes being considered in disciplines, such as articulating disciplinary expectations and performance standards and creating discipline-specific booklets that contain expectations, performance criteria, and case studies that contribute to doctoral students' understanding of the dissertation and the actual writing process.

Pointing to the fact that there is very little research that systematically explores doctoral student experiences with the often ill-defined dissertation, Leonard, in chapter 7, "Doctoral Students' Perspectives on the Dissertation," reports on her own research as part of the Lovitts study. As a doctoral student herself, she interviewed graduate students about their reactions to the performance expectations that emerged from Lovitts's project. She reports her results on three student-focused issues related to the dissertation: (1) students' understanding of the dissertation in their field, including their understanding of what makes a dissertation original and significant; (2) students' concerns about their dissertation; and (3) students' concerns about how their dissertation would be evaluated.

Though relatively new to doctoral programs, given their presence in K–16, portfolios are the focus of chapter 8, "Portfolios in Doctoral Education." Cyr and Muth consolidate what we know about the types, purposes, formats, structures, and overall benefits of this assessment method, and then provide a partial roadmap for others who wish to capitalize on the power of portfolios to engage students further in their learning as well as to provide faculty with chronological evidence of students' achievement of student learning outcomes. Descriptions of some representative examples of doctoral programs that currently integrate portfolios, an overview of the portfolio design process, and discussion of the value of portfolios for doctoral education, such as enhancing student awareness of strategies for thinking about, producing, and completing tasks, provide impetus for expanded use of portfolios in doctoral education.

The final chapter of this book, "Recasting Doctoral Education in an Outcomes-Based Framework," illustrates how an educational leadership program at Iowa State University redesigned itself based on a learning-centered paradigm that first articulated student learning outcome statements. Huba, Schuh, and Shelley chronicle this redesign process, the ways in which faculty recast assessment methods, and the ways the new program design provides ongoing data about student learning for continuous improvement of the program. Providing examples of multiple program assessment methods and criteria for scoring student work, this chapter represents how quantitative and qualitative data about student learning has guided decisions faculty and administrators have made to improve a doctoral program.

The highest degree awarded in our educational system, the Ph.D., educates students to become experts who shape and contribute to society. It seems reasonable, then, for those who educate doctoral students to want to direct their professional attention to examining the practices that do or do not contribute to preparing our next generation of experts. Sharing the results of these new avenues of examination will build knowledge about the efficacy of doctoral practices. Just as we educate doctoral students to contribute to and build knowledge, so should we contribute to and build knowledge about the efficacy of doctoral program educational practices.

PART ONE

EMERGING CRITERIA AND NEW MODELS FOR ASSESSING DOCTORAL PROGRAMS

CHANGING OUR THINKING ABOUT ASSESSMENT AT THE DOCTORAL LEVEL

Nancy A. Borkowski

Graduate education faces significant challenges in today's society. Concern about the quality and traditional narrowness of graduate education has prompted many stakeholders, external and internal to the academy, to question the relevance of the doctoral degree in preparing students to succeed in our increasingly complex labor market. In addition, the funding climate has changed for higher education in general and graduate education in particular. As a result, competition for scarce resources has grown at the institutional level, requiring departments and programs to justify the allocation of resources to doctoral-level efforts.

Numerous studies and projects on doctoral education agree that there has been a significant disparity between the training that doctoral students receive and the reality of the career options that await them. Increasingly, graduate deans and faculty members at research institutions are demonstrating a growing interest in helping their Ph.D. graduates perform and succeed as intellectual leaders in the wide range of settings inside and outside the academy. Such interest has resulted in changes in what constitutes a doctoral-level education, changes within specific doctoral programs, and the adoption of new practices to broaden the professional preparation of doctoral students.

As institutions make changes to better reflect the intentions of a relevant doctoral education, questions arise: "Are the changes working?" and "How do we know the changes are working?" These questions of accountability challenge institutions to provide evidence of their effectiveness to both internal and external constituents, especially regarding the value of a student's education in becoming a contributing citizen to society and a professional within a chosen discipline or field.

The purpose of this chapter is to create the landscape for assessment at the doctoral level. First, the important external and internal issues driving the broader need for assessment and accountability in doctoral education will be discussed, followed by an overview of the significant developments and national studies over the last decade that have led to a change in the thinking about what constitutes success in doctoral education.

The Push for Accountability

The concept of assessment has long been and continues to be a mainstay for K–12 public schools. Significant attention focused on K–12 education with the release of the government report *A Nation at Risk: The Imperative for Educational Reform* (National Commission on Excellence in Education, 1983) that outlined the state of "mediocrity" of American education. More recently, the federal government's No Child Left Behind Act (U.S. Department of Education, 2002) mandated (and continues to mandate) greater accountability and academic proficiency of today's K–12 students. Reports such as these have led to a higher level of federal and state involvement in measuring student learning outcomes at the K–12 level to a point where federal and state funding for student learning is linked to quality in performance standards.

As externally mandated standards became the norm in K–12 settings, national government reports called for similar improvements in assessment in higher education at the undergraduate level beginning in the mid-1980s. In response to the *A Nation at Risk* report, the National Institute of Education's 1984 report *Involvement in Learning: Realizing the Potential of American Higher Education* served as a hallmark study that addressed issues of accountability in higher education and advocated active learning as the key to improved student outcomes. More recently, the National Center for Postsecondary Improvement, supported by funding from the U.S. Department of Education, published a report in 1999 advocating improvements in undergraduate assessment efforts after comparing student assessment practices at the undergraduate level with those of other types of higher education institutions (Peterson, Einarson, Augustine, & Vaughan, 1999).

Perhaps the most notable recent legislation involves the yet-to-be-passed 2003–04 reauthorization of the Higher Education Act, a key government law that outlines rules and regulations for higher education, including graduate education. Concerns over accountability and budget balancing have delayed passage of this legislation, illustrating the growing lack of confidence by the U.S. Congress regarding higher education's ability to regulate itself and provide effectiveness in student learning outcomes (Lederman, 2006a). These concerns were further highlighted with the release of the *National Assessment of Adult Literacy* report by the Department of Education that found "proficient" literacy with only 25% of undergraduates and 31% of adults with some graduate education (National Center for Educational Statistics, 2005). Responding to the Department of Education report, the *New York Times* took the following stance:

> Colleges and universities should join in the hunt for acceptable ways to measure student progress, rather than simply fighting the whole idea from the sidelines. Unless the higher education community wakes up to this problem—and resolves to do a better job—the movement aimed at regulating colleges and forcing them to demonstrate that students are actually learning will only keep growing. (Proof of Learning, 2006, sec. 4, p. 11)

In addition to the national government reports and mandates advocating reform efforts in undergraduate higher education, the Council for Higher Education Accreditation (CHEA) serves as the largest nongovernmental national organization for higher education accreditation and an influential "national voice for voluntary accreditation and quality assurance to [the] U.S. Congress and U.S. Department of Education" (Council for Higher Education Accreditation, 2003a). In its 2003 *Statement of Mutual Responsibilities for Student Learning Outcomes*, CHEA articulated the increasing importance of assessment in American higher education, especially the use of student learning outcomes:

> evidence of student learning outcomes is becoming a principal gauge of higher education's effectiveness. Employers and elected officials have never been clearer in their demand that the graduates of U.S. colleges and universities should possess an increasingly specific set of higher-order literacies

and communication skills. Students, parents, and the public are looking not only at the price of a college credential, but also at the quality of general education and career education that lies behind the credential. In particular, they want to know what the learning gained in these programs will mean in the marketplace of employment and in their lives as citizens and community members. Inside the academy, conversations are widening about how to organize institutions of higher education to improve undergraduate teaching and learning. (2003b, p. 4)

These diverse external and internal factors continue to fuel the assessment movement in higher education.

External Factors Influencing the Assessment Movement

External demands by constituents and stakeholders in education have dominated the assessment landscape over the past two decades. Factors external to the academy driving higher education assessment include federal initiatives; state reports and legislation; accreditation directives at the national, regional, and disciplinary levels; and nonprofit, government, and corporate funding shifts. These factors—some of which are briefly described below—are important to note, as they have broadly shaped and influenced the need for improved assessment in doctoral education.

Federal Initiatives

In response to the national concerns of accountability in higher education, a number of changes have occurred. For example, the Fund for the Improvement of Postsecondary Education, known for supporting "innovative reform projects" in higher education, doubled the number of grant awards for assessment of student learning outcomes over the past 20 years, and has shifted its focus to program effectiveness (Office of Postsecondary Education, 2006). Most recently, the Commission on the Future of Higher Education was created in 2005 by the secretary of education to

consider how best to improve our system of higher education, to ensure that our graduates are well prepared to meet our future workforce needs and are able to participate fully in the changing economy. To accomplish this purpose, the Commission shall consider Federal, State, local, and institutional roles in higher education and analyze whether the current goals of higher education are appropriate and achievable. (U.S. Department of Education, 2005)

A key area of assessment the commission is exploring is the "testing" of skills (either voluntary or mandated) at the undergraduate level, citing a number of higher education initiatives successfully using testing as a primary assessment measure (Miller, 2006). One of these initiatives, the Collegiate Learning Assessment project—developed by the Rand Corporation and co-ordinated by the nonprofit policy research group Council for Aid to Education—aims to measure direct student outcomes of general education skills such as critical thinking, analytic reasoning, and written communication using a "value-added" approach (Benjamin & Chun, 2003). This assessment measure is gaining in popularity with commission members, legislators, and higher education institutions (Lederman, 2006b). Another initiative cited was the Western Governors University, an accredited online university initiative founded by the governors of 19 western U.S. states that focuses on com-petency-based skill attainment through the use of performance assessments, objective examinations, essay exams, and observations of skill acquisition (Johnstone, 2005). Unique initiatives such as the online university may be-come more prominent as technology and distance education grow in popu-larity in higher education.

State Initiatives

Over the last 25 years, states have experienced a one-third decline in funding from the federal government for higher education (Ehrenberg & Rizzo, 1994) because of a diversion of funds toward pressing issues related to na-tional health care and K–12 reform. In addition, states increasingly have fo-cused their attention on accountability for funding allocated to higher education. A national initiative of states, the State Higher Education Execu-tive Officers, has established a focus on learning assessment and created the National Commission on Accountability in Higher Education to "review ways that the states have improved performance in higher education and their experience in using accountability systems toward that end" (National Commission on Accountability in Higher Education, 2005). Another na-tional initiative, the National Forum on College Level Learning (sponsored by the Pew Charitable Trusts, http://www.teach.virginia.edu/centers/college levellearning/), compared the contributions of "college educated human capital" in each of five states (Illinois, Kentucky, Nevada, Oklahoma, and South Carolina) to gauge how well colleges were educating that capital to get both a "system-wide snapshot" and "cross-state comparisons" (Nettles, Perorazio, & Cole, 2002).

The Futures Project: Policy for Higher Education in a Changing World (http://www.futuresproject.org/) funded by a number of nonprofits (Atlantic Philanthropies, Lumina Foundation, GE Foundation, Pew Charitable Trusts, Ford Foundation, Carnegie Corporation, and Rockefeller Foundation) investigated the role of higher education in three areas: autonomy and accountability, accessibility, and responsibility for student learning. The report calls for a "new compact between higher education and the public, negotiated by higher education officials and state policymakers . . . to provide state control over public colleges and universities" (Couturier & Scurry, 2005).

According to the Education Commission of the States, an interstate compact that assists policymakers, the "emerging trend is to define postsecondary success in terms of broad state impacts in lieu of focusing solely on individual institutional performance" (Education Commission of the States, 2006). The Measuring Up initiative, coordinated by the National Center for Public Policy and Higher Education, provides just that with a state-by-state "report card" of higher education performance in five key areas. In the most recent report (*National Center for Public Policy and Higher Education*, 2005), all states received an "incomplete" in learning improvement, except for the five states involved in the previously mentioned National Forum on College Level Learning initiative (http://measuringup.highereducation.org/default .cfm).

In addition to national initiatives involving states, individual states have developed an assessment mandate for higher education as of 2004 (Business–Higher Education Forum, 2004). Most higher education assessment mandates use one or more of three main "performance models" for accountability as outlined by the Education Commission of the States: performance funding (funding tied to actual results), performance budgeting (campus achievement used as a factor in funding future allocation), and performance reporting (periodic reports on performance progress). States commonly measure levels of performance by (a) tracking progress over time, (b) benchmarking through comparison with peer institutions, and/or (c) comparing progress to predetermined sets of standards (Education Commission of the States, 2006).

Accreditation

National-Level Accreditation

Accreditation has been an ever-present force at the national and regional levels in higher education. To make known the increasing importance of assessment utilizing student outcomes, the Council for Higher Education published *Accreditation and Student Learning Outcomes: A Point of Departure* (Ewell, 2001). In his article, Ewell advocates that accreditation organizations become more assertive in their requirements for evidence of student learning outcomes.

Regional-Level Accreditation

While national accreditation serves a prominent role in higher education, individual institutions rely heavily on the mandates and expectations of six regional accrediting bodies. Based on geographic location, these bodies include the Middle States Association of Colleges and Schools (MSACS), New England Association of Schools and Colleges (NEASC), North Central Association of Colleges and Schools (NCACS), Northwest Commission on Colleges and Universities (NWCCU), Southern Association of Colleges and Schools (SACS), and Western Association of Schools and Colleges (WASC). Beginning in 1992 with changes to the Higher Education Act, the federal government required each of the six regional accrediting agencies to include student learning outcomes as part of their accrediting process (Business–Higher Education Forum, 2004). As a result, many of the associations have altered requirements and produced excellent guidebooks with methods for implementing assessment requirements. For example, the Middle States association published the *Framework for Outcomes Assessment* (1996) followed by *Assessing Student Learning and Institutional Effectiveness* (Higher Learning Commission, 2005). The North Central association's Higher Learning Commission approved the creation of a four-year Institute on Assessment of Student Learning in 1995 as a voluntary part of the accreditation process for institutions interested in improving student learning outcomes assessment. The Western association declared its assessment intentions with the publication of an *Evidence Guide*, stating "the Commission seeks to move accreditation from its current reliance on assertion and description toward a reliance on demonstration and performance" (Western Association of Schools and Colleges, 2002, p. 6). The Standards for Accreditation of both the New England and Northwestern associations identify specific outcome measures, including "gaining feedback from alumni, employers, and others situated to help in the description and assessment of student learning" (New England Association of Schools and Colleges, 2005, p. 13) and student information, mid-program assessment, alumni satisfaction and loyalty, and employment and/or employer satisfaction measures (Northwest Commission on Colleges and Universities, n.d., Policy 2.2).

A unique research study by the National Center for Postsecondary Improvement combined the assessment efforts of five state government agencies and three regional accreditation associations to determine relationships for student learning outcomes at undergraduate level. Using the states of Missouri, South Carolina, Florida, Washington, and New York, and the Middle States, Northwest, and North Central regional accrediting agencies, researchers found a lack of communication and a disconnect between the types of policies and criteria for assessment used by government agencies compared to the regional accreditation associations (Nettles et al., 2002).

Professional/Specialized Accreditation

Specialized and professional accreditation plays an important role in accountability in higher education, involving over 60 accrediting organizations. While national and regional accreditation focuses on accountability of the entire individual institution, specialized/professional accreditation focuses on the program level and its corresponding departments. Student learning outcomes and competencies have long been key components to programs involved in this type of accreditation, especially business, engineering, and teacher education. Palomba and Banta (2001) focused a publication on the student learning outcomes assessment practices of eight professional disciplines: business, computer science, engineering, nursing, pharmacy, social work, teacher education, and the visual arts.

Funders of Higher Education Initiatives

For decades up until 2001, generous funding from public and private non-profit organizations and philanthropic arms of corporations has permitted a variety of entities within higher education to conduct research that seeks to improve various aspects of postsecondary education related to access, affordability, and quality, especially at the undergraduate level. In fact, many of the state and national initiatives discussed thus far have been accomplished because of the funding assistance of major nonprofit and corporate foundations, including the William and Flora Hewlett Foundation, Lilly Endowment, Robert Wood Johnson Foundation, Ford Foundation, Andrew W. Mellon Foundation, Starr Foundation, Pew Charitable Trusts, and the David and Lucile Packard Foundation (Lawrence & Marino, 2003).

However, the level of support by nonprofit and corporate funding has decreased dramatically over the past five years due to economic downturns, stock market declines, increased funding to national and international relief efforts, and changing organizational priorities. According to the Foundation Center, funding support in 2001 increased at a faster rate for disease-specific health organizations, public/general health organizations, mental health agencies, and environmental organizations than for higher education institutions (Lawrence & Marino, 2003). Two major funders of higher education research, Atlantic Philanthropies and Pew Charitable Trusts, have shifted their focus away from financing higher education issues in favor of issues facing preschool and K–12 education and social service/health care areas. The Pew Charitable Trusts funded higher education endeavors including capital construction and research and cosponsorship of the initial National Survey of Student Engagement (http://nsse.iub.edu/index.cfm) and the Measuring Up initiative of the National Center for Public Policy and Higher Education.

Some foundations have chosen to channel funding specifically to student outcomes and assessment issues in higher education. For example, the Teagle Foundation working with the American Association of Colleges and Universities has developed a grant program, Initiatives in Value-Added Assessment, stating "the systematic measurement of the value added in various settings of higher education is an area in which more can be done. Nothing, we believe, has more potential to affect students' educational experience as much as sustained and appropriate assessment of what they learn" (Teagle Foundation, 2006). The Pew Forum on Undergraduate Learning, funded by Pew Charitable Trusts, seeks to "encourage and enable colleges and universities to take responsibility for helping their undergraduates attain demonstrable learning outcomes" through initiatives that internally improve student learning outcomes or externally develop new forms of accountability (http://www.pewundergradforum.org/).

External Rankings of Higher Education Institutions

Conducted by commercial third-party organizations usually in the print media, college rankings were created as an effort to assist consumers—namely, parents and students—with college decision-making information. The rankings include publications that rank institutions, such as *U.S.-News & World Report* and *The Princeton Review*, as well as those that rank specific professional/specialized programs, such as *Financial Times* and *BusinessWeek*.

Critics question the validity of these rankings based on the types and quality of assessment measures used or omitted in rankings research; many feel that the rankings communicate institutional and disciplinary reputations, not quality of learning. These criticisms have spawned various reactions from the higher education community, such as nonparticipation in future rankings processes (e.g., Reed College withdrawing from *U.S.News & World Report* rankings), intentional withholding of information to commercial magazines (such as Wharton and Harvard business schools with *BusinessWeek* in 2004), the creation of rankings focused on characteristics of colleges not evaluated previously (such as service-to-society rankings launched by *Washington Monthly* in 2005 at http://www.washingtonmonthly.com/fea tures/2001/0201.green.html; or *Yahoo! Internet Life Magazine's Most Wired Universities*, which no longer exists; or the *Journal of Black Higher Education Racial Diversity Rankings* at http://www.jbhe.com/features/36_leading_uni versities.htm), the publication of differing college "best-buy" guides, and the creation of organizations attempting to make changes to the culture of rankings (such as the admission reform efforts of the nonprofit Education Conservancy, which was created in 1994 (www.educationconservancy.org).

Even with the criticisms, rankings continue to prosper and hold the attention of the American public as a way to assess various aspects of quality in higher education for a few reasons. First, the commercial success and proliferation of such rankings and guides supports the claim that consumers crave such information. Second, not everyone agrees that rankings and guides have such a profound influence on consumer decision making. The Art & Science Group, a market-research and enrollment-management company, found that a minority of students applying to college claim that rankings influence them in their college decisions, and for most, the influence is no stronger than that of the popular guidebooks available (Gose, 2005).

Third, higher education rankings have become an international phenomenon in countries including Australia, Canada, and the United Kingdom. In fact, two ranking systems compare institutions globally—the *Academic Ranking of World Universities* (2003; http://ed.sjtu.edu.cn/ranking.htm) and the *World University Rankings* (2004; www.thes.co.uk/worldrankings/). A recent report from the Educational Policy Institute, an international organization that compares the various ranking systems of university "quality" in 16 different countries, concluded that

> As imperfect as they are, they [rankings] satisfy a public demand for transparency and information that institutions and governments have not been able to meet on their own. Moreover, as higher education becomes more costly for individuals and families, the demand for comparative information on universities will increase. (Usher & Savino, 2006, p. 38)

Internal Factors Influencing Assessment Movement

Although external calls for accountability have received much of the attention in higher education, internal calls for improving assessment have been expressed by the academic community. Increasingly, knowing about the efficacy of educational practices through the assessment of student work is viewed by internal constituents as a professional responsibility in faculty and administrative roles. While the external factors are providing the pressure to change our thinking about assessment, internal factors are providing the tools to accomplish those changes. Factors internal to the academy that broadly shape and influence doctoral-level assessment—briefly described below—include a shift in focus about learning and responsibility, changing faculty perspectives on assessment, nontransferability of K–12 directives to higher education, interest in the whole student, and professional and disciplinary association activities and directives.

Shift in Thinking about Learning and Responsibility

A key element in the rise of interest in assessment and accountability is the changing view within higher education of the concept of teaching and learning. In his groundbreaking *Scholarship Reconsidered* (1990), Ernest Boyer challenged higher education to rethink the role of teaching and learning by encouraging scholarship to include not only discovery, integration of knowledge and service, but also quality teaching. The Wingspread Group on Higher Education (1993) produced *An American Imperative: Higher Expectations for Higher Education* calling for strengthening in three key areas in education for a successful future workforce: taking values seriously, putting student learning first, and creating a nation of learners. In its report, the group encouraged higher levels of assessment:

> Indeed, the entire system is skewed in favor of the input side of the learning equation: credit hours, library collections, percentage of faculty with terminal degrees, and the like. The output side of the equation—student achievement—requires much greater attention than it now receives. That attention should begin by establishing improved measures of student achievement, measures that are credible and valued by the friends and supporters of education, by testing and accrediting bodies, and by educational institutions themselves.

A groundbreaking/seminal article by Barr and Tagg (1995) encourages undergraduate higher education to move away from an "instruction paradigm" that focuses on teaching toward a "learning paradigm" that focuses on the student. In this shift, a university's purpose is not to

> transfer knowledge but to create environments and experiences that bring students to discover and construct knowledge for themselves, to make students members of communities of learners that make discoveries and solve problems . . . within its framework, effective learning technologies are continually identified, developed, tested, implemented, and assessed against one another. The aim in the Learning Paradigm is not so much to improve the quality of instruction—although that is not irrelevant—as it is to improve continuously the quality of learning for students individually and in the aggregate. (p. 15)

This shift of thinking to a learning paradigm focuses on taking responsibility and incorporating the use of assessment of student learning outcomes:

> when one takes responsibility, one sets goals and then acts to achieve them, continuously modifying one's behavior to better achieve the goals. To take responsibility for achieving an outcome is not to guarantee the outcome, nor does it entail the complete control of all relevant variables; it is to make the achievement of the outcome the criterion by which one measures one's own efforts. (Barr & Tagg, 1995, p. 15)

Research by the National Research Council on improving undergraduate learning and assessment efforts reinforced the shift to a learning paradigm. The publication *How People Learn* (Bransford, Brown, & Cocking, 2000), funded by the Department of Education's Office of Educational Research and Improvement, focused on learning more about the science of learning in order to better assess learning, and was followed by *Knowing What Students Know: The Science and Design of Educational Assessment* (Pellegrino, Chudowsky, & Glaser, 2001) focused on identifying and sharing good assessment practices and models.

Also during this time, the Association of American Colleges and Universities (AACU), a national organization dedicated to improving undergraduate liberal education, published *Greater Expectations: A New Vision for Learning as a Nation Goes to College* (2002) that advocated improved learning outcomes for students while encouraging individual institutions to assume responsibility for the quality and environment for learning and assessment. Following that report, two AACU publications, *Our Students' Best Work: A Framework of Accountability Worthy of Our Mission* (2004) and *Liberal Education Outcomes: A Preliminary Report on Student Achievement in College* (2005), reinforce that departments and faculty are expected to be given the primary responsibility to define and assess the outcomes of the liberal arts education experience.

Changing Faculty Perceptions on Assessment

Traditionally, faculty as a group have expressed resistance to the assessment movement in higher education for a variety of possible reasons outlined in the *Academe* article "How Can Assessment Work for Us?" (Linkon, 2005). Many faculty believe that the internal accountability measures already in place within academia (tenure and peer review processes) sufficiently assess quality. Others believe that higher education and knowledge should not be viewed as external economic "commodities." Others are concerned with what they perceive as damaging effects of assessment in the K–12 system on the role and academic freedom of teachers. Even faculty who embrace the concept of assessment have issues and concerns with the lengthy process involved in assessment, their lack of knowledge on methods/tools for conducting assessment, and the lack of an institutional reward system that encourages the use of assessment.

Many faculty realize that the assessment movement is here to stay because of the many external and internal factors discussed in this chapter. A new approach to assessment is beginning to take shape—an approach that summons faculty to take control of molding assessment to fit their needs and reflect the values of higher education.

> Despite the real concerns that assessment raises for faculty, I want to argue that we should embrace the responsibility for critically evaluating our work as teachers. We should do so not only because we care about our students' learning, but also because our critical engagement may allow us to change the way assessment is practiced and understood. If we can claim assessment as the "property" of faculty, then we may be able to make it work for us rather than against us. (Linkon, 2005)

This new attitude is shared by the National Commission on Accountability in Higher Education, as reflected in its "national imperative for higher education" report:

> Faculty members must lead the way in devising more coherent programs of general education, more effective and efficient teaching techniques, and useful, authentic assessments of student learning. And institutional reward systems must provide more incentives and recognition for faculty contributions that increase student learning, retention, and success. (National Commission on Accountability in Higher Education, 2005, p. 22)

Finally, in their call for doctoral-level reform in the state of Texas, Cohen and Cherwitz (2006) state:

> Rather than wait for the chorus of calls for accountability to swell and lead to externally imposed, poorly designed solutions, we should take the initiative by working together to devise strategies for improving our doctoral program success rates, participation and program of study.

Interest in the Whole Student

As the learning paradigm takes hold at the undergraduate level, student perceptions and activities within their "whole college experience" become an important link to institutional efforts to create and improve student learning outcomes. Perhaps the longest-running research on college students is the Cooperative Institutional Research Program (CIRP), a survey collected annually for the past 40 years on cognitive and affective data about entering first-year students. To expand on the limitations of the CIRP, it's founder, Alexander Astin, studied student outcomes and the impact of college on students via a longitudinal study of over 25,000 students, producing an often cited resource about the whole college experience, *What Matters in College: Four Critical Years* (Astin, 1977) and its follow-up, *What Matters in College: Four Critical Years Revisited* (Astin, 1993). Another key publication on the effect of college on students included 20 years of research and 2,600 studies to produce *How College Affects Students* (Pascarella & Terenzini, 1991). Its follow-up, *How College Affects Students: A Third Decade of Research* (Pascarella & Terenzini, 2005), incorporates changes not only in student demographics and types of higher education institutions, but also changes in knowledge about how students learn and increasingly diverse ways of measuring learning.

The interest in learning more about student learning outcomes based on the whole college experience and assessing these outcomes led to the creation of the National Survey of Student Engagement (NSSE) in 1998. Initially funded by Pew Charitable Trusts and now housed at Indiana University, the NSSE conducts annual surveys that provide both national and institution-level information about students' views and opinions of various dimensions of their collegiate experience. To date, over 950 institutions have participated in the study, and the founders see potential for expanding the breadth and depth of information as another key internal source of assessment data.

Academic Association Initiatives

A number of higher education associations have gotten involved in the assessment movement at the undergraduate level, including the Association of American Universities and the Association of American Colleges and Universities. Perhaps the most influential organization focused on assessment in higher education was the American Association for Higher Education (AAHE), which served as a national voice for issues affecting higher education for over 35 years prior to its dissolution in 2005. AAHE was a pioneer in the higher education assessment movement, creating and coordinating an annual assessment forum beginning in the mid-1980s with funding from the Fund for Improvement of Postsecondary Education and continuing up until 2005. Faculty and administrator interest in assessment was high, as evidenced by the attendance at one forum of over 1,800. AAHE also produced the *Nine Principles of Good Practice for Assessing Student Learning* using the vision and collaboration of ten assessment "gurus" in higher education (Astin et al., 1996). These principles continue to serve as a cornerstone in developing assessment measures in higher education. *Change* magazine, a major publication about important trends and issues in higher education, was produced by AAHE, including a popular compilation of articles on improving teaching and learning, *Learning from* Change: *Landmarks in Teaching and Learning in Higher Education from* Change *Magazine 1969–1999*, that includes a section on assessment of learning (DeZure, 2000).

Another national organization promoting student learning outcomes and assessment at the undergraduate level is the Association of American Colleges and Universities, which has developed a number of projects in conjunction with the *Greater Expectations* report. Bridging the gap between academia and accreditation agencies, AACU developed the Greater Expectations Project on Accreditation and Assessment with accreditation agency involvement to emphasize student outcomes in accreditation standards focused on liberal learning. Another AACU initiative, the Strategies for Achieving Greater Expectations (SAGE) Group assists campuses with the implementation of recommendations from the report (http://www.aacu-.org/SAGE/index.cfm). In conjunction with the Carnegie Foundation for the Advancement of Teaching, AACU created the Integrative Learning Project (http://www.carnegiefoundation.org/programs/index.asp?key = 24) to assist campuses with "developing designs for comprehensive approaches aimed at providing students with purposeful, progressively more challenging, integrated educational experiences" (see http://www.aaup.org/publications/Aca deme/2005/05nd/05ndcohe.htm).

The Landscape for Doctoral-Level Assessment

As previously mentioned, many faculty do not believe that higher education can or should be held accountable in the same ways as K–12 directives. As external mandates continue to call for collective improvements in higher education accountability using the success of the K–12 system, a report from the Business–Higher Education Forum (2004) warns of higher education's lack of consensus in creating an externally driven accountability model for three main reasons:

- The K–12 model of linking student outcomes to centralized standards does not fit with higher education's diverse populations, goals, levels, and types of learning.
- Most assessment in higher education is conducted at the institutional level (instead of the individual student level), and results are not relayed to the public.
- The use of "broad measures" inherent in higher education is not compatible with the statistical language of K–12 results familiar to legislators.

These differences between higher education and K–12 reinforce the need for faculty involvement and initiative in creating a new assessment model for higher education.

The American graduate school system is generally viewed as the best in the world. In the United States, graduate education is valued as a key component of our higher education system. As outlined by the Council of Graduate Schools,

> the public tends to view undergraduate education as a right of citizenship. Graduate education is more often perceived as a privilege for those who have the time and resources to participate. Yet, numerous studies provide ample evidence that graduate education is increasingly important as preparation for an expanding range of career options and for the future economic and social well being of the country. (Sims & Syverson, n.d., p. 68)

In his plea for federal funding of graduate education in the *Change* article "Hey Capital Hill: Fund Graduate Education" (2005) Philip Cohen outlines the many public benefits of graduate education and the national crisis we face because of a lack of advanced degree graduates in the science disciplines. The importance of graduate education is reflected in his statement, "Increasingly, Americans will need graduate and professional degrees to get their first job and advance in their careers. Indeed, a master's degree is now the entry-level requirement for many professions" (p. 3). Also, as homeland security, global issues, and international competition become more prevalent, the quality of our workforce becomes increasingly important. In a paper advocating a renewal of the National Defense Education Act of 1950, the Council of Graduate Schools states "one of the lessons of the original NDEA

[National Defense Education Act] was that effective support for graduate education provides a necessary starting point for a comprehensive plan to address challenges across the educational spectrum as well as in industry and government sectors" (Council of Graduate Schools, 2005b, p. 9).

According to the Council of Graduate Schools, graduate education is seen as the "jewel in the crown of our educational system," but faces two major obstacles to its reputation and future. First, the decline of international students studying in the United States (and then possibly remaining here to work in research or industry) and the decline of domestic students—especially minorities and women—pursuing advanced degrees in the sciences will reduce the quality and level of the research and innovation needed to compete in the increasingly complex knowledge economy. Second, the institutional and external funding sources that graduate students rely on (research and teaching assistantships, traineeships, and fellowships) look to continue to be uncertain as government appropriations to higher education and external funders focus on funding other national issues outside of higher education. According to a report released by the National Academies' Committee on Science, Engineering, and Public Policy (COSEPUP; Committee on Science, Engineering, and Public Policy, 2006) on science and engineering,

> From a national perspective, global competition in higher education and research and in the recruitment of students and scholars means that the United States must invest in the development and recruitment of the best and brightest from here and abroad to ensure that we have the talent, expertise, and ideas that continue to spur innovation and keep our nation at the leading edge of science and technology. (p. 159)

The predominant focus on external accountability and internal assessment for improvement in higher education has been at the undergraduate level. But, with the increased visibility of the many external and internal agents surrounding higher education assessment and the concerns voiced about our ability to compete in the global economy, issues have been raised in particular about the quality of doctoral education. As the Association of American Universities' Committee on Graduate Education notes in its 1998 graduate education report (http://www.aau.edu/reports/GradEdRpt.html),

> Criticisms commonly heard today [about doctoral education] include overproduction of Ph.D.s; narrow training; emphasis on research over teaching;

use of students to meet institutional needs at the expense of sound education; and insufficient mentoring, career advising, and job placement assistance.

Effective assessment is necessary in graduate education to improve and meet the needs of our future global economy. Austin and Wulff (2004), in their chapter in *Pathways to the Professoriate*, identify four concerns adding to the increased attention on graduate education: (1) the role and preparation of the graduate teaching assistant, (2) the labor market and career options for graduates both in and outside of the academy, (3) attrition rates for graduate students, and (4) the importance of the graduate experience in preparing for a faculty career.

Key External Factors

Graduate education currently does have to provide assessment information to external sources. For example, public institutions must provide data to governing organizations, accrediting agencies, and legislative bodies. As noted earlier, many external nonprofit and corporate funders have strengthened guidelines and requirements for evidence of outcomes for projects involving graduate education initiatives. Government shifts in funding away from higher education, budget cuts, and calls for tying funding to performance deeply affect doctoral education. At the federal level, the government offers support for graduate fellowships and trainee internships, research assistantships, and student loans—all major contributing factors to the success of doctoral education. At the state level, individual governments provide teaching and research assistantships, and graduate fellowships. Accrediting agencies influence doctoral education through their requirements for evidence of quality in student learning beyond the baccalaureate level.

A number of external nonprofit and corporate funders that have long supported innovation and research in graduate education are also shifting funding because of agenda priorities. One in particular, the Andrew W. Mellon Foundation, recently announced the suspension of its graduate humanities fellowship program as it considers other ventures for supporting graduate education in the humanities. This potential shift is major, in that the foundation funded a 10-year $80 million project designed to improve doctoral humanities and social science programs by reducing time to degree and attrition (Groen, Jakubson, Ehrenberg, Condie, & Yung-Hsu Liu, 2005). Considered unique by many for tying assessment to funding, this initiative required participating departments to follow students' progress and show evidence of that progress as a condition of receiving any grant funding.

The future of external funding of doctoral education is not totally bleak. With the concern over our country's future competitiveness in science and technology, external funding has been renewed at the graduate level with initiatives targeting issues in the science, technology, engineering, and math (STEM) disciplines. The National Institutes of Health and the National Science Foundation support a number of key initiatives. For example, NSF sponsors the Alliances for Graduate Education and the Professoriate (AGEP) designed to increase the number of minority Ph.D. graduates (http://ehr-web.aaas.org/mge/); Integrative Graduate Education and Research Traineeship (IGERT), designed to assist in interdisciplinary and professional/ employment skill development training of future Ph.D.-level scientists and engineers (http://www.igert.org/); and the Center for the Integration of Research, Teaching, and Learning (CIRTL), housed at the University of Wisconsin, designed to enhance national graduate student faculty development for future STEM discipline faculty (http://cirtl.wceruw.org/). Funded by both NSF and the Ford Foundation, the Center for Innovation and Research in Graduate Education (CIRGE) at the University of Washington seeks to "establish empirical bases for trend assessment, policy decisions, and innovations in graduate education through studies on graduate and postdoctoral education at the local, national, and international levels" (Center for Innovation and Research in Graduate Education, 2006).

Embedded in the funding for each of these initiatives is evidence of assessment and learning outcomes in the forms of intellectual merit and broader impact on society. Continued funding from these types of organizations will "give a voice" to faculty and administrators interested in focusing attention on improving doctoral education and the assessment of learning outcomes.

Key Internal Factors

Internal to the academy, professional and disciplinary academic associations have been influential in promoting improvement and assessment in doctoral education. Many of these organizations now require data from member institutions concerning a variety of graduate-level issues. For example, the Association of American Universities (1998) formed the Committee on Graduate

Education that conducted an assessment of graduate education on its member campuses by looking at quantitative aspects, institutional policies, and financial support. The committee then provided recommendations for best practices in graduate education.

Some associations interested in doctoral education provide quantifiable statistical information about aspects of doctoral graduates and their programs. The National Opinion Research Center (NORC) oversees the Survey of Earned Doctorates, research on doctoral students conducted annually since 1920 about "educational histories, funding sources, and post-doctoral plans" (National Opinion Research Center, 2006). NORC also oversees the biennial Survey of Doctorate Recipients that uses descriptive information to track educational experiences and first-job status of doctoral graduates. As part of the National Academies, the National Research Council (NRC) conducts research on issues and trends in scientific and engineering disciplines and workforces, including the early careers of life scientists. The NRC is known widely for its rankings of doctoral programs published in 1982 and 1995 that employed reputational measures and secondary sources of data. According to the NRC,

> these data are presented to encourage the debate that is needed to assure all who have an interest in and concern about the quality of advanced study whether members of the academic or policy community, or of the general citizenry that the training provided to research scholars and scientists is strong enough to meet the challenges that face our nation and our world in the coming decades. (Goldberger, Maher, & Flattau, 1995)

Some associations focus their attention and efforts on pressing issues in higher education, including those that involve the doctoral level. The Carnegie Foundation for the Advancement of Teaching focuses research on improving education at the K–12 level and both the undergraduate and graduate levels in higher education. The organization has coordinated key higher education educational initiatives, including the Carnegie Academy for the Scholarship of Teaching and Learning (CASTL) initiative; Integrative Learning Project: Opportunities to Connect; Preparation for the Professions Program for clergy, engineering, legal, medical, and nursing education fields; and the Carnegie Initiative on the Doctorate.

Another association, the Council of Graduate Schools (CGS), is a national group comprising more than 450 colleges and universities focused solely on improving graduate education. Projects and conferences at the regional and national level address a wide range of issues in doctoral education, including assessment, financial support, admissions improvements, career services, the role of graduate dean, technology, international students, changing student demographics, and student crisis management. CGS cosponsors the annual U.S. National Survey of Graduate Enrollment with the Educational Testing Service (ETS). With support from external organizations such as the Ford Foundation, the Alfred P. Sloan Foundation, Pfizer Inc., the National Science Foundation, and the Office of Research Integrity, CGS has initiated a variety of best practices initiatives. The organization also publishes *CGS Communicator*, a monthly newsletter for graduate deans and those interested in graduate education, and the *Assessment and Review of Graduate Programs: A Policy Statement* guide (Council of Graduate Schools, 2005a).

The Preparing Future Faculty (PFF) program (http://www.preparing-faculty.org/), cosponsored by the Council of Graduate Schools and the Association of American Colleges and Universities, with support from Pew Charitable Trusts, the National Science Foundation, and Atlantic Philanthropies, was created in 1993 to prepare graduate students for the full range of duties as faculty members with a focus on teaching. Unique in its partnership with 11 disciplinary associations (representing biology, chemistry, communication, computer science, English, history, mathematics, physics, political science, psychology, and sociology) and diverse institutions within disciplinary clusters, PFF programs expose students to the different teaching and faculty duties within a variety of institution types. A highly successful program, as evaluated by an external nonprofit research firm, WestEd (2004), the PFF program completed four phases until external funding expired in 2002. However, many of the campus programs are still in existence today because of institutional commitment of support and funding.

International Influence

Improving doctoral and graduate education has become of international interest. The Bologna Declaration agreement, created in 1999, reorganized higher education in Europe and led to the creation of the European University Association (EUA). With 750 member universities in 45 countries, the EUA views doctoral-level education as the cornerstone of higher education, as evidenced from a report of research on the quality of doctoral education in Europe, *Doctoral Programmes for the European Knowledge Society: Report on the EUA Doctoral Programmes Project* (European University Association, 2005). Improving doctoral education has been in the forefront in the United Kingdom and Australia. For example, an alternative Ph.D. concept, the NewRoutePhD (http://www.newroutephd.ac.uk/) has gained interest in the United Kingdom because it incorporates professional skill development into the traditional curriculum through interdisciplinary studies and group work, while building media, technology, and business skills. UK researchers have also focused attention on identifying objective doctoral standards and investigating differences between the "ideal" and "passable" doctorate (Cantwell & Scevak, 2004). The 2005 meeting of the Improving Student Learning symposium in London focused entirely on assessment issues in doctoral education. In Australia, the government published *The Doctoral Education Experience: Diversity and Complexity* outlining issues in doctoral education (Neumann, 2003). In addition, the Australian Centre for the Study of Higher Education developed the Assessing Learning Project in 2002 to assist Australian colleges and universities in providing quality assessment practices at all levels, especially related to online delivery, large classrooms, plagiarism and academic honesty, effective group work, and student diversity issues (James, McGinnis, & Devlin, 2002).

Assessment Efforts at the Doctoral Level

Research about doctoral education has been conducted over many decades on various aspects of the doctoral experience. However, much of the earlier research has not focused on views on quality of the doctoral experience or its relationship to postgraduate success. For the purpose of this chapter, the focus will be on the more recent research studies beginning in the 1990s that have brought significant attention and clarity to many of the pressing issues in doctoral education and the need for assessment. For a more detailed synopsis of graduate education research conducted prior to 1990, refer to Kerlin and Smith Kerlin (1994) and Kerlin (1995), for overviews of research on doctoral education regarding issues such as student demographics, degrees awarded, attrition and time to degree, status of women and minorities, class/social status, finances, and career plans. Also, Appendix A contains a list of Web sites and resources that provide information about recent studies and links to those studies, including *Overview of Doctoral Education Studies and Reports 1990–Present* (Carnegie Foundation for the Advancement of Teaching, 2002) that provides a summary of findings and recommendations on doctoral education in four key areas (i.e., the doctoral pipeline, the process and content of doctoral study, career preparation, and feedback mechanisms), along with over 50 studies and reports connected to those issues, and an article written in *Change* by Jody Nyquist (2002) that summarizes the main issues in doctoral education and reviews the major initiatives over the past decade.

Based on their review of graduate education research from the 1970s and 1980s, Kerlin and Smith Kerlin (1994) identified the need for further and broader research and assessment in graduate education for the following reasons:

- Current focus of research is on the "what" and "how" in methodology, but there is limited or no focus on "why" in terms of student progress
- Limited institutionwide research is conducted about the graduate student experience
- Existing research is conducted primarily at the department/program level
- Fresh data is needed to study future supply and demand of degree recipients
- Lack of involvement in decision making by key internal stakeholders—faculty, students themselves, and administration
- The need to understand attrition issues via students themselves

In the 1990s research on doctoral education began to shift in focus. *In Pursuit of the Ph.D.* by Bowen and Rudenstine (1992) identified the current state of affairs in doctoral education and set the stage for more detailed and varied research. The study researched time to degree and attrition for over 35,000 students in 6 disciplines at 10 leading universities over a 24-year period. The authors recommended improved quality in doctoral education within departments and greater support for students by faculty.

One major report, *Reshaping the Graduate Education of Scientists and Engineers* (1995), commonly known as the COSEPUP report, created a stir at the national level with its recommendation that the Ph.D. experience change and reshape itself to be more adaptable, versatile, and technologically proficient. The report recommended for graduate students a wider range of academic options and skill development, better information and guidance about careers in academic and nonacademic settings, and a national human resource policy group to examine issues in graduate education.

Another key study sought to provide more research about the postgraduate plans of doctoral graduates. Using the results of alumni surveys of almost 6,000 Ph.D. graduates from 6 Ph.D. disciplines at over 61 universities, Nerad and Cerny (1999, 2000) examined career paths of Ph.D.s 10 to 14 years past graduation to determine employment patterns overall and for individual disciplines. One of the major findings was what was called "a culture of neglect" for students in terms of job search and career assistance. Chapter 4 in this volume provides more background and detail about the study and its potential uses today.

Students' views of their doctoral experiences were an area of focused research for a few very important studies conducted in the late 1990s. The National Association of Graduate-Professional Students (NAGPS) conducted a study of over 32,000 current students and recent Ph.D.s in 1,300 programs across the country in 2001 using the National Doctoral Program Survey (http://cresmet.asu.edu/nagps/index.php). Funded by the Alfred P. Sloan Foundation, the researchers sought information about students' satisfaction with their doctoral experience. Results of the survey found that although students were satisfied with their overall doctoral experience, they were not satisfied with their preparation for nonacademic careers, the extensiveness of the curriculum, training for their teaching roles, and minority representation within the doctoral programs.

Perhaps one of the more widely publicized and cited research studies about student perceptions is *At Cross Purposes: What the Experiences of Doctoral Students Reveal about Doctoral Education* (Golde & Dore, 2001) funded by the Pew Charitable Trusts. Using the results of over 4,000 doctoral students who completed a Survey of Doctoral Education and Career Preparation, Golde and Dore's study revealed some similarities with the results of the NAGPS survey. Although students were satisfied overall with their curriculum and advisors, most were not satisfied with or did not understand the graduate process or outcome options, creating what the researchers termed an "information deficit" (p. 34) about the graduate process itself and a "three-way mismatch" (p. 5) with the doctoral program training, student aspirations, and career and employment options.

Another study during this time about students' experiences, *Leaving the*

Ivory Tower: The Causes and Consequences of Departure from Doctoral Study (Lovitts, 2001), addressed the issue of high attrition in doctoral education and researched the causes for early departure from doctoral programs. Lovitts concluded that the differences between "completers" and "non-completers" of doctoral programs related to the level of integration and connection with the doctoral program, including socialization and financial aid support.

Another group of significant studies focused on the development of teaching assistants and preparation for future faculty careers within the academy. Such publications as *Working Effectively with Graduate Assistants* (Nyquist & Wulff, 1996), "On the Road to Becoming a Professor: The Graduate Student Experience" (Nyquist & Associates, 1999), *Building the Faculty We Need: Colleges and Universities Working Together* (Gaff, Pruitt-Logan, & Weibl, 2000), and "Paradise Lost: How the Academy Converts Enthusiastic Recruits into Early-Career Doubters" (Trower, Austin, & Sorcinelli, 2001) brought attention to the issues surrounding the inadequate training of graduate students to teach within their teaching assistant duties and inadequate preparation for the full spectrum of duties as a future faculty member. A more recent study by Wulff, Austin, Nyquist, and Sprague (2004) tracks the lives of 65 doctoral students over a four-year period to view their development as teaching scholars.

Re-envisioning the Ph.D. Project

One project in particular, Re-envisioning the Ph.D., led by Jody Nyquist at the University of Washington and funded by the Pew Charitable Trusts, is credited by many as being a major attempt to put a national spotlight on reforming doctoral education. Over 365 producers and consumers of the Ph.D. were interviewed, including representatives from research-intensive universities, comprehensive and doctoral universities, liberal arts and community colleges, doctoral students, business and industry, foundations, government, disciplinary and educational associations, K–12 education, and accrediting agencies. These interviews led to the identification of themes and patterns of concern for doctoral education (Nyquist & Woodford, 2000a) and "promising practices" in process at the time to address those concerns. At a conference in April 2000, a cross-section of producers and consumers of the Ph.D. were brought together to voice their concerns about doctoral education and review themes already identified, as well as to identify strategic partnerships to address those issues. Seven "meta-themes" were derived from the conference to improve doctoral education (Nyquist & Woodford, 2000b). Although the Re-envisioning the Ph.D. project officially ended in June 2003, its effect on doctoral education resounds today, and its Web site (http://www.depts.washington.edu/envision) continues to be a key source of information for those interested in doctoral education reform.

The Responsive Ph.D. Initiative

The Responsive Ph.D. Initiative, organized by the Woodrow Wilson National Fellowship Foundation (WWNFF) and funded by the Pew Charitable Trusts and the Atlantic Philanthropies, led an effort to sharpen the findings from the Re-envisioning the Ph.D. project into major recommendations for change. The five-year initiative, organized around four themes—crafting new paradigms, exploring new practices, recruiting and retaining new people, and forming new partnerships—conducted a variety of activities involving various stakeholders in doctoral education, including campus roundtables at 14 participating campuses, a diversity forum, a sectors forum for diverse constituents, a graduate student leadership conference, an assessment conference, and a deans conference attended by over 50 deans to assess the initiative and plan for the future in 1995.

The initiative culminated in the publication of *The Responsive Ph.D.: Innovations in U.S. Doctoral Education* (Woodrow Wilson National Fellowship Foundation, 2005b) that supports four principles to support change in doctoral education: (1) strong graduate schools and graduate deans with real budgets and scope, (2) a continuing interchange with the worlds beyond academia, (3) a higher priority on attracting, cultivating, and retaining Ph.D.s of color, and (4) conducting assessment with reasonable consequences. The report also includes brief summaries of 41 promising practices gleaned from the Ph.D. Professional Development Assessment Project, an internally conducted study at WWNFF and the first nationally organized attempt to assess the effectiveness of promising practices in the professional development of doctoral students. Another report released by the initiative, *Diversity and the Ph.D.: A Review of Efforts to Broaden Race and Ethnicity in U.S. Doctoral Education* (Woodrow Wilson National Fellowship Foundation, 2005a), reviews select national programs designed to increase the number of doctoral candidates of color.

Current Initiative Efforts in Doctoral Assessment

Research and assessment of doctoral education gained momentum over the last decade, and the future appears to be continuing at the same pace or to be gaining steam. Currently, a number of significant initiatives are under way to improve aspects of doctoral education. For example, in December 2004, the Council of Graduate Schools created a research initiative, Graduate Education 2020, an undertaking with the Educational Testing Service that will research a different issue in graduate education each year through 2020 to shed light on the need for continued research in graduate education (Jaschik, 2005). CGS is also launching a study about entrepreneurship in graduate education that seeks to provide models of successful incorporation of entrepreneurship into the graduate curriculum. The Ph.D. Completion Project launched in 2004 by CGS with funding collaboration from the business (Pfizer) and nonprofit (Ford Foundation) communities, recently compiled preliminary results of its three-year research project to identify and assess different approaches to reduce doctoral attrition in STEM disciplines (Denecke & Frasier, 2005). The Commission on Graduate Education at Stanford University has completed its report on how to improve graduate education at the university. The commission expects to conduct a multiyear plan, including such ideas as "the creation of a new position to supervise graduate education, new programs to encourage interdisciplinary work in graduate school, and new funds to encourage the graduate student body" (Jaschik, 2005). The National Research Council is beginning its long-awaited new assessment of research doctoral programs ratings project (National Research Council, 2006) with significant changes and updates based on the review of methodology used in the previous 1982 and 1995 research (Ostriker & Kuh, 2003). And last, the Carnegie Initiative on the Doctorate (CID), discussed in chapter 2 (p. 53), focuses on preparing "stewards of the discipline" through training students to become researchers and scholars in a cross-section of departments and has recently announced the publication of its findings, *Envisioning the Future of Doctoral Education: Preparing Stewards of the Discipline* (Golde & Walker, 2006).

The Future for Doctoral-Level Assessment

Three trends about the future of assessment in higher education expressed in the opening plenary from the 1999 AAHE Assessment Forum are proving to be accurate as we survey the landscape six years later. In that plenary session, Peter Ewell of the National Center for Higher Education Management Systems; Tom Angelo, coauthor of the widely used *Classroom Assessment Techniques* handbook (Angelo & Cross, 1993), and Cecilia Lopez of the North Central Association Commission on Institutions of Higher Education projected that the demand for assessment in higher education would continue and that the call for implementing assessment in the culture of doctoral education should be heeded as the following "trends" for the future become a reality now:

1. Increase in accountability demands
    - *engagement* of campuses in accrediting process
    - *linking* of assessment results to state resources
    - *responsibility* for assessment placed on individual institutions
2. Increase diversification of postsecondary education
    - *individual students* used as unit of analysis instead of institution
    - *core-competencies* focus
    - *authentic* performance assessments valid across diverse populations and sectors of higher education
    - *integrity* of college degree demanded by employers
3. Shift to student-centered learning paradigm
    - *value-added* focus on assessment
    - *technology* incorporated into learning and assessment of learning
    - *embedding* of assessment in campus culture

As stated throughout this chapter, much of the push for assessment of student learning outcomes has been externally imposed; however, internal factors are creating a climate for doctoral-level faculty and administrators to consider and implement good assessment practices. As of now, doctoral education has the autonomy to decide how best to assess student learning outcomes. If we can use the assessment process, improve our programs based on stated results, and then articulate our results to our publics and stakeholders, we will bridge what many have considered a widening gap between the governments, accrediting agencies, and consumers and the academic community. Appendix B provides a list of assessment resources for doctoral educators, including a list of general resources, how-to assessment guides, and assessment resources created by accreditation agencies and funding agencies.

It is our professional responsibility as educators to learn about and improve student learning to develop a culture of evidence that seeks to answer the following kinds of questions: What do we know about the efficacy of our current educational practices in preparing students for success beyond graduation? What obstacles prohibit students from continuing their studies? How do we know what and how students are learning and experiencing their educational journey? To assist with that process, the remaining chapters in this book offer innovative efforts that help us to learn and know more about the efficacy of our practices in doctoral education.

References

Angelo, T. A., & Cross, K. P. (1993). *Classroom assessment techniques: A handbook for college teachers*. San Francisco: Jossey-Bass.

Association of American Colleges and Universities. (2002). *Greater expectations: A new vision for learning as a nation goes to college*. Washington, DC: Author. Retrieved from http://www.greaterexpectations.org/

Association of American Colleges and Universities. (2004). *Our students' best work: A framework of accountability worthy of our mission*. Washington, DC: Author. Retrieved from http://www.aacu.org/publications/pdfs/StudentsBestReport.pdf

Association of American Colleges and Universities. (2005). *Liberal education outcomes: A preliminary report on student achievement in college*. Washington, DC: Author. Retrieved from http://www.aacu.org/advocacy/pdfs/LEAP_Report_FINAL.pdf

Association of American Universities. (1998). *Committee on Graduate Education Report and Recommendations*. Washington, DC: Author. Retrieved from http://www.aau.edu/reports/GradEdRpt.html

Astin, A. W. (1977). *What matters in college: Four critical years*. San Francisco: Jossey-Bass.

Astin, A. W. (1993). *What matters in college: Four critical years revisited*. San Francisco: Jossey-Bass.

Astin, A. W., Banta, T. W., Cross, K. P., El-Khawas, E., Ewell, P. T., Hutchings, et al. (1996). *Nine principles of good practice for assessing student learning*. Washington, DC: American Association for Higher Education Assessment Forum. Retrieved from http://www.assessment.tcu.edu/assessment/aahe.pdf

Austin, A. E., & Wulff, D. H. (2004). The challenge to prepare the next generation of faculty. In D. H. Wulff & A. E. Austin & Associates (Eds.), *Paths to the professoriate: Strategies for enriching the preparation of future faculty* (pp. 3–16). San Francisco: Jossey-Bass.

Barr, R. B., & Tagg, J. (1995, November/December). From teaching to learning: A new paradigm for undergraduate education. *Change, 27*(6), 13–25. Retrieved from http://critical.tamucc.edu/~blalock/readings/tch2learn.htm

Benjamin, R., & Chun, M. (2003, Summer). A new field of dreams: The Collegiate Learning Assessment project. *Peer Review, 5*(4), 26–29. Retrieved from http://www.aacu.org/peerreview/pr-su03/pr-su03feature2.cfm and http://www.cae.org/default.asp

Bowen, W. G., & Rudenstine, N. L. (1992). *In pursuit of the Ph.D.* Princeton, NJ: Princeton University Press.

Boyer, E. L. (1990). *Scholarship recondsidered: Priorities of the professoriate.* Princeton, NJ: Carnegie Foundation for the Advancement of Teaching.

Bransford, J. D., Brown, A. L., & Cocking, R. R. (Eds.). (2000). *How people learn: Brain, mind, experience, and school.* Washington, DC: National Academy Press. Retrieved from http://newton.nap.edu/html/howpeople1/

Business–Higher Education Forum. (2004). *Public accountability for student learning in higher education: Issues and options.* Position paper. Washington, DC: Author. Retrieved from http://www.bhef.com/includes/pdf/2004_public_accountability.pdf

Cantwell, R. H., & Scevak, J. (2004, November). *Discrepancies between the "ideal" and "passable" doctorate: Supervisor thinking on doctoral standards.* Paper presented at the annual conference of the Australian Association for Research in Education, Melbourne. Retrieved from http://www.aare.edu.au/04pap/can04980.pdf

Carnegie Foundation for the Advancement of Teaching. (2002). *Overview of doctoral education studies and reports 1990–Present.* Stanford, CA: Author.

Center for Innovation and Research in Graduate Education. (2006). *About CIRGE: Mission.* Seattle: University of Washington. Retrieved February 20, 2006, from http://depts.washington.edu/coe/cirge/html/aboutus.html

Cohen, P. (2005, November/December). Hey Capitol Hill: Fund graduate education. *Change, 91*(6), 24–26. Retrieved from http://www.aaup.org/publications/Academe/2005/05nd/05ndcohe.htm

Cohen, P., & Cherwitz, R. (2006, January 17). In doctoral education, it's time for an overhaul. *Austin American-Statesman.* Retrieved from http://www.statesman.com/opinion/content/editorial/stories/01/17gradschool_edit.html

Committee on Science, Engineering, and Public Policy. (1995). *Reshaping the graduate education of scientists and engineers.* Washington, DC: National Academy Press. Retrieved from http://newton.nap.edu/html/grad/

Committee on Science, Engineering, and Public Policy. (2006). *Rising above the gathering storm: Energizing and employing America for a brighter economic future.* Washington, DC: National Academy Press. Retrieved from http://darwin.nap.edu/books/0309100399/html

Council for Higher Education Accreditation. (2003a). *CHEA at a glance*. Washington, DC: Author. Retrieved from http://www.chea.org/pdf/chea_glance_2003 .pdf

Council for Higher Education Accreditation. (2003b). *Statement of mutual responsibilities for student learning outcomes: Accreditation, institutions, and programs*. Washington, DC: Author. Retrieved from http://www.chea.org/pdf/StmntStu dentLearningOutcomes9-03.pdf

Council of Graduate Schools. (2005a). *Assessment and review of graduate programs: A policy statement*. Washington, DC: Author.

Council of Graduate Schools. (2005b, November). *NDEA 21: A renewed commitment to graduate education*. Washington, DC: Author. Retrieved from http://www .cgsnet.org/pdf/NDEA21RevNov05.pdf

Couturier, L. K., & Scurry, J. E. (2005). *Correcting course: How we can restore the ideals of public higher education in a market-driven era*. Providence, RI: The Futures Project: Policy for Higher Education in a Changing World. Retrieved from http://www.futuresproject.org/publications/Correcting_Course.pdf

Delgado, R. (2005, December 7). *Graduate education under microscope: Commission presents its findings to senate*. Stanford Report. Palo Alto, CA: Stanford University. Retrieved from http://news-service.stanford.edu/news/2005/december7/gradu ate-120705.html

Denecke, D. D., & Frasier, H. S. (2005, November). Ph.D. Completion project: Preliminary results from baseline data. *CGS Communicator, 38*(9), 1–2, 7–8.

DeZure, D. (2000). *Learning from* Change: *Landmarks in teaching and learning in higher education from* Change *magazine 1969–1999*. Sterling, VA: Stylus.

Education Commission of the States. (2006). *Student learning: Accountability (postsec.)*. Retrieved from http://www.ecs.org/html/issue.asp?issueID = 202&subIs sueID = 137

Ehrenberg, R. G., & Rizzo, M. J. (1994, July/August). Financial forces and the future of higher education. *Academe, 90*(4), 25–31. Retrieved from http://www.aa up.org/publications/Academe/2004/04ja/04jaehre.htm

European University Association. (2005). *Doctoral programmes for the European knowledge society: Report on the EUA Doctoral Programmes Project*. Brussels, Belgium: Author.

Ewell, P. T. (2001). *Accreditation and student learning outcomes: A proposed point of departure*. Washington, DC: Council on Higher Education Accreditation. Retrieved from http://www.chea.org/award/StudentLearningOutcomes2001.pdf

Ewell, P., Angelo, T., & Lopez, C. (1999). *Assessment at the millennium: Now what?* Opening plenary at American Association for Higher Education Assessment Forum, June 19, 1999, Denver, CO. Slides available at www.nchems.org/ Millennium.ppt

Gaff, J., Pruitt-Logan, A. S., & Weibl, R. A. (2000). *Building the faculty we need: Colleges and universities working together.* Washington, DC: Association of American Colleges and Universities and the Council of Graduate Schools.

Goldberger, M. L., Maher, B. A., & Flattau, P. E. (1995). *Research-doctorate programs in the United States: Continuity and change.* Washington, DC: National Academy Press. Retrieved from http://www.nap.edu/readingroom/books/researchdoc/

Golde, C. M., & Dore, T. M. (2001). *At cross purposes: What the experiences of doctoral students reveal about doctoral education.* Philadelphia, PA: Pew Charitable Trusts.

Golde, C. M., & Walker, G. E. (Eds.). (2006). *Envisioning the future of doctoral education: Preparing stewards of the discipline* (Carnegie essays on the doctorate). San Francisco: Jossey-Bass.

Gose, B. (2005, February 25). Battling the hype and student stress. *Chronicle of Higher Education, 51*(25), B6. Retrieved from http://chronicle.com/weekly/v51/i25/25b00601.htm

Groen, J., Jakubson, G., Ehrenberg, R., Condie, S., & Yung-Hsu Liu, A. (2005). *Program design and student outcomes in graduate education.* Washington, DC: Bureau of Labor Statistics.

Higher Learning Commission. (2005). *Commission Institute on the Assessment of Student Learning.* Chicago: North Central Association of Colleges and Schools. Retrieved from http://www.ncahigherlearningcommission.org/download/AssessInstituteOvrvw.pdf

James, R., McGinnis, C., & Devlin, M. (2002). *Assessing learning in Australian universities.* Victoria, Australia: Centre for the Study of Higher Education. Retrieved from http://www.cshe.unimelb.edu.au/assessinglearning/about.html

Jaschik, S. (2005, December). New research on graduate education. *Inside Higher Ed.* Retrieved from http://insidehighered.com/news/2005/12/14/grad

Johnstone, D. (2005, July/August). A competency alternative: Western Governors University. *Change, 37*(4), 24–33. Retrieved from http://www.findarticles.com/p/articles/mi_m1254/is_4_37/ai_n15966199 and http://www.wgu.edu/index.asp

Kerlin, S. P. (1995). Pursuit of the Ph.D.: "Survival of the fittest," or is it time for a new approach? *Education Policy Analysis Archives, 3*(16). Retrieved from http://epaa.asu.edu/epaa/v3n16.html

Kerlin, S. P., & Smith Kerlin, B. (1994, October). *Electrifying stories: Virtual research communities in graduate education.* Paper presented at the annual meeting of the Pacific Northwest Association for Institutional Research and Planning Portland, OR. Retrieved from http://kerlins.net/bobbi/research/myresearch/estories.html

Lawrence, S., & Marino, L. (2003). *Update on funding for higher and graduate educa-*

tional institutions. Washington, DC: Foundation Center. Retrieved from http://fdncenter.org/research/trends_analysis/pdf/hiedupdt.pdf

Lederman, D. (2006a, January 12). Is Higher Ed Act renewal dead? *Inside Higher Ed.* Available from http://insidehighered.com/news/2006/01/12/hea

Lederman, D. (2006b, February 15). No college left behind? *Inside Higher Ed.* Retrieved from http://insidehighered.com/news/2006/02/15/testing

Linkon, S. L. (2005, July/August). *How can assessment work for us? Academe, 91*(4). Retrieved from http://www.aaup.org/publications/Academe/2005/05ja/05jalink.htm

Lovitts, B. E. (2001). *Leaving the ivory tower: The causes and consequences of departure from doctoral study.* Lanham, MD: Rowman & Littlefield.

Miller, C. (2006, January 24). Memo from the chairman. *Inside Higher Ed.* Retrieved from http://insidehighered.com/views/2006/01/24/miller

National Center for Educational Statistics. (2005). *National assessment of adult literacy: A first look at the literacy of America's adults in the 21st century.* Washington, DC: Author. Retrieved from http://nces.ed.gov/NAAL/PDF/2006470_1.pdf

National Center for Public Policy and Higher Education. (2004). *Measuring Up 2004: The national report card on higher education.* San Jose, CA: Author.

National Commission on Accountability in Higher Education. (2005). *Accountability for better results: A national imperative for higher education.* Boulder, CO: State Higher Education Executive Officers. Retrieved from http://www.sheeo.org/account/comm-home.htm

National Commission on Excellence in Education. (1983). *A nation at risk: The imperative for educational reform.* Washington, DC: Author. Retrieved from http://www.ed.gov/pubs/NatAtRisk/index.html

National Institute of Education. (1984). *Involvement in learning: Realizing the potential of American higher education.* Washington, DC: U.S. Government Printing Office.

National Opinion Research Center. (2006). *Survey of earned doctorates.* Retrieved from http://www.norc.uchicago.edu/issues/docdata.htm

National Research Council. (2006). *Assessment of research doctorate programs.* Washington, DC: The National Academies. Retrieved from http://www7.nationalacademies.org/resdoc/index.html

Nerad, M., & Cerny, J. (1999, Fall). From rumors to facts: Career outcomes of English Ph.D.s. *CGS Communicator, 32*(7), 1–11. Washington, DC: Council of Graduate Schools. Retrieved from http://www.mla.org/ade/bulletin/N124/124043.htm

Nerad, M., and Cerny, J. (2000). Improving doctoral education: Recommendations from the Ph.D.s Ten Years Later Study. *CGS Communicator, 33*(2), 2.

Nettles, M. T., Perorazio, T. E., & Cole, J. J. K. (2002). *Case studies of five selected state government and three regional accreditation association's higher education assessment policies and practices.* Ann Arbor, MI: National Center for Postsecondary Improvement. Retrieved from http://www.stanford.edu/group/ncpi/unspecified/assessment_states/pdf/Fi nal%20State%20Policy%20Report.pdf

Neumann, R. (2003). *The doctoral education experience: Diversity and complexity.* Canberra, Australia: Department of Education, Science, and Training. Retrieved from http://www.dest.gov.au/NR/rdonlyres/873B3698-F3BA-4D86-869C-0C3 C6DB95658/804/03_12.pdf

New England Association of Schools and Colleges. (2005). *Standards for accreditation.* Bedford, MA: Author. Retrieved from http://www.neasc.org/cihe/stan dards_for_accreditation_2005.pdf

Northwestern Commission on Colleges and Universities. (n.d.). *Accreditation standards: Policy 2.2.* Redmond, WA: Author. Retrieved from http://www.nwccu.org/ Standards%20and%20Policies/Standard%202/Standard%20Two.htm

Nyquist, J. D., & Associates. (1999, May/June). On the road to becoming a professor: The graduate student experience. *Change, 31*(3), 18–27.

Nyquist, J., & Woodford, B. (2000a). *Re-envisioning the PhD: What concerns do we have?* Seattle, WA: Center for Instructional Development and Research, University of Washington. Retrieved from http://www.grad.washington.edu/envision/ PDF/ConcernsBrief.pdf

Nyquist, J., & Woodford, B. (2000b). *Re-envisioning the PhD: Seven propositions from the national conference.* Seattle, WA: Center for Instructional Development and Research, University of Washington. Retrieved from http://www.grad.wash ington.edu/envision/project_resources/metathemes.html

Nyquist, J., & Wulff, D. (1996). *Working effectively with graduate assistants.* Thousand Oaks, CA: Sage.

Office of Postsecondary Education. (2006). Lessons learned from FIPSE projects II: September 1993. Retrieved from http://www.ed.gov/about/offices/list/ope/fipse/ lessons2/assess.html

Ostriker, J. P., & Kuh, C. V. (Eds.). (2003). *Assessing research doctorate programs: A methodology study.* Washington, DC: National Academies Press. Retrieved from http://fermat.nap.edu/books/030909058X/html

Palomba, C. A., & Banta, T. W. (Eds.). (2001). *Assessing student competence in accredited disciplines: Pioneering approaches to assessment in higher education.* Sterling, VA: Stylus.

Pascarella, E. T., & Terenzini, P. T. (1991). *How college affects students.* San Francisco: Jossey-Bass.

Pascarella, E. T., & Terenzini, P. T. (2005). *How college affects students: A third decade of research.* San Francisco: Jossey-Bass.

Pellegrino, J. W., Chudowsky, N., & Glaser, R. (2001). *Knowing what students know: The science and design of educational assessment*. Washington, DC: National Academy Press. Retrieved from http://newton.nap.edu/books/0309072727/html

Peterson, M. W., Einarson, M. K., Augustine, C. H., & Vaughan, D. S. (1999). *Designing student assessment to strengthen institutional performance in doctoral and research institutions*. Stanford, CA: National Center for Postsecondary Improvement.

Proof of learning at college. (2006, February 26). *New York Times*, sec. 4, p. 11.

Sims, L. B., & Syverson, P. D. (n.d.). Utilizing data for effective administration of graduate education. *Higher Education Strategist, 1*(1), 65–94. Retrieved from http://www.cgsnet.org/Default.aspx?tabid=184

Teagle Foundation. (2006). Initiatives in value added assessment. Retrieved from http://www.teaglefoundation.org/learning/outcome.aspx

Trower, C. A., Austin, A. E., & Sorcinelli, M. D. (2001, May). Paradise lost: How the academy converts enthusiastic recruits into early-career doubters. *AAHE Bulletin, 53*(9), 3–6.

U.S. Department of Education. (2002). No child left behind. Washington, DC: Author. Retrieved from http://www.ed.gov/nclb/landing.jhtml

U.S. Department of Education. (2005). *Charter: A national dialogue: The secretary of education's Commission on the Future of Higher Education*. Washington, DC: Author. Retrieved from http://www.ed.gov/about/bdscomm/list/hiedfuture/charter.pdf

Usher, A., & Savino, M. (2006). *A world of differences: A global survey of university league tables*. Toronto, Ontario, Canada: Educational Policy Institute, Canadian Education Report Series. Retrieved from http://www.educationalpolicy.org/pdf/World-of-Difference-200602162.pdf

WestEd. (2004). Preparing future faculty in mathematics and science. *R&D Alert, 6*(2), 4.

Western Association of Schools and Colleges. (1992). *Evidence guide: A guide to using evidence in the accreditation process: A resource to support institutions and evaluation teams*. Alameda, CA: Author. Retrieved from http://www.wascsenior.org/wasc/Doc_Lib/Evidence_Guide.pdf

Wingspread Group on Higher Education (1993). *An American imperative: Higher expectations for higher education*. Retrieved from http://www.johnsonfdn.org/AmericanImperative/puttinglearning.html

Woodrow Wilson National Fellowship Foundation. (2005a). *Diversity and the Ph.D.: A review of efforts to broaden race and ethnicity in U.S. doctoral education*. Princeton, NJ: Author. Retrieved from http://www.woodrow.org/newsroom/News_Releases/report_on_doctoral_innovation.html

Woodrow Wilson National Fellowship Foundation. (2005b). *The responsive Ph.D.: Innovations in U.S. doctoral education.* Princeton, NJ: Author. Retrieved from http:// www.woodrow.org/ newsroom / News_Releases/report_on_doctoral_inno vation.html

Wulff, D. H., Austin, A. E., Nyquist, J. D., & Sprague, J. (2004). The development of graduate students as teaching scholars: A four-year longitudinal study. In D. H. Wulff, A. E. Austin, & Associates (Eds.), *Paths to the professoriate: Strategies for enriching the preparation of future faculty* (pp. 46–73). San Francisco: Jossey-Bass.

Appendix A

Web Sites and Resources Highlighting Doctoral Education Reform Initiatives

Carnegie Foundation for the Advancement of Teaching. (2002). *Overview of doctoral education studies and reports 1990–present.* Stanford, CA: Author. Retrieved from http://www.carnegiefoundation.org/dynamic/downloads/file_1_9.pdf

Center for Innovation and Research in graduate education. (2006). *Publications.* Seattle, WA: Author. Retrieved from http://depts.washington.edu/coe/cirge/html/publications.html

Gaff, J. G. (2002, Summer). The disconnect between graduate education and the realities of faculty work: A review of recent research. *Liberal Education.* Retrieved from http://www.aacu.org/liberaleducation/le-su02/le-su02feature.cfm

National Association of Graduate-Professional Students. (2001). The 2000 national doctoral survey: Recommended practices. Columbia, MO: Author. Retrieved from http://cresmet.asu.edu/nagps/about/recpractices.php

Nyquist, J. D. (2002, November/December). The Ph.D.: A tapestry of change for the 21st century. *Change, 34*(6),13–20. Retrieved from http://www.grad.washing ton.edu/envision/PDF/Change.pdf

Nyquist, J. & Wulff, D. H. (n.d.). *Re-envisioning the Ph.D.: Re-envisioning project resources. Recommendations from national studies on doctoral education.* Seattle, WA: University of Washington. Retrieved from http://depts.washington.edu/en vision/project_resources/national_recommend.html

Phds.org. (2006). Phds.org: Science, math, and engineering career resources. Reforming graduate education. Retrieved from http://www.phds.org/graduate-school-success/reforming-graduate-education/

Re-envisioning the Ph.D. (n.d.). Re-envisioning project resources. Selected bibliography on doctoral education sorted chronologically. Seattle, WA: University of

Washington. Retrieved from http://depts.washington.edu/envision/project_re
sources/biblio_chron.html

Siegel, L. M. (2005). Rethinking the doctorate. Durham, NC: Duke University. Retrieved from http://www.gradschool.duke.edu/about_us/key_articles/rethink
ing_the_doctorate.html

Woodrow Wilson National Fellowship Foundation. (2005). *Responsive Ph.D. resources*. Princeton, NJ: Author. Retrieved from http://www.woodrow.org/respon
sivephd/responsive_phd.html

Wulff, D. H., & Austin, A. E. (Eds.). (2004). *Paths to the professoriate: Strategies for
enriching the preparation of future faculty*. San Francisco: Jossey-Bass.

Major Initiatives:

- career preparation (Golde & Dore, 2001)
- developing teacher-scholars (Wulff, Austin, Nyquist, & Sprague, 2004)
- National Doctoral Survey (Fagen & Suedkamp-Wells)
- retaining students (Lovitts, 2001)
- Ten Years Later study (Nerad, Aanerud, & Cerny)
- strategy reform efforts for the professoriate
- scholarship of teaching and learning (Hutchings & Clark)
- Preparing future faculty program (Pruitt-Logan & Gaff)
- Re-envisioning the Ph.D. initiative (Nyquist & Woodford)
- Responsive Ph.D. initiative (Weisbuch)

Appendix B

Assessment Resources for Doctoral Educators

General Assessment Resources

Achacoso, M. V., & Svinicki, M. D. (Eds.). (2005, Winter). Alternative strategies
for evaluating student learning. *New Directions for Teaching and Learning*, 100.

Allen, M. J. (2004). *Assessing academic programs in higher education*. Bolton, MA:
Anker Publishing.

American Association for Higher Education. (2001). *Enacting a scholarship of assessment: A research agenda*. Washington, DC: American Association for Higher Education Assessment Forum. Retrieved from http://depts.alverno.edu/ere/PDF
%20Files/2001%20June%20AAHE%20Agenda.pdf

Assessment update: Progress, trends, and practices in higher education. A quarterly newsletter. San Francisco: Jossey-Bass.

Astin, A. W. (2002). *Assessment for excellence: The philosophy and practice of assessment
and evaluation in higher education*. Phoenix, AZ: Oryx Press.

Baird, L. L. (Ed.). (1993, Winter). Increasing graduate student retention and degree attainment. *New Directions for Institutional Research*, 80.

Banta, T. W. (Ed.). (2004). *Hallmarks of effective outcomes assessment* (Assessment Update Collections). San Francisco: Jossey-Bass.

Banta, T. W., & Associates. (Eds.). (1993). *Making a difference: Outcomes of a decade of assessment in higher education*. San Francisco: Jossey-Bass.

Banta, T. W., Lund, J. P., Black, K. E, & Oblander, F. W. (1996). *Assessment in practice: Putting principles to work on college campuses*. San Francisco: Jossey-Bass.

Bilder, A. E. C., & Clifton F. (1996). Challenges in assessing outcomes in graduate and professional education. *New Directions for Institutional Research*, *92*, 5–15.

Boyer Commission on Educating Undergraduates in the Research University. (1998). *Reinventing undergraduate education: A blueprint for America's research universities*. Retrieved from http://naples.cc.sunysb.edu/Pres/boyer.nsf/

Burke, J. C., & Associates. (Eds.). (2005). *Achieving accountability in higher education*. San Francisco: Jossey-Bass.

Gardiner, L. F., Anderson, C., & Cambridge, B. L. (Eds.). (1997). *Learning through assessment: A resource guide for higher education*. Washington, DC: American Association for Higher Education.

Haworth, J. G. (Ed.). Assessing graduate and professional education: Current realities, future prospects. *New Directions for Institutional Research*, 92.

Huba, M., & Fried, J. (2000). *Learner-centered assessment on college campuses. Shifting the focus from teaching to learning*. Needham Heights, MA: Allyn & Bacon.

Maki, P. (2002a). Developing an assessment plan to learn about student learning. *Journal of Academic Librarianship*, *28*(1), 8–13. Retrieved from http://www.usc.edu/programs/cet/private/pdfs/Develop_Learning_Plan.pdf

Maki, P. (2002b). Moving from paperwork to pedagogy: Channeling intellectual curiosity into a commitment to assessment. *AAHE Bulletin*, *54*(9), 3–5. Retrieved from http://www.aacsb.edu/resource_centers/assessment/Maki-Reprint.asp

Maki, P. (2004). *Assessing for learning: Building a sustainable commitment across the institution*. Sterling, VA: Stylus.

Mentkowski, M., Astin, A. W., Ewell, P. T., & Moran, E. T. (Eds.). (1991). *Catching theory up with practice: Conceptual frameworks for assessment*. Washington, DC: American Association for Higher Education Assessment Forum. Retrieved from http://eric.ed.gov/ERICDocs/data/ericdocs2/content_storage_01/0000000b/80/24/b4/bo.pdf

Nichols, J. O., & Nichols, K. W. (1995). *The departmental guide and record book for student learning outcomes assessment and institutional effectiveness*. Flemington, NJ: Agathon Press.

Palomba, C. A., & Banta, T. W. (1999). *Assessment essentials: Planning, implementing, and improving assessment in higher education*. San Francisco: Jossey-Bass.

Palomba, C. A., & Banta, T. W. (Eds.) (2001). *Assessing student competence in accredited disciplines: Pioneering approaches to assessment in higher education.* Sterling, VA: Stylus.

Suskie, L. (Ed.). (2001). *Assessment to promote deep learning: Insight from AAHE's 2000 and 1999 assessment conferences.* Washington, DC: American Association for Higher Education.

Suskie, L. (2004). *Assessing student learning: A common sense guide.* Bolton, MA: Anker Publishing.

Upcraft, M. L., & Schuh, J. H. (1996). *Assessment in student affairs: A guide for practitioners.* San Francisco: Jossey-Bass.

Walvoord, B. (2004). *Assessment clear and simple: A practical guide for institutions, departments, and general education.* San Francisco: Jossey-Bass.

How-To Assessment Guides

Angelo, T., & Cross, K. P. (1993). *Classroom assessment techniques: A handbook for faculty.* San Francisco: Jossey-Bass.

Pfatteicher, S. K. A., Bowcock, D., & Kushner, J. (1998). *Program assessment tool kit: A guide to conducting interviews and surveys.* Madison: University of Wisconsin, Learning through Evaluation, Adaptation, and Dissemination (LEAD). Retrieved from http://homepages.cae.wisc.edu/~lead/pages/products/toolkit.pdf

Stassen, M. L. A., Doherty, K., & Poe, M. (2001). *Program-based review and assessment: Tools and techniques for program improvement.* Amherst: University of Massachusetts: Office of Academic Planning and Assessment. Retrieved from http://www.umass.edu/oapa/oapa/publications/online_handbooks/program_based.pdf

University of Wisconsin. (2000). *Using assessment for academic program improvement.* Madison: University of Wisconsin Office of the Provost and Vice Chancellor of Academic Affairs. Retrieved from http://www.provost.wisc.edu/assessment/manual/

Accreditation-Related Assessment Resources

Council of Regional Accrediting Agencies. (2003). *Regional accreditation and student learning: A bibliography.* Philadelphia, PA: Middle States Commission on Higher Education. Retrieved from http://www.msache.org/msache/content/pdf_files/Regnlbib.pdf

Lopez, C. L. (1999). *A decade of assessing student learning: What we have learned; what's next?* Chicago: North Central Association of Colleges and Schools. Retrieved from http://www.ncahigherlearningcommission.org/AnnualMeeting/archive/ASSESS10.pdf

Middle States Association of Colleges and Schools. (1996). *Framework for outcomes assessment*. Philadelphia, PA: Middle States Commission on Higher Education. Retrieved from http://autoestudio.uprrp.edu/publicacionspdf/msafram.pdf

Middle States Association of Colleges and Schools. (2002). *Best practices in outcomes assessment*. Philadelphia, PA: Middle States Commission on Higher Education. Retrieved from http://www.msache.org/msache/content/pdf_files/best-oa.pdf

Middle States Association of Colleges and Schools. (2005). *Assessing student learning and institutional effectiveness: Understanding Middle States' expectations*. Philadelphia, PA: Middle States Commission on Higher Education. Retrieved from http://www.msche.org/publications/Assessment_Expectations051222081842.pdf

Ratcliff, J. L., Lubinescu, E. S., & Gaffney, M. A. (Eds.). (2001). How Accreditation influences assessment. *New Directions for Higher Education*, 113.

Western Association of Schools and Colleges. (2002). *Evidence guide: A guide to using evidence in the accreditation process: A resource to support institutions and evaluation teams*. Akameda, CA: Author. Retrieved from http://www.wascsenior.org/wasc/Doc_Lib/Evidence_Guide.pdf

National Funding Organization Assessment Resources

Frechtling, J. (Ed.). (2002). *The 2002 user-friendly handbook for project evaluation*. Arlington, VA: National Science Foundation, Division of Research, Evaluation, and Communication. Retrieved from http://www.nsf.gov/pubs/2002/nsf02057/start.htm

Frechtling, J., & Sharp, L. (Eds.). (1997). *User-friendly handbook for mixed-method evaluation*. Arlington, VA: National Science Foundation, Directorate for Education and Human Resources, Division of Research, Evaluation, and Communication. Retrieved from http://www.ehr.nsf.gov/EHR/REC/pubs/NSF97-153/START.HTM

National Science Foundation. *OERL: Online Evaluation Resource Library*. Retrieved from http://www.oerl.sri.com/home.html

W. K. Kellogg Foundation. (1998). *Evaluation handbook*. Battle Creek, MI: Author. Retrieved from http://www.wkkf.org/pubs/Tools/Evaluation/Pub770.pdf

Internet Assessment Resource Compilations

American University: Selected Bibliography of Graduate Student and Program Assessment: http://www.american.edu/academic.depts/provost/oir/grad_bibliography.htm

Clemson University Institutional Effectiveness and Assessment Web site: http://assessment.clemson.edu/links/arbiblo.htm

North Carolina State University Planning and Analysis Web site: http://www2.acs.ncsu.edu/UPA/assmt/resource.htm

2

THE CHALLENGES OF DOCTORAL PROGRAM ASSESSMENT

Lessons from the Carnegie Initiative on the Doctorate

Chris M. Golde, Laura Jones, Andrea Conklin Bueschel, and George E. Walker

M any parties have a vested interest in the evaluation of doctoral programs, and the stakes are high. Prospective graduate students want to know where they can get the "best" education. Prospective faculty members want to be affiliated with a "high quality" program. Deans and department chairs want to improve the quality of programs to attract the "best and brightest" students and faculty in a time when international competition is stiffening. Judgments about program quality affect resource allocation within the university and may also affect grant funding and other external resource decisions. Unfortunately, important decisions about doctoral-level programs are often based on informal, anecdotal appraisals. Formal, systematic, evidence-based assessment of the quality of a doctoral program is an important challenge for universities.

Beginning with an overview of four major approaches currently used to assess program quality, including a discussion of their limitations, we then offer an alternate assessment strategy that we have developed for departments participating in the Carnegie Initiative on the Doctorate (CID). This five-year project, coordinated by the Carnegie Foundation for the Advancement of Teaching, is designed to help improve doctoral programs by challenging departments to be more reflective about how well they create the next generation of scholars. This chapter describes and advocates a more holistic approach to assessment: the regular self-examination of the doctoral program by faculty and students with the aim of continual refinement to realize a mutually agreed-upon vision. Sustained self-examination leading to action is unusual and difficult, so this chapter also discusses five challenges to such activities. We conclude the chapter with the case study of a department that has undertaken this process successfully.

Overview of Currently Used Program Assessments

National Rankings

The two best-known assessments of research doctoral programs focus almost exclusively on the "quality" of the faculty, a reputational measure based on the perceptions of other faculty members. Every year an assessment of graduate programs in the United States is conducted by *U.S.News & World Report*, leading to a ranking of programs by discipline. In arts and sciences Ph.D. programs, the rankings are solely based on ratings on a five-point scale of "program quality," completed by deans, program directors, and senior faculty (Morse & Flanigan, 2005).

A much more thorough and comprehensive assessment of doctoral programs in the United States is the periodic review conducted by the National Research Council (NRC; Goldberger, Maher, & Flattau, 1995). The resulting ranking of departments by discipline is used extensively by faculty members and administrators across the country. In the 1982 and 1995 assessments, the quantitative measures included faculty research productivity and awards garnered. Equally important were reputational ratings of the scholarly quality of program faculty and of program effectiveness, as determined by a large survey of graduate faculty.

Although these rankings measure some important characteristics of the faculty who are critically important contributors to doctoral education, reputational rankings certainly do not comprehensively assess the quality of the educational program. As the NRC book itself points out, there are limitations to reputational measures:

> The reputational rating of a program is related to the level of involvement of faculty in research and scholarly activities. Reputational ratings do not tell us how well the program is structured, whether it offers a nurturing

environment for students, or if the job placement experiences of its graduates are satisfactory. . . . Reputational standing does not take into account other elements in the "quality of faculty performance," such as contributions to teaching of graduate and undergraduate students or contributions to the welfare of the departments, the institution, or the larger academic community. (Goldberger et al., 1995, pp. 22–23)

Assessment of Students

A second strategy for assessing doctoral programs focuses on students' experiences and achievements. At the university or department level, these assessments typically look at the career trajectories of alumni. "Graduates of our program go on to have stellar careers!" is the message on many departmental Web sites that then list the names of alumni currently holding faculty positions. There are two implications of this kind of message: The experiences students have in graduate school are responsible for their future success, and a faculty position is the most desirable outcome of graduate studies. We all recognize, of course, that "better" programs attract more talented and better prepared students, resulting in "more successful" alumni. A positive reputation becomes a self-fulfilling prophecy.

It would be more useful, but is much more difficult, to measure the growth and development of students during the doctoral program. The department that provides great added value surely does an outstanding job of educating students. No national studies or evaluations of this type exist; instead, evaluations typically rely on student self-assessments, usually at a single point in time. Two well-known evaluations of student development are both one-time surveys. The Survey of Doctoral Education and Career Preparation asked students to assess the extent to which the program developed their skills in a number of areas, particularly pinpointing perceived gaps in preparation for teaching and research (Golde & Dore, 2001). The National Association of Graduate and Professional Students survey (2001) provided department-level analyses of program effectiveness. Both surveys were limited because they did not assess the same students at two points in time and because they relied on students' self-assessments of their preparation. Nevertheless, they provided data across institutions and disciplines that were previously unavailable.

One of the only longitudinal studies of graduate student development was conducted by Jody Nyquist and her colleagues (Nyquist et al., 1999).

This research team asked graduate students to describe with words or pictures their "personal journey as a graduate student" at several points during their doctoral careers. The students' responses revealed a growing understanding of the norms and values of academe, and all students had an account of their efforts to demystify the values and align those values with their own. Although the purpose of the study was not program assessment, the project proved valuable in making explicit students' confusion about graduate education and their perception that there are few supports to help them on their path. The study also piloted an innovative assessment tool, asking students to depict their journey with drawings and stories, examples of which are included in the article.

Quantitative Measures

A third strategy for program assessment uses quantitative measures as proxies for the effectiveness of a program as a whole. The two most widely collected and reported measures are graduation/attrition rates and average time to degree. Even if these data are accurate (a point we will return to in a moment), they are often difficult to interpret because they are time-lagged. Doctoral education is a lengthy process: it can take a dozen years for all members of a cohort to conclude their education—either via graduation or attrition. Over time, departmental requirements and staff members change, making it difficult to impute causality between practices and outcomes. There are other measures—time through qualifying exams, time to attrition, completion rates for the first two years—that can be captured in a briefer period, but are less commonly used in program assessment. Even if these data are collected, drawing meaningful statistical inferences from a limited group of students is difficult. With a small number of students, variation can be very wide, making it difficult to make inferences about a program's effects. The small size of a cohort of students hampers data analysis in all but the largest programs. There are statistical techniques (like rolling averages) that can be adopted for small samples, but these can require a greater level of computational savvy to generate.

Many university graduate schools, in partnership with registrars and offices of institutional research, have begun to make a concerted effort to monitor and consistently compute completion and time to degree data. However, when the CID asked participating departments to provide data on enrollment, time to degree, attrition and graduation rates—data we assumed were accessible—this request presented a considerable challenge to department staff. The reality is that these data are simply not readily available to most faculty members.

Career placement data are also commonly collected and reported. But they too suffer from problems of time lag and small n. Career placement data are delayed as program graduates progress through postdoctoral, instructor, and other temporary positions. Moreover, these data are rarely collected by a central university office. Until universities commit resources to units such as the university development and alumni affairs office, career planning and placement centers, or graduate schools to track graduate students after they leave the university, departmental staff and faculty are the only ones in the position to collect this information. When a willing faculty member or staff member tries to track down alumni, it can be very difficult, particularly if there has been no consistent effort to do so in the past.

Even when such data are consistently collected and widely available, they only serve as gross indicators of program effectiveness. Unfortunately, they are not calibrated with shared understanding of what reasonable time to degree figures, attrition rates, and placement patterns should be. They cannot provide strong indicators of the effect of graduate programs on their students' intellectual development or career success.

External Review Committees

A fourth common strategy for program-level assessment is scheduling an external review. External reviews are often conducted at the departmental level, usually at the request of the department chair or a dean. At some institutions, external reviews of each doctoral-granting department are conducted every five or ten years. The external review team works like an institutional accreditation body: conducting a site visit, reviewing data, interviewing key players, and writing a report. Arguably, a holistic picture of the effectiveness of the doctoral program can be created by a team of experienced faculty from outside that collects a variety of evidence from a wide range of sources.

Unfortunately, these evaluations are all too often cases of "high stakes—low yield" assessments: the results affect critical resources without providing suggestions that can lead to program improvement. Members of these teams are often nominated by the department, including faculty from prestigious universities whose names are bound to impress and who understand the system. Some data, only indirectly related to the educational quality of the program—such as number of grants, publications, and faculty awards—are sent in advance. During the site visit the team will meet with faculty and students who are fully aware of the high stakes and have been well briefed on how to describe the department positively. Because review team members want to help the discipline and their colleagues, the resulting report will usually stress how increased resources will lead to a noticeable improvement of the department's prestige and effectiveness. All too often, these reports seem limited, documenting the positive and obscuring real problems. Even if a frank verbal report is offered to the chair, a candid, written report to the dean is viewed as too risky, likely to result in adverse consequences befalling the department.

One unintended consequence of these well-intentioned efforts to be positive is that the department loses an opportunity to learn about itself. Every department, however successful, has things to learn from friendly critics with an outside perspective. Another consequence is that faculty members may become cynical and conclude that evaluations are largely time-consuming, meaningless exercises.

To summarize, rigorous, thorough, and holistic reviews of doctoral programs are uncommon. There may be isolated examples of comprehensive evaluations of departments, but in most cases departments have not had opportunities to engage in the type of assessment that can provide feedback that is genuinely valuable for improving the overall quality of a doctoral program.

A Different Approach to Assessment

While there may be a role for external review as part of an assessment tool kit at the department level, we argue that there is more value in a department assessing the quality of its own doctoral program regularly and continuously, particularly when done in reference to a clearly agreed-upon vision for the program and its students. This process is not a habit of most departments. Internal reviews of the doctoral program typically only result from crisis or administrative fiat. However, much as reflective teachers continuously collect evidence and evaluate the effectiveness of their teaching (with the goal of improving student learning), it behooves a doctoral program to regularly assess the effectiveness of its work in preparing the next generation of scholars and researchers. Building the collective habits of mind required for continuous self-reflective evaluation is not easy, but it is possible, and it is a strategy that is likely to ensure high program quality over the long term.

The purpose of the Carnegie Initiative on the Doctorate was and is to improve North American doctoral education at the departmental level—the center of action for doctoral education. To do that, we provided an organizing idea: the purpose of doctoral education is to develop students as "stewards of the discipline." Our strategy for doing so was to issue an Invitation for Participation to doctoral-granting departments in six disciplines: chemistry, education, English, history, mathematics, and neuroscience. In all, we selected 84 doctoral-granting departments or programs to join the CID (we called them participating departments). All told, 44 universities are represented. The most concentrated interactions between the participating departments and the Carnegie Foundation CID staff were between January 2003 and December 2005, although the work in many departments continues, sometimes formally under the name of Carnegie or the CID.

Participating departments received no money, but rather the Foundation provided intellectual grist for the mill; feedback, support, and encouragement; annual convenings at the Foundation; and a network of colleagues to engage in a process of self-reflection and deliberation leading to action. The project was relatively loosely structured; departments were *not* told how to design their local process, which aspects of their doctoral program to focus on, what particular practices they ought to implement, or what kind of evidence they ought to collect. Instead, we asked participating departments to identify a leadership team of faculty and students. Leadership teams were expected to deliberate seriously, suggest and implement appropriate changes in the program, and to assess their efforts. Accountability did not come from reporting to the Foundation out of a fear of losing money, but rather from a spirit of shared inquiry. Participating departments continue to share the vision of developing students as stewards of their discipline; they believe that doctoral education is important and could be more effective. They are committed to sharing and learning from their peers. (For more information on the Carnegie Initiative on the Doctorate see www.carnegiefoundation.org/cid.)

While departments are primarily concerned with improving the situation locally, the Foundation is interested in knowledge and field building. These departments serve as "existence proofs," and provide models for other departments within their discipline and their universities. Ultimately, both the process of the CID and effective practices will be shared widely, with the intention of spreading them within and across disciplines.

During the three years in which the Foundation staff worked most closely with participating departments, we persistently encouraged faculty and students to ask and answer three sets of fundamental questions:

1. What is the *purpose* of the doctoral program? What does it mean to develop students as stewards of the discipline? What are the desired outcomes of the program?
2. What is the *rationale and educational purpose of each element* of the doctoral program? Which elements of the program should be retained and affirmed? Which elements could usefully be changed or eliminated?
3. How do you know? What *evidence* aids in answering those questions? What evidence can be collected to determine whether changes serve the desired outcomes?

Although this process sounds simple, at first, department members found it difficult to suspend skepticism about the value of taking time to discuss things taken for granted. Over time, however, this deliberative process proved liberating and intellectually exciting. In some cases, this process led to incremental changes, such as adding students to departmental committees and instituting optional workshops. In others, wholesale revisions were begun, such as adding or dropping required courses. In some departments, small changes led to larger questions, such as debating the purpose and structure of the qualifying exams; more serious deliberations sometimes followed initial reforms. In all cases participating departments took advantage of annual convenings at the Carnegie Foundation to share their work, including their successes and setbacks, with other departments in a spirit of candor and the camaraderie of a shared mission. At the same time, they used the ideas and experiences of others to inform their own work. Assessment and evidence were a leitmotif that ran through departments' work. Rather than seeing data collection as something imposed by administrators whose motives were suspect, departments began to create and collect their own evidence, motivated by the questions they wanted to answer. They turned their research lenses and skills onto themselves.

The CID strongly advocates that departments take a holistic approach, assessing their performance in doctoral education against their stated goals and purposes. This approach requires interpreting many assessments, of specific elements of the doctoral program itself and of individual students, and combining the resulting information into a holistic package. Deriving meaning—engaging in analysis and interpretation—requires the application of judgment and is best undertaken collectively.

This process is not perfect, of course. To some, it seems that only modest changes have been proposed, and only a few have been implemented. And it is true that the necessary assessment of these changes has generally not yet occurred; data collection over a period of years will be required to achieve reliable findings. However, we believe that the changed habits of mind are, in fact, revolutionary. In particular, it is important to recognize that many doctoral students have been involved with this process. In most departments students were fully participating members of the CID leadership team. And in many cases students took responsibility for developing and implementing new elements of the doctoral program. Consequently, those who become graduate faculty members themselves will take with them a more reflective approach to the conduct of doctoral education.

Nor was this process smooth. In the next section of this chapter, we discuss the challenges that departments faced in assessing their own effectiveness. Because the participating departments included willing participants, and each department had a team of faculty and students committed to the process (rather than the traditional, marginalized solo do-gooder), they avoided many of the problems described earlier. The focus on faculty reputation as a proxy for program quality, or on simplistic quantitative measures such as time to degree, or on one-shot review committees was avoided by placing the focus on student development and on involvement of all of the departments' members.

This structure allowed us to see a different category of problems and obstacles, most of them resulting from narrow and habitual thinking. Several of these challenges derived from a commonly held belief that it is not sufficiently important for an individual or department to spend serious time thinking critically about the doctoral program. These challenges are not easily solved, but must be confronted with good humor and persistence.

Challenges for Holistic Departmental Assessments

Based on our work with the departments participating in the CID, we know that holistic assessment at the departmental level is a daunting enterprise.

Success depends on recognizing and surmounting a series of challenges. We have identified five that recurred in the participating departments:

1. defining program goals
2. unfamiliarity with social science research techniques
3. attitudes about assessment
4. developing the will to change
5. the culture of privacy

These challenges are significant and in many cases are not amenable to easy solutions. Nevertheless, they must be confronted, both by acknowledging them and by thinking creatively about how to change negative attitudes, if programs are to change and improve. After we describe each challenge, we suggest some strategies for addressing it.

Defining Doctoral Program Goals

It is challenging to articulate and then agree upon clear goals for a doctoral program. For some faculty and students the task of "creating a mission statement with explicit goals" smacks of recent accountability movements in education that are perceived as efforts to curb academic autonomy. Even when undertaken with an open mind, articulating goals can rapidly degenerate into meaningless text crafting, resulting in bland clichés. "The goal of our department is to help all students reach their potential as future researchers and scholars" is an example of a worthy, but overly general, goal.

Some participating departments resisted engaging in this discussion because they believed that broad deliberation would lead to conflicts, reopening old wounds and causing damage to the department. Departmental leaders told us, "There are some differences it is better not to discuss." We argue that it may be important in this process for a department simply to say, "We cannot discuss who we are, what we do well, and why we do it." In some cases, the very act of making the out-of-bounds areas explicit with a statement like this one can shock enough faculty members that the department ultimately becomes unstuck.

It is important to find new ways to enter the conversation about the mission and goals of the doctoral program. One promising strategy for defining more specific purposes of a graduate program is to ask faculty and students to engage in the exercise of constructing an image of a prototypical Ph.D. recipient—either a description of the typical current graduate or a prospective vision of a desired graduate. Whether constructed individually or in small groups, this process creates more specific statements to stimulate discussion by the department as a whole. Sidebar 2.1 is an exercise to create a profile of the Ph.D. recipient from a particular program.

Activities like this one allowed the University of Nebraska mathematics department to agree upon a list of eight characteristics that define a Ph.D. holder in mathematics. These are listed in sidebar 2.2. The department also developed a more explicit description of the anticipated career outcomes for Ph.D. recipients from the department. The document including both lists was approved by the department's CID committee and was circulated to all faculty and graduate students for discussion. The department chair, John Meakin, reports, "There is strong support for the document in our department, although we have not formally 'adopted' it as a departmental document. We may do so in the future, but we are in a sense experimenting with it right now" (personal communication, 2005). All incoming graduate students are given a copy during orientation with the understanding that their first homework assignment is to read and critique the document. The chair gives them a liberal five years to complete this assignment, but says he will be asking for progress reports at the end of each semester when he meets with graduate students. Meakin also said that he routinely conducts exit interviews with graduate students who are leaving the program, whether they are graduating with a Ph.D. or a master's degree, or leaving for any reason. He plans to ask them "whether we are delivering the kind of educational experience that the document promises." Rather than being yet another artifact that gets filed away, the department has created a document that is a touchstone for students and faculty against which students' expectations, experiences, and progress can be measured.

Unfamiliarity with Social Science Research Techniques

A second challenge is that faculty members and graduate students may be skeptical of the value of educational research, in particular, and social science techniques more generally. Survey and other quantitative data are sometimes greeted with skepticism. Qualitative techniques, such as interviews, focus groups, and analysis of open-ended survey questions are sometimes dismissed as "anecdotal evidence." Educational research is conducted in real-life settings in which controlled experiments with side-by-side comparison groups are often not possible. In addition to the elements being studied, there are

SIDEBAR 2.1.
Profile of a Ph.D. Recipient

The purpose of this exercise is to focus on the goals and purposes that a doctoral program serves. The structure and content of the doctoral program—all of the elements and experiences that are included in it—should serve ends that department members have agreed upon and that they have clearly communicated to students. The process of writing goals for the Ph.D. program may suggest areas to expand, refine, or initiate.

Write a description of a prototypical doctoral recipient from the department—either a typical *current* graduate or a *desired* graduate:

1. What skills, knowledge, and habits of minds does the candidate possess upon graduation?
2. What career is the graduate entering?
3. How has the graduate changed over the course of her studies in the program?

Answering these three questions in detail might be aided by considering these areas:

- the breadth and depth of content knowledge expected of a Ph.D. graduate in the discipline and how a Ph.D. recipient might be expected to be able to use that knowledge
- the scholarly and research skills a Ph.D. recipient will have mastered, including the ability to recognize and generate interesting and tractable questions, to evaluate the work of others, to employ appropriate techniques, to analyze evidence and make an argument, and to present conclusions to others in written and oral forms
- the ability to teach effectively in various settings
- familiarity with and the appropriate preparation for the breadth of career opportunities in the discipline
- experience collaborating with others within the discipline and in other associated disciplines
- familiarity with expected professional behavior, ability to balance individual intellectual behavior and responsibility to the discipline and to society as a whole, and more generally the habits of mind for making professional, ethical decisions

---

SIDEBAR 2.2.
Purpose of the Doctorate in Mathematics
Department of Mathematics, University of Nebraska-Lincoln

The purpose of doctoral education in mathematics is to produce the next generation of mathematicians, scholars who will maintain the integrity and vitality of the discipline. Doctoral graduates in mathematics should become *stewards of the discipline*, people who are entrusted with advancing mathematical knowledge, with preserving and developing the mathematical literature, with communicating mathematical knowledge to others, and with understanding and advancing the role of mathematics in society.

A doctoral graduate in mathematics should possess

- a broad knowledge of the mathematical literature, its historical development, and how diverse parts of mathematics relate to each other
- a general understanding of the centrality of mathematics in society, the impact that mathematics has in many fields of human endeavor, and the impact that other disciplines have on mathematics
- a deep knowledge of some area of mathematics, and have made a significant contribution to the literature in that area
- an understanding of and commitment to the ethical principles that underlie professional work in the discipline of mathematics
- a sense of membership in the community of current and former mathematical scholars, and an understanding of the historical roots of this community
- a commitment to the profession, engaging in professional service, both within the graduate's immediate community, and within the broader community of mathematical scholars
- the ability to communicate the beauty and power of mathematical ideas to audiences as diverse as the general public and experts in the graduate's area
- the ability to help others learn to combine creativity and imagination with the rigor, logic, and precision of mathematics

---

uncontrollable, confounding variables. Consequently, the standards of data validity and reliability are quite different from those of many science fields. Drawing inferences from a small response rate on a survey is something many scientists are dubious about. Humanities scholars, on the other hand, may not be comfortable with studying numerical data about their programs. Humanists may be particularly attuned to the nuance of phrasing in a survey question and thus distrust the results.

Patience and imagination are allies in addressing this challenge. There is sufficient variety in data collection methods and instruments—as described in other chapters in this book—to allow departments to choose methods that provide reasonably familiar forms of evidence. For example, a survey of students, faculty, or alumni can contain open-ended text response items for disciplines whose scholarship is centered on texts, or can include a rigorous sampling and reporting procedures for disciplines more focused on quantitative analysis. In any case, use of more than one approach to collect evidence ("triangulation using mixed methods," to use educational jargon) is palatable and credible to more people. Using multiple methods to answer questions also provides a fuller picture that increases the reliability of the conclusions drawn. (The case of the University of Pittsburgh Department of English described later in this chapter is an example.) Over time, faculty members, regardless of their discipline, come to recognize that data provide ways to understand the strengths and shortcomings of the department. Matters that do not yield to precise measurement are still worth discussing; imprecise data can still be useful, if only to provoke discussion and spur further inquiry. Once a problem is understood, it is possible to bring judgment to bear in developing solutions.

Relatedly, many faculty members and graduate students are not familiar with using these research techniques themselves. Even with goodwill and interest in conducting social science—and many departments want us to gather information from students, alumni, and faculty—few faculty or graduate students have ever designed a survey or facilitated a focus group. In an effort to address this challenge, some of our CID programs have successfully consulted their campus's School of Education or Teaching and Learning Center for assistance in data collection design and data analysis. Many of the CID departments worked with Carnegie staff to refine the survey instruments they administered to students, faculty, and alumni. Working with knowledgeable but disinterested others is also useful in overcoming issues of bias in research design, a serious issue in self-assessment.

Attitudes about Assessment

External departmental reviews of the type described earlier not only are viewed by many as meaningless activities, but they also may have taught faculty members some unfortunate lessons: reviews are an exercise that can be gamed, reviews are done to please others, rhetorical platitudes are appropriate, reviews are risky endeavors since resources can be lost to others who play the game more successfully, and improvements are only motivated by the competition for resources. All of these lessons, of course, harden faculty members' attitudes against any kind of departmental review, program evaluation, or anything including the word "assessment," and, thus, represent a third challenge.

Participating departments that have invested time in generating, analyzing, and sharing data about the department to serve their own purposes (rather than an externally imposed review) have been able to make progress with their faculty. Attitudes can be changed by providing examples of how to use data about the department. Hypothetically, a faculty member might observe to a colleague that three women have left the doctoral program in the past year. When someone follows up that casual observation with questions about attrition patterns, an informal assessment has begun, and a more natural transition to formal assessment can follow. More formally, a well-written report prepared by students presented to the faculty can help to move a conversation about the doctoral program forward. A well-facilitated departmentwide town hall meeting can be a setting to present and discuss the meaning of data about the department. It is critical for faculty members to recognize that improvement is in their own interest, as well as the interest of their department and their students.

We believe there is great potential in the practice of peer review; however, new forms may need to emerge that transcend the superficiality that plagues the common convention. In the CID we have found that departments can engage in honest criticism and sincere support of the reform efforts of programs they compete with. We paired departments attending convenings as "Friendly Critics." By spending a few hours discussing their programs and challenges in detail with one another, program representatives received from their Friendly Critics targeted feedback and ideas about how to be persuasive upon their return to campus. This feedback and advice is helpful because it is sensitive to the local context and politics. The reciprocal nature of this process diffuses feelings of being evaluated. We were told that this strategy, at least in the context of a Foundation-sponsored convening, was helpful.

Using competitive peers as friendly critics and creating a visiting committee of alumni are two examples of the "low stakes–high yield" approach to assessment. Whether within a single department or across departmental boundaries, it is important to create a process that is informal, values based, inclusive, data driven, and conducted with colleagues in a way that minimizes defensiveness. Conversations conducted in a spirit of openness create opportunities to discuss problems rationally. In the low stakes–high yield environment problems can be aired and appropriate solutions considered.

Developing the Will to Change

A fourth challenge programs face is developing the will to make necessary changes. The first step toward addressing this challenge is making assessment a priority for departments and already overworked faculty, staff, and students. Even if department members demonstrate interest and willingness, they know that time spent on this kind of work is not often rewarded. In the existing institutional structure, service—especially service that may expose problems in a program—is unlikely to be given support or resources for those engaged in it. The political challenges of making change are daunting, and the participatory democracy that is the hallmark of academic decision making is often discouragingly slow and incremental.

Departments participating in the CID had the advantage of the Carnegie name (even without monetary resources) to provide prestige, momentum, and urgency to the deliberative process. Motivation to act is an area where the university administration must show leadership in creating new incentives and rewards for departments that demonstrate commitment to rigorous review and renewal of their graduate curriculum and programs. Publicizing exemplary efforts to trustees and other faculty and students is one important and inexpensive step administrators can take to encourage such labor-intensive work.

Departmental leadership and institutional support are critical in this regard. A department chair and director of graduate studies, working in tandem toward the goal of improving the doctoral program, can set a tone that invites others to join this enterprise. One CID department chair described the formula for a successful leadership team as

> a group of energetic associate professors, who now have the confidence and desire to improve the department, augmented by senior faculty with institutional memory and clout, and assistant professors and students with energy and interesting ideas. (personal communication, March 2004)

In addition, graduate student leadership is an important force for change. Graduate students have a vested interest in improving not only their own experiences, but also the lot of those who follow after them. Importantly, they are not wedded to or limited by present paradigms. Alexis Jeannotte, a neuroscience student at Georgetown University reporting on the program's work in 2004–05, said, "Our committee has the most energy from students. Faculty support student ideas. Students no longer see themselves as 'the taught.' Now faculty members see us as people with something to offer."

The Culture of Privacy

The fifth and final challenge to implementing reflective and holistic changes in doctoral programs is the habits of individualism and autonomy that pervade many practices in doctoral education. The air of mystery that shrouds the rationale and structures of the doctoral program are akin to the culture of privacy accorded to teaching, justified by appeals to academic freedom, autonomy, and tradition. Most doctoral programs lack transparency. Students come to believe that the rationales for educational practices are being deliberately withheld from them. Imagine their surprise when they learn, for example, that most faculty members cannot explain why the qualifying exams are structured the way they are. It is considered impolite and inappropriate to ask questions such as, "Why do we do it this way?" and "Is there a better way?" This lack of transparency can help create an us-versus-them mentality between students and faculty, rather than a group of junior and senior colleagues working together as part of a robust intellectual community.

There are challenges that go beyond a lack of transparency in the program. It may be difficult to hold a meaningful conversation about topics that have systemic roots and seem intractable at the department level. Shared problems like growing time to degree, recruitment of underrepresented minority student groups to graduate study, insufficient student finances, and a changed job market, may seem unsolvable and thus not worth discussion. However, avoiding these issues may inadvertently result in a disengaged social and intellectual climate in a department.

During our CID convenings, we deliberately create a safe space with clear norms. One cardinal rule imposed on the two- or three-member team of faculty and students is, "During this convening, you *are* the department." This rule means that concerns about how to deal with recalcitrant faculty members or mysterious bureaucratic processes can be suspended in favor of creative thinking and openness to new ideas. Another rule is that participants must discuss everything—successes and obstacles, exemplary elements and troublesome requirements—with equal candor. They must be willing to accept feedback and probing questions from colleagues in other departments, as well as Carnegie staff and other observers. And, faculty must listen to students. The model of the Gordon Research Conferences was in our mind as we developed a framework for convenings (Gordon Research Conferences, n.d.). We stress that an atmosphere of trust must be maintained. Our experience demonstrates that it is possible to facilitate honest discussion of internal program issues with your closest academic competitors in an atmosphere of trust and anticipated mutual benefit. Our participants are also motivated to participate in this semipublic exposure of their program's weaknesses by a commitment to the advancement of their discipline as a whole.

Of course, some faculty members will continue to resist self-examination. Some argue that looking carefully at their Ph.D. program, which seems to them to be working fine, is not a good use of their time. Others will argue that examining and exposing the program's weaknesses will harm the department's reputation and adversely affect recruitment of top faculty and students. And even once genuine discussions begin, the absence of documentation of promising practices for doctoral education means that there's often a high incidence of "reinvention." One of the important contributions of the CID has been the opportunity to share well-established practices among departments in the same discipline. It can be occasionally dismaying to recognize that seemingly obvious strategies (a panel of alumni discussing nonacademic careers, a peer mentoring program to help first-year students make a smooth transition into the department, an annual review of each student's progress) are not widespread. Instituting practices that have been successful in other departments is a simple strategy for improving practice over all. Practices that are routine in some disciplines, such as journal clubs or weekly research group meetings, can be revolutionary when applied in other disciplines. The lessons learned about successful implementation can be shared, saving a great deal of time and energy on the part of the departments that adopt the practices. Convenings have become critical "trading zones" for effective practices.

There are resources for improving doctoral education, but they do not often reach into the silos of individual departments. The Promising Practices listed in the Re-envisioning the Ph.D. Web site, for example, is a very useful resource (Re-envisioning the Ph.D., 2000). To assist with such documentation, the CID has also encouraged departments to use the Carnegie Foundation Web authoring tool to document and share their work. The Knowledge Exchange Exhibition and Presentation tool, known as the KEEP Toolkit, is described in the next section of this chapter. The next step after documentation is collecting evidence of whether practices are effective. The Ph.D. Professional Development Assessment Project, a component of the Responsive Ph.D., is a compilation of efforts to determine effectiveness (The Responsive Ph.D., 2004). The scholarship of teaching and learning work that has taken hold in undergraduate education is another useful model and framework to adapt to the doctoral level (Gale & Golde, 2004).

There is an individual face to the culture of privacy, as well. Many faculty members resist policies (or even requests for information) that imply accountability for the progress of their advisees in the program. This attitude runs counter to the situation in some mathematics departments, in which advisers must routinely explain why their advisees are enrolled after the fifth year, and describe the plan to move them to a satisfactory completion of the degree. Departmental leadership and a critical mass of faculty who proceed even in the absence of complete consensus can be useful. Some departments have crafted statements of mutual expectations between advisers and advisees, including topics such as frequency of meetings, suggested topics for discussion, and the role of other dissertation committee members (e.g., Gross, 2002).

Going Public Using the KEEP Toolkit

One way to encourage openness and share information across programs is to provide easy-to-use and readily accessible means for sharing changes departments have made in their doctoral programs and the strategies they have used to design and implement these changes. The Carnegie Foundation believes that the documentation of scholarly work about teaching and learning is an important strategy for improvement.

Although difficult for some, opening a graduate program to regular review will ultimately strengthen the reputation and competitive standing of a department. These benefits can be more quickly realized by publishing the results of the reform effort. In addition to highlighting departmental strengths, sharing reform lessons strengthens the discipline as a whole and can open up rewarding new areas of scholarship for faculty and students. Extending the scholarship of teaching and learning from undergraduate education to the graduate level is a natural expansion of this interdisciplinary movement.

To support scholarly inquiry into teaching and learning, the Knowledge Media Lab at the Carnegie Foundation has created a Web authoring tool called the KEEP Toolkit. The CID departments use the KEEP Toolkit to share their work with one another. KEEP users create Web pages (called "snapshots"), usually working from predesigned templates, so that the resulting snapshots provide information about similar topics. Once they are completed, CID-related snapshots are mounted in an electronic gallery so that viewers can see the work of departments across all six disciplines. Initially, access to the collection of snapshots has been restricted to members of participating departments, but now selected snapshots are public and can be seen at http://gallery.carnegiefoundation.org/cid.

For CID-participating departments, the CID staff created CID-specific templates to make it easy for departments to share their efforts at changing their doctoral programs. One template provides a space for departments to describe an innovation they are considering or have implemented. (Each department describes many innovations, each on a separate snapshot.) The innovation template asks a department to describe its own work by responding to the following six prompts (departments were readily able to modify the template to suit their needs—and many did):

- What is the issue we are trying to address?
- How do we know that this is an issue?
- What is the change or innovation that is intended to address this issue?
- What is the intended effect of the innovation?
- Why did we select that approach? Describe the deliberative process that led to selection of the innovation or change described above. What other strategies or changes were considered and rejected? Why? Does this innovation help solve a variety of problems?
- What data or evidence will demonstrate the effect of our innovation? Describe plans to assess the innovation. What kinds of data or forms of evidence will demonstrate whether, and in what ways, our innova-

---

SIDEBAR 2.3
The KEEP Toolkit

Since 2000, a main focus of the Knowledge Media Laboratory (KML) of The Carnegie Foundation has been to help faculty and educational institutions document, share, and reflect on their efforts to transform teaching and student learning. The Foundation's experience suggests that creating succinct yet appealing representations and sharing them effectively remains an intellectually and technically daunting task. Despite the increasing desire of faculty, students, programs, and institutions to develop and use these kinds of representations for collective knowledge sharing and building, in many cases there is limited support available for them to explore the possibilities and initiate their own efforts.

The Knowledge Exchange Exhibition and Presentation (KEEP) Toolkit is a set of open-source, Web-based tools that help teachers, students, and institutions quickly create compact and engaging knowledge representations (snapshots) of aspects of teaching and learning so they can be shared with others. The KEEP Toolkit is available to educators and students at all levels as a free service.

Users can also create templates that provide both conceptual organizing frameworks and visual layouts. By guiding users through framing questions, directions, and rubrics, these templates help them organize materials—course materials and artifacts; student work examples; audio, image, and video files—in a manner that best represents and contextualizes the content and linked resources.

The CID use of KEEP is described in a case study illustrated with examples from the Indiana University education school in the Gallery of Teaching and Learning, a showcase for a variety of multimedia examples and electronic portfolios (http://gallery.carnegiefoundation.org/).

---

tion has the intended effect? Link to actual data or samples of evidence (e.g., survey results, focus group summaries).

In a similar way, we created a template in which departments can describe exemplary elements of their existing program. This template allows departments to share aspects of their program that others may desire to adopt. In this snapshot template we embedded the following prompts:

- Describe the exemplary element.
- What educational purpose does this element serve? In what ways does it contribute to student learning?

- Describe details of the element:
  - When does this element appear in the doctoral program?
  - Who is responsible for conducting or implementing it?
  - Is it required or optional?
  - Why and when was it instituted?
- Describe the intended and actual effect or impact of this element. What forms of evidence demonstrate the ways in which this feature had the effect you describe above?
- Reflection from a faculty member. Describe your experience of this element in practice from your point of view as a faculty member. How has this changed your work as a graduate faculty member (teaching, supervising research, advising, and mentoring)? How has it changed students' experiences and behaviors? Do you believe that this is a positive change in the doctoral program? Why?
- Reflection from a student. Describe your experience of this element in practice from your point of view as a student. How has this affected your experiences and behaviors (completing requirements; conducting research and scholarship; preparing for your future career; acquiring knowledge, habits of mind, and skills to succeed in the discipline)? Do you believe that this is a positive aspect of the doctoral program? Why?

One advantage of using the KEEP Toolkit and snapshots that highlight efforts to improve doctoral programs is that questions of change are bracketed into a separate space from official Web pages about the department. This organizational structure helps make it safer to talk about what might in other cases be somewhat politically fraught questions. Displaying the innovation and exemplary element snapshots in the same gallery also provides an opportunity for departments to document and share the excellent work and the positive contributions to doctoral education that are already taking place. Moreover, the snapshots provide an easy way to append documents and other evidentiary material in a way that can be easily shared by others. Snapshots have included copies of surveys, graphs of data, drafts of proposals, minutes of meetings, PowerPoint presentations used at department meetings, and mission statements.

The University of Pittsburgh's Department of English: Putting CID-Inspired Assessment Tools into Practice

Many of the departments participating in the CID have engaged in the deliberative, evidence-based, holistic, self-reflective assessment process outlined earlier. What does this process look like in practice? What actual tools and strategies do departments employ? This section provides a detailed description of the work of one participating department, the University of Pittsburgh's English Department, which has creatively and effectively used evidence to inform deliberations and changes in the doctoral program. This case illustrates the promise of some of the strategies we have outlined earlier in this chapter.

As described in sidebar 2.4, the University of Pittsburgh's English Department has a national reputation for its innovative program in cultural and critical studies introduced in 1985–86. However, by the year 2000 it was clear to many in the department that some aspects of the program were not working well. The department conducted a mini review of itself that led to a series of programmatic changes, motivated by five beneficial outcomes, as described in the sidebar. (These steps preceded the department's application to the CID.) Significantly, the department sought evidence that the changes would have the desired impact as part of its work in the CID. Led by the director of graduate studies, Eric Clarke, the department has been collecting and reviewing three quite different kinds of data as the department seeks to assess the effectiveness of the programmatic changes it implemented. Because the department had identified five anticipated benefits of the changes, it was able to determine which kinds of evidence would be convincing.

Admissions Data

One measure of the success of the changes made to the Pittsburgh English Department Ph.D. program is admissions data. The graph in Figure 2.1 shows an increase in the number of applicants (the bars), and a decrease in the proportion of applications accepted (the lines), coupled with increases in the yield rate (the proportion of admitted students who choose to enroll). (The same data, disaggregated by the three program specialties, are also shared with all faculty.) The director of graduate studies also compiles lists of the universities that students turn down in favor of Pittsburgh and lists of

SIDEBAR 2.4
The University of Pittsburgh's English Department

Beginning in 2001, the English Department at the University of Pittsburgh initiated a series of structural and curricular changes in response to a perceived mismatch between its "cultural and critical studies" program requirements (started in 1985–86) and time to degree and the overall structure of the program. Despite the innovative intellectual reorientation of its Ph.D. program in the mid-1980s, the department had retained the M.A. in English as the gateway to this program for those students applying with a B.A.; these students were then required to reapply to enter the Ph.D. program. Department members believed that this outdated structure decreased the department's attractiveness to the best students and placed them at a disadvantage to those programs they routinely competed with for students. More important, it compromised their students' ability to undertake a coherent intellectual development in a timely way. The old structure required students to spend at least 7 years earning the M.A. and the Ph.D. Between 1991 and 2001 the average time to degree was 8.5 years.

In 2000–2001 the department instituted four changes to the M.A. and Ph.D. programs:

- Direct admission to the Ph.D. program. Applicants with a B.A. are now admitted directly into the Ph.D. program. All students who are making satisfactory progress are eligible for an M.A. after their first two years in the program by completing a master's research paper, or after completing the Ph.D. Project in their fourth year.
- Increased faculty advising and evaluation. All Ph.D. students undergo a review at the end of their first year in the program. This review begins faculty evaluation and advising of Ph.D. students at a crucial early phase of their studies.
- Streamlined Ph.D. Project structure. In lieu of a qualifying exam, doctoral students are expected to create a Ph.D. Project. The time students spend working on the Ph.D. Project was reduced from a loosely suggested four terms to a mandated three terms (spring, summer, fall), with each phase of the project having a clearly defined schedule. Currently, this shortens time to degree by one year.
- Reduced seminar requirement. The number of seminars required for completion of the degree was decreased from 17 to 13.

Five beneficial outcomes of these changes are expected:

1. improved time to degree
2. more flexibility in using funds for graduate student support
3. greater parity and competitiveness with other Ph.D. programs
4. better clarity and structure for the Ph.D. Project
5. programmatically coherent faculty advising

FIGURE 2.1

Admissions data from the University of Pittsburgh English Department

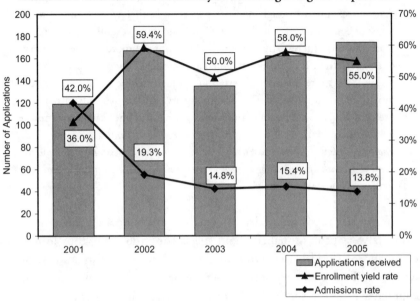

the universities chosen by students who are admitted to Pittsburgh but enroll elsewhere. Clarke said, "There are a few schools we lose students to across the board, every year. And recently people are turning other institutions down for us!" These data provide concrete evidence that the department is meeting its third desired outcome: greater parity and competitiveness with other Ph.D. programs.

Ph.D. Project and Dissertation Prospectus Titles

Since the 1985–86 academic year, the department has fulfilled the university requirement for a comprehensive examination with the Ph.D. Project. The project had been a 30-page paper, followed by written and oral exams conducted by the student's Project Committee. The 2004 departmental handbook, available at http://gallery.carnegiefoundation.org/collections/cid/english.pitt/innovation. html, described the project as

> an occasion to integrate various aspects of the changing disciplinary practices of English studies and to define a broad area of inquiry for subsequent work. It is a historical and theoretical investigation of a topic that can be

demonstrated by the student to be of long-term significance for critical study. It offers a way of making connections among various interests a student has explored through seminar papers and other work from a broad range of courses taken. The Project allows students to examine and synthesize a range of interests that ordinarily lead into the more detailed inquiry of a dissertation. It could be imagined as providing context or background to the later, more focused, dissertation work. It can be more tentative or provisional than a dissertation, examining a variety of methods or parallel projects. The Project Examinations replace what was once called a comprehensive examination. *While we no longer insist on "comprehensiveness" as knowledge of all literature written in English, the project is meant to demonstrate a breadth of knowledge as well as the ability to work on a single problem* [italics in original].

In the late 1990s many departmental members became concerned that students were professionalizing and specializing too early, thus losing the command of breadth that often marks scholars in English studies. Some wondered if the Ph.D. Project was serving its intended goal of providing a counterbalance to a specialization of the dissertation. Departmental leaders engaged in an innovative assessment strategy. Clarke recalls:

> As part of our initial deliberations for the CID, we compiled a list of Ph.D. Project titles along with Dissertation Prospectus titles for each of our doctoral students for as many years back as we could. Comparing project and prospectus titles for each student from 1998 to 2003 was revealing. Over 70% of them were either identical or nearly identical. This confirmed for many the sense that project work had narrowed significantly beyond what the department had intended when it moved to the Ph.D. Project format in 1986. (personal communication, May 17, 2005)

These data were compelling enough to launch discussions about changing the Ph.D. Project; revised project regulations were adopted in March 2005. Along with greater emphasis on breadth in the project guidelines, students must now write two shorter papers, each of which serves a different function. Clarke notes that the department will continue

> to discuss ways that we can start tracking the effects of these changes. We understand that these effects are long term in nature and assessment will likely rely on placement data we compile over the next five to ten years.

More immediately, however, we will discuss different types of surveys to administer to our students—likely both after the exam and after placement—that will help us to understand what relationship our revised examination has to the experiences our Ph.D.s have while at Pitt and after they begin their careers.

The department is clearly meeting the fourth goal listed in the sidebar: better clarity and structure for the Ph.D. Project.

Dissertation Committee Membership

A student's dissertation adviser has the primary responsibility for working with the student to shape that student's dissertation. In English studies, other members of the committee play important roles as well. Students consult with them on a regular basis as their ideas and writing evolve. Often, however, committee membership is relatively unrecognized and unrewarded work. Under the auspices of the CID, the Pittsburgh English Department compiled a list of the number of dissertation committees each faculty member had chaired and served on between 1992 and 2003. Collecting this information was part of the department's desire to know how dissertation advising related to faculty rank and areas of expertise. Few were surprised to learn that senior faculty members, particularly those with a visible research career, usually serve as dissertation chairs. But untenured and associate professors serve disproportionately as committee members. This information is particularly noteworthy because activities such as advising at the dissertation level and the distribution of advising responsibilities often is invisible, even within a particular department. Examining these data was an important step to achieving the fifth goal: programmatically coherent faculty advising.

The English Department at the University of Pittsburgh is now committed to a culture of evidence and to an iterative process of data collection and program assessment that is most evident in the 2004–05 Faculty Seminar series. The department held three two-hour events, attended by an average of 30 faculty and graduate students. Each event focused on one of the three departmental programs areas: literature, film studies, and composition and rhetoric. At each seminar, a panel of faculty members presented evidence about what kind of intellectual work had been fostered in the doctoral program since the early 1990s (documented by data such as dissertation titles), how this work was carried out (courses by area, and faculty advising on doc-

toral committees), and the specific outcomes of this work (placement). Eric
Clarke reported on the areas of interest listed in applications for admissions,
which revealed perceived departmental strengths. The presentations allowed
faculty members and students to discuss issues informed by evidence about
the program. The seminars resulted in additional improvements in each program area: renaming one program area to reflect changes in faculty hiring
and expertise, proposing changes to the graduate curriculum committee, and
identifying suggestions for what to emphasize on the departmental Web site.

This department is engaged in assessment activities as a result of faculty's
own concerns about the direction of the department. Because the process
emerged and evolved organically—with the interest and cooperation of at
least some of the faculty—the department uses evidence to help make
changes in its program. There have been other important drivers of the
change, such as university-mandated internal and external reviews, but it is
clear that a commitment to assessment and data has informed discussion in
ways that have proved to be positive. And there are now baseline data for
continued evaluation. Creating a culture of openness and evidence, such as
the English Department has developed, leads to deliberation and change—
one important goal of the Carnegie Initiative on the Doctorate.

Using Evidence to Improve Doctoral Programs

At the Carnegie Foundation we believe that ongoing, public, holistic, evidence-based deliberation that includes many members of the department is
a route to improving doctoral education. This process is not easy, but it is
remarkably effective. The Carnegie Initiative on the Doctorate is creating
existence proofs.

Our approach in the CID capitalizes on the habits of scholarship (honesty, curiosity, competitiveness) that are embedded in graduate programs
and applies those strengths to the challenges of assessment and reform of
doctoral programs. It is important to remember that a department must be
ready to embark on a journey that requires leadership, time, energy, and
goodwill. Characteristics of departments that have found the CID fruitful
include

- leadership by committed faculty and graduate students
- sincere efforts to include all faculty and graduate students in the
  process

- a focus on shaping the future of students' fields of study
- creative use of assessment tools

Assessment and evaluation are only meaningful when done for a genuine purpose. As we have described, there are tools and strategies that are effective. Creating a low stakes–high yield environment allows people to collect evidence and engage with the data. Encouragement, support, and resources help overcome reluctance.

The next step for the CID (or for any department that makes meaningful changes) is for faculty and graduate students to publish the results of their inquiry into the problems that lie submerged in all graduate programs and to document their efforts to address these issues. Our experience has demonstrated that programs that engage in critical self-examination informed by evidence are directly rewarded with a better doctoral program. Equally important are the indirect benefits of an intellectually vital departmental culture committed to shared goals. Such communities are humane and productive environments in which faculty and graduate students can flourish.

References

Gale, R., & Golde, C. M. (2004). Doctoral education and the scholarship of teaching and Learning. *Peer Review, 6*(3), 8–12.

Goldberger, M., Maher, B. A., & Flattau, P. E. (Eds.). (1995). *Research-doctorate programs in the United States. Continuity and change.* Washington, DC: National Academy Press.

Golde, C. M., & Dore, T. M. (2001). *At cross purposes: What the experiences of doctoral students reveal about doctoral education.* Philadelphia, PA: A report for The Pew Charitable Trusts. Retrieved from http://www.phd-survey.org

Gordon Research Conferences. (n.d.). *What is GRC?* Retrieved from http://www.grc.uri.edu/whatis.html

Gross, R. A. (2002, February 28). The adviser-advisee relationship. *Chronicle of Higher Education.* Retrieved from http://chronicle.com/jobs/2002/02/2002022802c.htm

Morse, R. J., & Flanigan, S. (2005). *The ranking methodology.* Retrieved from http://www.usnews.com/usnews/edu/grad/rankings/about/06method_brief.php

National Association of Graduate and Professional Students. (2001). *The 2000 national doctoral program survey (NAGPS).* Retrieved from http://survey.nagps.org

Nyquist, J. D., Manning, L., Wulff, D. H., Austin, A. E., Sprague, J., Fraser, P. K., et al. (1999). On the road to becoming a professor: The graduate student experience. *Change, 31*(3), 18–27.

Re-envisioning the Ph.D. (2000). *Promising practices.* Retrieved from http://www.grad.washington.edu/envision/practices/index.html

The Responsive Ph.D. Initiative. (2004). *The Ph.D. professional development assessment project.* Retrieved from http://www.woodrow.org/responsivephd/assessment.html and http://www.woodrow.org/responsivephd/ListofPractices.pdf

3

USING AN ALIGNMENT
MODEL AS A FRAMEWORK IN
THE ASSESSMENT OF
DOCTORAL PROGRAMS

Donald H. Wulff and Maresi Nerad

How often have we asked questions and gathered information about the sequencing, content, or number of courses in a doctoral program to determine how we might adjust course work to improve doctoral students' learning? When is the last time we sought improvement-based input from our current students and faculty/staff about the process and use of exams in our doctoral programs? What approaches have we used most successfully, not only to evaluate students' individual dissertations but also to provide students with ongoing professional development during the dissertation stage? How can the roles that faculty/staff serve during various phases of students' doctoral programs be improved to help students achieve the outcomes that have been identified for their programs?

Addressing such questions is essential for improving programs in doctoral education. Yet, these are the kind of questions that those of us involved in doctoral education have not been examining adequately in our assessment efforts. Although we have compiled data about doctoral student progression in terms of time to degree and completion rates, we have not yet developed thorough assessment processes for improving our doctoral programs while students are enrolled in them.

The authors wish to express their appreciation to Carla W. Hess, Chester Fritz Distinguished Professor Emerita of Communication Sciences and Disorders at the University of North Dakota, Grand Forks, for her feedback on earlier drafts of this manuscript.

In the meantime, doctoral educators continue to struggle with challenges related to retention, attrition, and the loss of some of the best students, including underrepresented minority students (Antony & Taylor, 2004; Denecke & Frasier, 2005; Golde, 1996, 1998; Lovitts, 2001, 2004; Nerad & Miller, 1996); student dissatisfaction with various parts of the doctoral education process (Wulff, Austin, Nyquist, & Sprague, 2004); insufficient mentoring and lack of systematic, developmental preparation for future roles (Aanerud, Homer, Nerad, & Cerny, 2006, chapter 4 in this volume; Wulff et al., 2004); and often a mismatch between what students are prepared to do at various stages of their doctoral education and what they actually do in their careers (Aanerud et al., 2006; Gaff, Pruitt-Logan, & Weibl, 2000; Golde & Dore, 2001; Wulff et al., 2004).

To help in addressing such challenges in doctoral education, we present in this chapter a particular framework for successful doctoral programs and discuss implications of that framework for program assessment. Our framework, which we call an alignment model, suggests that successful doctoral programs involve a process of aligning program activities, students, and faculty/staff in their specific contexts in order to achieve desired outcomes of helping students complete the degree in a reasonable time, with a satisfactory experience, and with the knowledge and skills necessary for a range of careers.

Because our beliefs about assessment are thoroughly grounded in the alignment model for successful doctoral programs, we begin the chapter by discussing the model—first what the basic components of doctoral education in the model are and then how alignment of these basic components can contribute to improving doctoral programs. Once we present our alignment model for doctoral programs, we explain why formative assessment—an improvement-based, internally centered, ongoing assessment process—is essential in the model. We do so by identifying basic premises related to alignment and by explaining the importance of formative assessment for addressing each of the premises. We conclude the chapter with sample questions and approaches that illustrate the application of formative assessment within the alignment model.

The Basic Components—What Are the Basic Components in Our Model of a Successful Doctoral Program?

The basic components in our model of a successful doctoral program include:

1. program activities
2. students
3. faculty and staff
4. desired outcomes
5. the context

Each of these components is an essential consideration in the success of doctoral programs.

Component 1: Program Activities

Program activities in doctoral education consist of both the formal curriculum and the various activities of a doctoral program purposely designed to prepare students as intellectuals with the knowledge and skills appropriate for careers in their fields or disciplines. With the support of faculty/staff, students proceed sequentially through program activities, such as orientation, course work, laboratory research, fieldwork, examinations, internships/assistantships, and the dissertation (e.g., Baird, 1972; Isaac, Quinlan, & Walker, 1992; Nyquist, Abbott, & Wulff, 1989; Nyquist & Wulff, 1996). Various scholars have identified phases of progress as doctoral students work their way through these program activities (Golde, 1996; Nerad & Cerny, 1993; Nyquist & Sprague, 1998; Nyquist & Wulff, 1996; Sprague & Nyquist, 1989). For our purposes in this chapter, we use three distinct phases in these doctoral program activities.

Phase I

In the first phase, students' activities include participating in orientations, taking courses, reading books, and acquiring appropriate research skills, often by performing supporting research tasks. In moving through these activities, students are primarily dependent knowledge consumers, or, as Sprague and Nyquist (1989) suggest, "senior learners." The faculty/staff in this phase serve as sources of information. Working in rather structured learning environments, the faculty/staff engage with students in the initial series of activities designed to ensure the learning of appropriate knowledge.

Phase II

In the second phase, students take exams to demonstrate the mastery of the literature, concepts, and methods they need in their disciplines. Through the exam activities, students move into a period of transition in which they prepare to demonstrate their expertise as knowledge consumers. At the same time, they assume a new level of independence as scholars, or what Sprague and Nyquist (1989) call "colleagues in training." In this phase, faculty/staff continue to support the students but become more collegial in encouraging the students to be increasingly independent in taking responsibility for their learning and for their ability to demonstrate it.

Phase III

In the third phase of their programs, students undertake their own research for their dissertations or theses and design approaches for producing knowledge in addition to consuming knowledge. As knowledge producers, or what Sprague and Nyquist (1989) call "junior colleagues," the students have responsibility for understanding original research and conducting studies that advance thinking in their fields. During this less structured phase, faculty ideally become senior peers in increasingly collegial relationships with the students.

During each of these three major phases, the programmatic activities are different; the students are undergoing changes in their own development as they respond to faculty expectations; faculty/staff are playing changing roles in their support of doctoral students; and various factors in the departmental, institutional, and national/international contexts for doctoral education are continually changing and evolving. These changing dynamics contribute to a process of socialization during which students learn the language, norms, culture, and expectations of their specific fields (e.g., Antony, 2002; Antony & Taylor, 2004; Austin, 2002a, 2002b; Boyle & Boice, 1998; Ellis, 2001; Golde, 1998; Staton & Darling, 1989; Tinto 1997; Turner & Thompson, 1993; Weidman & Stein, 2003; Weidman, Twale, & Stein, 2001).

This component of doctoral education, consisting of programmatic activities sequenced in three phases that gradually socialize students, is significant because it suggests that doctoral education is an evolving process that includes changing activities and varied roles for the participants. It emphasizes the complexity of the doctoral experience for all involved and reinforces the need for assessment approaches that can help to determine how to make such a complex process successful.

Component 2: Students

Students, including doctoral students enrolled part-time or full-time in on-campus or off-campus programs, represent the second basic component of doctoral education. Increasingly, students themselves have been included as an essential component in thinking about the quality of doctoral programs. Although in the past the National Research Council used primarily the scholarly reputation of the faculty as an indicator of doctoral program quality (Goldberger, Maher, & Flattau, 1995), the council's Committee to Examine the Methodology for the Assessment of Research-Doctorate Programs recently recommended that students be included (Ostriker & Kuh, 2003). Others have supported this need to include students in program assessment, suggesting that "the quality of an academic program can be judged by the quality of its students" (Haworth & Conrad, 1996, p. 46).

It is especially important to include students because of the changes that are taking place in the graduate population. Scholars have noted, for instance, the changing student demographics resulting from increasing numbers of women and students of color pursuing Ph.D.s (e.g., Austin, 2002b; Berg & Ferber, 1983; Ellis, 2001; Isaac, Pruitt-Logan, & Upcraft, 1995; Maher, Ford, & Thompson, 2004; Nerad & Cerny, 1999; Nerad, June, & Miller, 1997; Syverson, 1996; Turner & Thompson, 1993). Along with these trends have come idiosyncratic and changing needs, expectations, goals, and perceptions of careers and potential jobs in certain disciplines (Golde & Dore, 2001, 2004; Nerad, Aanerud, & Cerny, 2004; Syverson, 1996; Wulff, Austin, Nyquist, & Sprague, 2004). Often the goals of students are very different from the goals and intentions with which they are being prepared (Wulff et al., 2004). In some cases, the students may not be expressing those goals openly to advisors and mentors with whom they are interacting most closely, thus creating challenges for faculty/staff who work closely with students in the socialization process during the three phases of doctoral education.

Given this variety of student-related factors that affect the success of doctoral programs, we have included students as one of the most basic components in doctoral programs. It is important that we capitalize on the varied backgrounds of students and seek ways to make their personal goals and expectations more explicit and open to discussion and negotiation. To do so, we need assessment approaches that can help us to understand students' diverse backgrounds and changing perspectives and determine how that information can be balanced against the needs, expectations, and goals of institutions and faculty/staff to improve our doctoral programs.

Component 3: Faculty and Staff

The third major component of doctoral programs consists of faculty and staff. In our model, the faculty/staff component, first of all, consists of graduate faculty responsible for designing a doctoral program, teaching in classrooms or laboratories, advising, supervising students in their research, and overseeing service experiences. In addition, we include among our faculty/staff any nonfaculty and professional staff who serve as administrators and function in other support roles. Such administrative members are knowledgeable about difficulties doctoral students encounter, often advise them, and serve as key sources of information for students (Nerad & Cerny, 1993).

Faculty/staff always have been key figures in graduate students' success, and, as our model for doctoral programs suggests, faculty/staff are significant, especially because of their changing roles as students move through various phases of the program activities in doctoral education. Specifically, the faculty/staff begin in teaching and advising roles and gradually guide students in formulating research ideas with concrete research questions. In the process, faculty/staff ultimately focus less on being knowledge experts and more on enabling students' independence.

Just as the demographic characteristics of our contemporary students are changing, so are the characteristics for faculty (Finkelstein & Schuster, 2001; Gappa, Austin, & Trice, 2005). Finkelstein and Schuster (2001) point out, for example, that the native-born white men who traditionally were the core of the profession now represent less than one-half of the new faculty cohort (p. 4). Increasingly, then, we are working with a more diverse faculty, and with that diversity has come a greater range of expectations and roles (Gappa et al., 2005). These diverse faculty not only bring new goals and expectations based on their awareness of societal needs but also have to balance those against some of the more traditional expectations that have been an ongoing part of doctoral education.

Adapting to this change of expectations and roles is not always easy for faculty members in doctoral programs, as such adaptation requires an array of approaches for interacting with students who also have diverse needs and expectations as they move through the phases of their education. At the same time faculty members are adjusting to changing advisory roles, they are also at various stages of thinking about and embracing changes that are emerging in doctoral education. Although some are acutely aware of the need to make adaptations, for example, preparing students for varied roles beyond the professoriate, others are concerned about changes that appear to challenge the rigor and research orientation of the traditional doctoral education as a research degree. Those concerns, then, are manifested in their approaches to doctoral education. As one example, faculty members in some disciplines still do not accept that there is a widening range of career paths for contemporary students (Nerad & Cerny, 2000; Nerad et al., 2004). Instead, those faculty continue to prepare their students as though all the students are going to become faculty, while in reality only about half of all Ph.D. recipients ultimately do so (Nerad et al., 2004).

Understanding what faculty/staff do and do not contribute to a doctoral program during various phases of it can add significantly to an examination of the quality of the program. Therefore, it is essential to design assessment approaches that seek greater understanding of the varied faculty/staff experiences, commitments, and perspectives that advance or constrain efforts to achieve successful doctoral programs.

Component 4: Outcomes

A fourth major component of our model includes the overarching outcomes desired for a doctoral program. These outcomes provide the guidelines against which we can judge success or failure (Gardner, 1994).

What are those outcomes? At one time, we could have answered this question with a straightforward response, suggesting that doctoral students needed to emerge solely as content experts with appropriate research skills that they could apply in their careers, primarily as professors in research institutions. However, as LaPidus (1998) notes:

> We have come a long way from the one student, one professor, one research project concept of doctoral education and are beginning to understand that doctoral study is an educational experience designed to prepare students for a variety of roles and responsibilities, all centered on the applications of scholarship. This means more than simply adding on components; it requires examination of the basic purpose and goals of doctoral education. (p. 102)

Indeed, recently there has been emphasis on preparing doctoral students for a greater variety of career possibilities and a broader range of knowledge and skills in such areas as teaching scholarship, community engagement, teamwork, organizational development, ethics, and time management (e.g., Austin, 2002a; Gaff, 2002; Gaff et al., 2000; Golde & Dore, 2001; LaPidus, 1995; Nerad, 2005; Nerad, Aanerud, & Cerny, 2004; Nyquist, 2002; Wulff & Austin, 2004). We also believe that we should be striving to achieve such outcomes if the preparation of graduate students is to be successful. At the same time, though, we believe that the major outcomes for a doctoral program must be the completion of the program in a reasonable amount of time with a reasonable degree of satisfaction and preparation of students as creative, independent scholars (Lovitts, 2005). In addition, we would emphasize that students must have adequate preparation for a variety of career options. The challenge, then, is to find ways to include the broader range of knowledge and skills while simultaneously achieving the major outcomes desired for time to degree, levels of satisfaction, and preparation of students as independent scholars.

We can seek that successful balance, partially, as LaPidus (1998) suggests, through the ongoing examination of the purposes and outcomes of each doctoral program. We acknowledge, of course, that those outcomes and the specific methods for achieving them will vary depending on individual institutional and program contexts. In our framework, however, such ongoing efforts to identify and examine the outcomes of a specific doctoral program are essential to the success of the program.

Component 5: The Context of Doctoral Programs

The fifth component in our model of successful doctoral education is context, or those factors in the departmental and institutional environment as well as outside forces that affect the quality of education in a doctoral program. The components of doctoral programs previously discussed—programmatic elements, students, faculty/staff, and outcomes—all exist in a specific context that affects—and can be affected by—what happens within the program. Three levels of influence shape the context:

1. influences outside the institution
2. influences within the institution
3. influences within an individual program

Lovitts (2005) discusses such contextual influences in terms of two general categories. The broader culture of doctoral education (macro environment) includes "the social-cultural and institutional contexts in which students live and work" (p. 150). Lovitts explains that "the social-cultural context embodies the norms, values, and beliefs of the surrounding culture" and "the institutional context is the cultural context of graduate education writ large and the cultural context of one's discipline" (p. 150). In contrast, the micro environment, according to Lovitts, "is the immediate setting—university, department, laboratory—in which a graduate student works and the interactions that take place in that setting" (p. 149). Influences from outside institutions, such as funding agencies, disciplinary associations, and hiring organizations/ institutions, exert indirect and sometimes very direct influences at the macro level, often affecting such things as the kinds of skills needed for various jobs or future directions and emphases in doctoral programs. At the micro level of the immediate institution, such varied factors include the availability and type of financial support; campus facilities, such as the library; centralized support, such as fellowships offered through graduate schools; campus teaching and learning centers; housing; and child care. Also at the micro level, but at the level of a specific program, are factors, for example, such as the departmental/ program climate, departmental funding and support, office space, lab space, computer access, and the network of peers that contribute to the kinds of interactions that take place in the departmental context.

In recent years, there has been increased interest in the changing contextual factors in doctoral education—at both macro and micro levels—and their influences on quality (e.g., Anderson, 1996; Clark, 1995; Golde, 1996; Golde & Dore, 2004; Julius & Gumport, 2003; Lovitts, 2005; Nerad & Cerny, 1993). At the macro level, for example, there recently has been much discussion about changes needed in the preparation of Ph.D.s (Nyquist, 2002) and about more specific issues such as the implications of increasing focus on interdisciplinary work in doctoral education. At the micro level there are increasing emphases on preparing students within their departments not only for roles as researchers and teachers, but also as engaged scholars who can provide service and translate their expertise into information that can benefit their communities. Such changes at all levels have implications not only for the quality of doctoral student preparation, but also for issues of attrition and time to degree. We believe that any assessment intended to improve a doctoral program must examine the impact of this variety of contextual factors and ways to mitigate or expand their influence.

As we have suggested in this part of this chapter, the programmatic activities, the students, the faculty/staff, the outcomes, and the context encompass the major components of doctoral programs. Colleagues who have worked in doctoral education for some time are most likely not surprised by our suggestion that these basic factors are all important in assessing a program. What is different in our model of successful doctoral programs, however, is the way we have conceptualized these factors fitting together to contribute to desired doctoral outcomes.

The Alignment Model—How Do the Components Fit Together in Successful Doctoral Programs?

The five components previously discussed fit together in what we call an alignment model for successful doctoral programs. Although scholars have used the term "alignment" in a variety of ways in higher education, our framework in this model is consistent with the way Wulff (1985, 2005) uses the term to discuss teaching effectiveness. In his original case study research on teaching effectiveness, Wulff (1985) concludes that instructors who are effective in achieving their instructional goals engage in an ongoing process of aligning the content, themselves, and students in specific instructional contexts. When we shift this approach to doctoral programs, success in achieving desired outcomes involves the ongoing process of aligning program activities, students, and faculty/staff within their specific contexts (Figure 3.1). The overlap of the program activities, students, and faculty/staff in the specific context of a doctoral program represents *alignment,* the degree of congruence between and/or among these components. The greater the alignment between and among these components, the more successfully the desired outcomes can be achieved.

The box in the middle of the model represents the importance of a particular kind of assessment—formative assessment—in examining, as well as improving, the alignment to achieve desired outcomes in doctoral programs. To demonstrate more fully why formative assessment is so important in the alignment process for doctoral programs, we need to explain some of the basic premises underlying the alignment model for doctoral programs.

Alignment Premises—What Are the Underlying Premises of the Alignment Model for Successful Doctoral Programs?

Three basic premises underlying our alignment model help us to clarify why formative assessment is essential in doctoral programs.

FIGURE 3.1

A model for aligning components of doctoral programs to achieve desired outcomes

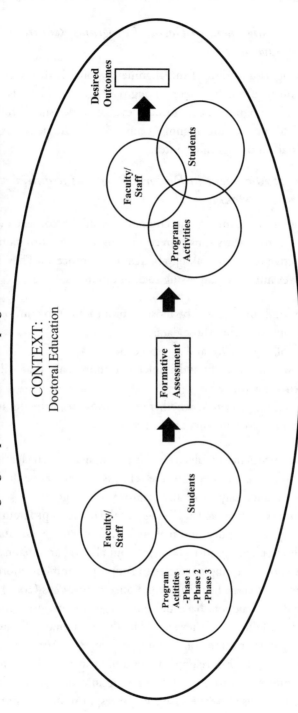

Adapted from "Using the Alignment Model of Teaching Effectiveness," by D. H. Wulff in *Aligning for Learning: Strategies for Teaching Effectiveness* (pp. 3–15), by D. H. Wulff, Ed., 2005, Bolton, MA: Anker. Reprinted with permission of Anker Publishing.

Premise No. 1: Alignment in Doctoral Programs Requires a Focus on Improvement

The underlying assumption of the alignment model is that successful doctoral education requires alignment among the basic components of the program. Thus, if a program is going to achieve outcomes successfully, it must take actions to improve the alignment among program activities, students, and faculty/staff in the specific context.

Premise No. 2: Alignment in Doctoral Programs Requires Internal Decision Making

To achieve alignment among the components in the context of a specific program, the constituents most directly involved in the program must engage in reflective decision making about how to proceed. They have to be involved, for example, in addressing such questions as:

- What kinds of data will be most helpful to our program review?
- How will we gather those data?
- How will we analyze and interpret the data?
- How will we identify and implement approaches that will work for needed adjustments?
- How will we determine whether or not those adjustments are working to align the components of our program?

Ultimately, constituents involved in the program must engage in ongoing communication that is essential to the reflective, cooperative decision making that will enhance alignment and improve the program.

The faculty/staff involved at all stages of the doctoral program, of course, are the primary internal decision makers in this process. Students, however, also have roles to play, not just as subjects, but also as participants, providing information and suggesting strategies to support alignment efforts (Hutchings & Clarke, 2004). In fact, Fagen and Suedkamp Wells (2004) argue that "because graduate students have the most to gain—or lose—from discussions of graduate education, they should be the most vital and integral participants in any conversations on the subject" (p. 87). Although individuals from campus or faculty development certainly can provide additional support in determining approaches and gathering information, faculty and students as internal decision makers have major responsibility for implementing the alignment process.

Premise No. 3: Alignment in Doctoral Programs Requires Ongoing, Cyclical Efforts

This premise begins with the recognition that basic components of a program—program activities, students, professors/staff, outcomes, and context—interact in a dynamic process that is in constant flux. As our model suggests, program activities change, both as a result of the contextual influences and as part of the socialization process that moves students through the three phases from knowledge consumers to knowledge producers. Students are changing as they move from one phase to another to become socialized as independent, creative knowledge producers. Faculty/staff change their roles as they support students through various parts of their educational experience. Desired outcomes change as needs and expectations of students are balanced against those of the institution and individual faculty/staff. The context changes with ongoing conversations about future directions in doctoral education at national, institutional, and programmatic levels. Most important, each of these components interacts with and affects the other components during various phases of the doctoral education process. Therefore, we do not achieve alignment at one point in our program and then stop the process. Rather, we engage in ongoing efforts to make the adjustments necessary to improve and maintain alignment as the process of graduate education evolves. Deciding when and how to make those adjustments requires an ongoing cycle of gathering information to inform the decisions necessary to improve the program and achieve the desired outcomes.

The alignment process, then, requires efforts to *improve* a specific program through *internal decision making* in an *ongoing, cyclical* process. Given this framework for successful doctoral programs as an alignment process, we believe that the assessment process for doctoral programs must address the criteria related to the alignment premises. For us, formative assessment is essential in the success of doctoral programs because, by definition, it addresses the criteria from these premises.

Formative Program Assessment—How Does Formative Assessment Address the Premises of the Alignment Model for Successful Doctoral Programs?

While the alignment model provides our framework, formative assessment, as Figure 3.1 suggests, provides the methods to achieve alignment in the process of improving doctoral education. To explain more fully what formative assessment is and why formative methods are so important in addressing the premises for alignment, we focus on the purpose, audience, and timing that are central to formative assessment.

Purpose—To Improve

Formative assessment is conducted for the purpose of improvement. Scriven (1967) was the first to emphasize this point when he made the distinction between formative and summative evaluation. He suggested that formative methods provide information to improve an ongoing program, while summative approaches provide information to judge worth, merit, or value at the completion of a program. Formative assessment, then, focuses on the broad issues of what is working and what needs to be changed in order to provide the improvement or development for the program and provides "feedback that can be used to modify or 'form' the ongoing program and thus improve its outcomes" (Gardiner, 1994, p. 67). Certainly, both formative and summative approaches are essential in evaluating doctoral programs, but formative assessment is more consistent with the improvement-based approach of the alignment model for successful doctoral education.

Audience—Internal Decision Makers

As opposed to summative evaluation that is more likely conducted for the benefit of external decision makers such as central administrators, government officials, or accrediting bodies, formative assessment is conducted to support the faculty/staff and students as decision makers most directly involved in the program (Davis, 1994). In order to improve a specific doctoral program, the constituents most directly involved must engage in reflective decision making about how to proceed, and the assessment choices that are made within the process must reflect that assessment is contextual, depending on the people involved and their specific situation (Patton, 1997, p. 126).

There are a number of important reasons for making sure that the individuals most directly involved are at the heart of the formative assessment. For one thing, these students and faculty/staff are the direct beneficiaries of improvements that are made. Having faculty at the center of the internal decision-making process ensures that their expertise and experiences are included in the decisions about whether the program is on track and whether adjustment can or should be made. At the same time, the experiences and expertise of those faculty/staff can be balanced with the needs and expectations of students. Having the students involved both as providers and as users of the formative data provides opportunities for them to see how the program can acknowledge what they bring to it and help them feel that they are directly involved in contributing to its directions. That integration can be a step toward retaining students and addressing some of the alienation and isolation they often experience when they find that the campus or departmental culture is not responsive to their needs, perceptions, and expectations (Lovitts, 2004; Nerad et al., 1997, p. xi). At the same time, students can use the process to help them determine how successfully they are proceeding through their programs and what kinds of adjustments they need to make to enhance the alignment as they strive to accomplish both their goals and the intended outcomes of the program.

For us, the focus on these internal decision makers in an alignment model shapes the kinds of questions we might ask about the use of formative assessment in our programs. For example:

- Who are the internal decision makers who should be most directly involved in the process?
- How can expectations for formative program assessment be identified and shared with these internal decision makers from the beginning?
- What approaches will encourage students and faculty/staff to recognize that their needs, beliefs, and expectations have to be balanced in relation to needs, beliefs, and expectations of others involved in the process?
- What procedures are in place for including all constituents in the decision making about the kinds of adjustments that need to be made as the program progresses?
- What kinds of processes are in place to make adjustments when backgrounds, needs, goals, expectations, and perceptions of constituents need to be balanced against each other?
- How will those adjustments be implemented by the constituents and how will the effects be reassessed in ongoing ways?

These questions are particularly relevant since both faculty and students have significant roles and responsibilities in the formative assessment process (Pruitt-Logan & Isaac, 1995). Addressing the logistical considerations in such questions can identify the individuals who will be most directly involved in the assessment process, clarify procedures for their involvement, and help to determine the ways in which the results will be used.

Timing—Ongoing, Cyclical Process

Formative assessment is typically an ongoing process that cycles important information back into a program to improve it. As Gardiner (1994) explains, formative assessment takes place *"during the active life* of a program, project or course"* (p. 67). Thus, we do not wait until the end of a course or program activity as we are likely to do with summative evaluation. Instead, we increase the number of points at which we gather information while the program is in progress and use that information to make the adjustments designed to improve the program for current stakeholders.

When faculty/staff and students receive feedback as they proceed, they have the opportunity to make adjustments that can help them be more successful in achieving the intended outcomes. At the same time, the students benefit from being able to participate as the program is in progress. Because doctoral education is a socialization process that can lead to either persistence or attrition, it is particularly important that we understand how students are experiencing the process as they proceed through it. Once they have dropped out of the program, they are no longer available to provide feedback through either formative or summative approaches. The best chance of addressing concerns and challenges that might contribute to attrition lies in the potential for improvements during the program.

Now that we have shown how important formative assessment is in the alignment model, we can begin to illustrate its use within that framework. In the next section of the chapter, we focus on the application of formative program assessment in an alignment model.

Application—How Can We Begin to Use Formative Assessment in an Alignment Model for Doctoral Programs?

In order to use formative assessment to increase alignment, we, first of all, have to identify questions that examine the individual components of a current program. We now know that such questions have to be designed to obtain information that can increase alignment of program components as the program is in progress. In Table 3.1 we list some representative kinds of questions that could engage faculty/staff and students in examining the basic

TABLE 3.1.
Sample Questions for Assessing Individual Components of Doctoral Programs

Component	Questions
Program Activities	• What are the activities that make up the three phases in the current program?
	• What and how are the activities in various phases contributing individually and collectively to current students' socialization and to successful program outcomes?
	• What are the roles and responsibilities of the current students and faculty/staff during each phase?
	• What special opportunities or challenges do each of the phases present for current students and/or faculty/staff?
	• How can the phases be improved to enhance their impact on the success of a program for the current students and faculty/staff?
	• How might understanding of the effectiveness of the individual phases be used to address such challenges as attrition, diversity, time to degree, and other challenges for current students and the faculty/staff?
Students	• Who are the current students?
	• What backgrounds, needs, concerns, beliefs, goals, and expectations do current students have that will contribute to or constrain success in the program?
	• What makes needs, goals, expectations, and/or perceptions of current students interesting, special, or challenging for them or for others who work with them?
	• To what extent do those needs, goals, expectations, and/or perceptions change as the current student progresses through the program?
	• How successfully do various phases of the program address these changes?
	• What is the impact of such changes on current students' success in the program?
	• To what extent do the needs, goals, expectations, and/or perceptions of current students need to be balanced against those of the institution or current faculty/staff?
Faculty/Staff	• Who are the key faculty/staff?
	• What backgrounds, needs, concerns, beliefs, goals, and expectations do current faculty/staff have that will contribute to or constrain success in the program?

(continues)

TABLE 3.1.
Continued

Component	Questions
	• What makes needs, goals, expectations, and/or perceptions of current faculty/staff interesting, special, or challenging for them and for others they work with? • To what extent do the needs, goals, expectations, and/or perceptions of faculty/staff change as students progress through the program? • How successfully do various phases of the program address these changes? • What is the impact of such changes on the success of current faculty/staff? • To what extent is it possible, or necessary, to balance the needs, goals, expectations, and/or perceptions of faculty and staff against those of current students and the institution?
Outcomes	• To what extent are the current goals realistic and appropriate for the program activities? • How well are the outcomes being achieved in the current program? • What is contributing to that success during various phases of the current program? • What can be done to enhance the achievement of goals at various phases when efforts in the current program are not adequate?
Context	• What are the current contextual factors that are affecting what happens in the program? • At which level are those factors most influential in the current program? • Which of those are helpful during various phases of the current program activities? • Which are constraining? • To what extent can any of the constraining factors be altered for the current program? • What approaches can be most helpful in addressing driving and constraining contextual factors as the current program proceeds?

components of a doctoral program. Our alignment model for doctoral programs suggests that none of these components alone dictates how goals for a doctoral program will be achieved. Although one of these components may receive more emphasis than another at a given point, addressing questions for all the components is essential in determining how alignment, and, ultimately, desired outcomes, can best be achieved.

As important as understanding each of these individual components is, it is even more important to examine the intersections between and among these major components of the program within their contexts. These interactions are relevant at each phase of the doctoral program. For instance:

- What effect does a program orientation during the initial phase have on a particular cohort of students in a doctoral program?
- What parts during the process of preliminary exams in the second phase of program activities are most helpful in assisting students to make the transition into their dissertation research and their future careers? How are those parts affected by the context?
- What can be done to improve the dissertation experience in the third phase of the program as a process that prepares students for a range of careers?

At the intersections of program activities, students, faculty/staff, outcomes, and the contexts of doctoral programs, then, lie important questions that create the need for formative program assessment and, thus, the need for ongoing attention to the alignment necessary for successful doctoral programs. To illustrate how formative assessment can be integrated across our alignment model, we have provided in Table 3.2 examples of sample questions, data sources, and procedures for improvement-based study of the intersections of some of the program components.

Clearly, there are other data-gathering methods we could have included in the examples, such as observations and assessment of representative student work, but there are excellent resources that explain fully what such methods are and how they can be incorporated in an overall assessment plan (see, for instance, Selim & Pet-Armacost, 2004; Westat, Frierson, Hood, & Hughes, 2002, as well as chapters 2, 5, 7, and 9 in this book). For our purposes in this part of the chapter, we simply wanted to illustrate briefly how formative assessment might be used to examine the components of doctoral programs and the interrelationships among those components.

TABLE 3.2.

Sample Questions, Data Sources, and Procedures for Using Formative Program Assessment Designed to Align the Components of Individual Doctoral Programs

Intersections	Assessment Questions	Data Sources and Procedures
Context—Program Activities: national agenda and program elements	Is our doctoral program curriculum designed as preparation for a range of careers?	• Student focus groups • Faculty interviews • Program director interview
Context—Students: graduate school services for students	Do the graduate school services meet the needs of our diverse student body?	• Student questionnaire • Graduate dean and program director individual interviews
Students—Program Activities: student satisfaction with program elements	How satisfied are our current students with their progress through the phases of the program?	• Student focus groups • Student satisfaction questionnaire
Faculty—Program Activities: faculty satisfaction with program elements	How satisfied are our current faculty with the use of required exams in the program?	• Faculty focus groups • Faculty satisfaction questionnaire
Faculty—Students: faculty-student interactions	Are our faculty members successfully implementing strategies that promote student development from directed knowledge consumers to independent knowledge producers?	• Student focus groups • Ongoing analysis of student portfolios • Faculty focus groups

Faculty-Students—Program Activities: advisement during various program elements	How can our student advising be adapted during each program element to fulfill current student and faculty needs/expectations more successfully?	• Student focus groups/satisfaction questionnaire • Academic and research advisor survey/individual interviews • Observation of advising meetings
Context—Faculty-Students Program Activities: faculty use of resources to support students in the program	How can our faculty best deploy departmental resources to support current students in moving successfully through the program?	• Program documents content analyses • Student focus groups/interviews • Faculty focus groups/interviews • Graduate dean and program director interviews

Conclusion

Our main goal in this chapter has been to present an alignment model as a framework for use in assessing doctoral programs and to explain the importance of formative assessment within that framework. As our explanation has suggested, the benefits of the approach are numerous. First, it positions us to examine not only important individual components of a doctoral program but also the intersections of those components. Thus, rather than viewing those components only in a hierarchical way—with some always more important than others—we can recognize that at various phases of doctoral programs any of the individual components may require additional examination and that exploring the interrelationships among the components can provide especially rich insights about when and how to improve programs. Second, integrating formative assessment into our alignment model reinforces the importance of ongoing, cyclical methods, shifting that review to a continuous improvement process as opposed to a process that is only conducted every five years or so. Finally, formative assessment in an alignment model focuses on the importance of involving the individuals who are most directly engaged in doctoral programs as participants, both in obtaining information to base decisions on and in deciding what adjustments can be most helpful for enhancing alignment. Ultimately, using formative assessment to increase alignment in doctoral programs engages all of us more comprehensively and productively in assessing individual doctoral programs in ways that contribute to the achievement of desired outcomes.

References

Aanerud, R., Homer, L., Nerad, M., & Cerny, J. (2006). Paths and perceptions: Assessing doctoral education using career path analysis. In P. L. Maki & N. Borkowski (Eds.), *The Assessment of doctoral education: Emerging criteria and new models for improving outcomes* (pp. 109–141). Sterling, VA: Stylus.

Anderson, M. S. (1996). Collaboration, the doctoral experience, and the departmental environment. *Review of Higher Education, 19*(3), 305–326.

Antony, J. S. (2002). Reexamining doctoral student socialization and professional development: Moving beyond congruence and assimilation orientation. *Higher Education: Handbook of Theory and Research, 17,* 349–380.

Antony, J. S., & Taylor, E. (2004). Theories and strategies of academic career socialization: Improving paths to the professoriate for Black graduate students. In D. H. Wulff, A. E. Austin, & Associates, *Paths to the professoriate: Strategies for enriching the preparation of future faculty* (pp. 92–114). San Francisco: Jossey-Bass.

Austin, A. E. (2002a, November). *Assessing doctoral students' progress along developmental dimensions.* Paper presented at the annual conference of the Association for the Study of Higher Education, Sacramento, CA.

Austin, A. E. (2002b). Preparing the next generation of faculty: Graduate school as socialization to the academic career. *Journal of Higher Education, 73*(1), 94–121.

Baird, L. L. (1972). The relation of graduate students' role relations to their stage of academic career, employment, and academic success. *Organizational Behavior and Human Performance, 7,* 428–441.

Berg, H. M., & Ferber, M. A. (1983). Men and women graduate students: Who succeeds and why? *Journal of Higher Education, 54*(6), 629–648.

Boyle, P., & Boice, B. (1998). Best practices for enculturation: Collegiality, mentoring, and structure. *New Directions for Higher Education, 101,* 87–94.

Clark, B. R. (1995). *Places of inquiry: Research and advanced education in modern universities.* Berkeley: University of California Press.

Davis, B. G. (1994). Demystifying assessment: Learning from the field of evaluation. In J. S. Stark & A. Thomas (Eds.), *Assessment and program evaluation* (pp. 45–57). Boston: Pearson Custom Publishing.

Denecke, D. D., & Frasier, H. S. (2005, November). Ph.D. completion project: Preliminary results from baseline data. *Communicator, 38*(9), 1–2, 7–8.

Ellis, E. M. (2001). The impact of race and gender on graduate school socialization, satisfaction with doctoral study, and commitment to degree completion. *Western Journal of Black Studies, 25*(1), 30–45.

Fagen, A. P., & Suedkamp Wells, K. M. (2004). The 2000 National Doctoral Program Survey. In D. H. Wulff, A. E. Austin, & Associates, *Paths to the professoriate: Strategies for enriching the preparation of future faculty* (pp. 74–91). San Francisco: Jossey-Bass.

Finkelstein, M. J., & Schuster, J. H. (2001). Assessing the silent revolution: How changing demographics are reshaping the academic profession. *AAHE Bulletin, 54*(2), 3–7.

Gaff, J. G. (2002). The disconnect between graduate education and faculty realities. *Liberal Education, 88*(3), 6–13.

Gaff, J. G., Pruitt-Logan, A. S., & Weibl, R. A. (2000). *Building the faculty we need: Colleges and universities working together.* Washington, DC: Association of American Colleges and Universities.

Gappa, J. M., Austin, A. E., & Trice, A. G. (2005). Rethinking academic work and workplaces. *Change, 37*(6), 32–39.

Gardiner, L. F. (1994). Assessment and evaluation: Knowing and judging results. In J. S. Stark & A. Thomas (Eds.), *Assessment and program evaluation* (pp. 65–78). Boston: Pearson Custom Publishing.

Gardner, D. E. (1994). Five evaluation frameworks: Implications for decision making in higher education. In J. S. Stark & A. Thomas (Eds.), *Assessment and program evaluation* (pp. 7–21). Boston: Pearson Custom Publishing.

Goldberger, M. L., Maher, B. A., Flattau, P. E. (Eds.). (1995). *Research-doctorate programs in the United States: Continuity and change.* Washington, DC: National Academy Press.

Golde, C. M. (1996). How departmental contextual factors shape doctoral student attrition. Doctoral dissertation, Stanford University, 1996. *Dissertation Abstracts International, 57*(08), 3415A.

Golde, C. M. (1998). Beginning graduate school: Explaining first year doctoral attrition. *New Directions for Higher Education, 101,* 55–64.

Golde, C. M., & Dore, T. M. (2001). *At cross purposes: What the experiences of doctoral students reveal about doctoral education.* Philadelphia, PA: A report prepared for The Pew Charitable Trusts. Retrieved from http://www.phd-survey.org

Golde, C. M., & Dore, T. M. (2004). The survey of doctoral education and career preparation: The importance of disciplinary contexts. In D. H. Wulff, A. E. Austin, & Associates, *Paths to the professoriate: Strategies for enriching the preparation of future faculty* (pp. 19–45). San Francisco: Jossey-Bass.

Haworth, J. G., & Conrad, C. F. (1996). Refocusing quality assessment on student learning. *New Directions for Institutional Research, 92,* 45–60.

Hutchings, P., & Clarke, S. E. (2004). The scholarship of teaching and learning: Contributing to reform in graduate education. In D. H. Wulff, A. E. Austin, & Associates, *Paths to the professoriate: Strategies for enriching the preparation of future faculty* (pp. 161–176). San Francisco: Jossey-Bass.

Isaac, P. D., Pruitt-Logan, A. S., & Upcraft, M. L. (1995). The landscape of graduate education. *New Directions for Student Services, 72,* 13–21.

Isaac, P. D., Quinlan, S. V., & Walker, M. M. (1992). Faculty perceptions of the doctoral dissertation. *Journal of Higher Education, 63*(3), 241–268.

Julius, D. J., & Gumport, P. J. (2003). Graduate student unionization: Catalysts and consequences. *Review of Higher Education, 26*(2), 187–216.

LaPidus, J. B. (1995). Doctoral education and student career needs. *New Directions for Student Services, 72,* 33–41.

LaPidus, J. B. (1998). If we want things to stay as they are, things will have to change. *New Directions for Higher Education, 101,* 95–102.

Lovitts, B. E. (2001). *Leaving the ivory tower: The causes and consequences of departure from doctoral study.* Lanham, MD: Rowman & Littlefield.

Lovitts, B. E. (2004). Research on the structure and process of graduate education: Retaining students. In D. H. Wulff, A. E. Austin, & Associates, *Paths to the professoriate: Strategies for enriching the preparation of future faculty* (pp. 115–136). San Francisco: Jossey-Bass.

Lovitts, B. E. (2005). Being a good course-taker is not enough: A theoretical perspective on the transition to independent research. *Studies in Higher Education, 30*(2), 137–154.

Maher, M. A., Ford, M. E., & Thompson, C. M. (2004). Degree progress of women doctoral students: Factors that constrain, facilitate, and differentiate. *Review of Higher Education, 27*(3), 385–408.

Nerad, M. (2005). From graduate student to world citizen in a global environment. *International Higher Education, 40,* 8–9.

Nerad, M., Aanerud, R., & Cerny, J. (2004). So you want to be a professor! Lessons from the Ph.D.s Ten Years Later Study. In D. H. Wulff, A. Austin, & Associates, *Paths to the professoriate: Strategies for enriching the preparation of future faculty* (pp. 137–158). San Francisco: Jossey-Bass.

Nerad, M., & Cerny, J. (1993). From facts to action: Expanding the graduate division's educational role. *New Directions for Institutional Research, 80,* 27–40.

Nerad, M., & Cerny, J. (1999). Widening the circle: Another look at graduate women students. *Communicator, 32*(6), 1–7. Washington, DC: Council of Graduate Schools.

Nerad, M., & Cerny, J. (2000). From rumors to facts: Career outcomes of English Ph.D.s. Results from the Ph.D.s Ten Years Later Study. *ADE Bulletin, 124,* 43–55. New York: Association of Departments of English, Modern Language Association.

Nerad, M., June, R., & Miller, D. S. (1997). The cyclical problems of graduate education: Institutional responses in the 1990s. In M. Nerad, R. June, & D. S. Miller (Eds.), *Graduate education in the United States* (pp. vii–xiv). New York: Garland.

Nerad, M., & Miller, D. S. (1996). Assessment in graduate and professional programs: Demand, processes, outcomes. *New Directions for Institutional Research, 92,* 61–76.

Nyquist, J. D. (2002). The Ph.D.: A tapestry of change for the 21st century. *Change, 34*(6), 13–20.

Nyquist, J. D., Abbott, R. D., & Wulff, D. H. (Eds.). (1989). Teaching assistant training in the 1990s. *New Directions for Teaching and Learning, 39.*

Nyquist, J. D., & Sprague, J. (1998). Thinking developmentally about TAs. In M. Marincovich, J. Prostko, & F. Stout (Eds.), *The professional development of graduate teaching assistants* (pp. 61–88). Bolton, MA: Anker.

Nyquist, J., & Wulff, D. H. (1996). *Working effectively with graduate assistants.* Thousand Oaks, CA: Sage.

Ostriker, J. P., & Kuh, C. V. (Eds.). (2003). *Assessing research-doctorate programs: A methodology study.* Washington, DC: National Academies Press.

Patton, M. Q. (1997). *Utilization-focused evaluation: The new century text* (3rd. ed.). Thousand Oaks, CA: Sage.

Pruitt-Logan, A. S., & Isaac, P. D. (1995). Looking ahead. *New Directions for Student Services, 72,* 123–128.

Scriven, M. (1967). The methodology of evaluation. In R. Tyler, R. Gagne, & M. Scriven (Eds.), *Perspectives of curriculum evaluation* (pp. 39–83). AERA Monograph Series on Curriculum Evaluation, No. 1. Chicago: Rand McNally.

Selim, B. R., & Pet-Armacost, J. (2004). *Program assessment handbook: Guidelines for planning and implementing quality enhancing efforts of program and student learning outcomes.* Orlando: University of Central Florida. Retrieved from http://iaaweb.ucf.edu/oeas2/pdf/acad_program_assessment_handbook...revo227 04.pdf

Sprague, J., & Nyquist, J. (1989). TA supervision. *New Directions for Teaching and Learning, 39,* 37–53.

Staton, A. Q., & Darling, A. L. (1989). Socialization of teaching assistants. *New Directions for Teaching and Learning, 39,* 15–22.

Syverson, P. D. (1996). Assessing demand for graduate and professional programs. *New Directions for Institutional Research, 92,* 17–29.

Tinto, V. (1997). Toward a theory of doctoral persistence. In M. Nerad, R. June, & D. S. Miller (Eds.), *Graduate education in the United States* (pp. 322–335). New York: Garland.

Turner, C. S. V., & Thompson, J. R. (1993). Socializing women doctoral students: Minority and majority experiences. *Review of Higher Education, 16*(3), 355–370.

Weidman, J. C., & Stein, E. L. (2003). Socialization of doctoral students to academic norms. *Research in Higher Education, 44*(6), 641–656.

Weidman, J. C., Twale, D. J., & Stein, E. L. (Eds.). (2001). Socialization of graduate and professional students in higher education: A perilous passage? *ASHE-ERIC Higher Education Report, 28*(3).

Westat, J. F., Frierson, H., Hood, S., & Hughes, G. (2002). *The user-friendly handbook for project evaluation* (NSF 99-12175). Arlington, VA: National Science Foundation. Retrieved from http://www.nsf.gov/pubs/2002/nsf02057/nsf02 057_1.pdf

Wulff, D. H. (1985). *Case studies of the communication of university instructors.* Unpublished doctoral dissertation, University of Washington, Seattle.

Wulff, D. H. (2005). Using an alignment model of teaching effectiveness. In D. H. Wulff, W. H. Jacobson, K. Freisem, D. H. Hatch, M. E. Lawrence, & L. R. Lenz (Eds.), *Aligning for learning: Strategies for teaching effectiveness* (pp. 3–15). Bolton, MA: Anker.

Wulff, D. H., & Austin, A. E. (2004). Future directions: Strategies to enhance paths to the professoriate. In D. H. Wulff, A. E. Austin, & Associates, *Paths to the professoriate: Strategies for enriching the preparation of future faculty* (pp. 267–292). San Francisco: Jossey-Bass.

Wulff, D. H., Austin, A. E., Nyquist, J. D., & Sprague, J. (2004). The development of graduate students as teaching scholars: A four-year longitudinal study. In D. H. Wulff, A. E. Austin, & Associates, *Paths to the professoriate: Strategies for enriching the preparation of future faculty* (pp. 46–73). San Francisco: Jossey-Bass.

4

PATHS AND PERCEPTIONS

Assessing Doctoral Education Using Career Path Analysis

Rebecca Aanerud, Lori Homer, Maresi Nerad, and Joseph Cerny

O ver the past few years, doctoral education has faced criticism about its relevance in preparing students for the careers they pursue following graduation. Critics both within academia and in industry (e.g., business, government, and nonprofit [BGN] sectors) argue that new educational approaches are needed to prepare doctoral students for the jobs and jobs skills that await them.[1] Those in BGN have argued that doctoral students are educated too narrowly and are not prepared to work collaboratively in teams. Those in the academy have argued that doctoral students are not prepared to teach, publish, write grants, or present their work in professional settings. Others assert that while doctoral education is sufficient, there are simply too many doctoral students for the job market that awaits them (Goldman & Massy, 2001). As a result of these criticisms, researchers such as Nerad, Cerny, Golde, and Dore have studied the relationship between doctoral education and Ph.D. career paths. In addition, Nerad and Cerny have studied Ph.D. holders' perceptions of the relevance and value of their doctoral education. It is, after all, the Ph.D. recipients who are in the best position to judge the relevance and value of their doctoral education in relation to their careers and lives.

Certainly that is the logic that informed Nerad and Cerny's national study, *Ph.D.s Ten Years Later* (Nerad & Cerny, 1999a, 1999b), which in turn inspired Golde and Dore's 2001 survey of doctoral students currently in U.S.

doctoral programs. The interest in and value of these studies subsequently inspired the National Research Council to recommend that student perspectives be included in future doctoral program assessments (Ostriker & Kuh, 2003). Nerad and Cerny (1999a) and Golde and Dore (2001) argue that student and former student (Ph.D. recipient) perspectives need to be included when assessing doctoral education. Whereas Golde and Dore focused their survey on current students who had not yet entered the job market and thus were not certain about their future employment, Nerad and Cerny surveyed former students and asked them about their education in light of their actual careers, thus providing an additional perspective.

Drawing from the Nerad and Cerny survey, this chapter focuses on the results of student responses in two disciplines, English and mathematics, to demonstrate the assessment value of understanding student career paths and student evaluations of doctoral programs in light of their career paths. We chose to focus on these two disciplines because they represent traditional arts and science fields, yet they differ in a number of ways. The job markets in English are different from the job markets in math. Math has a postdoctoral phase that, although not mandatory, does function as part of the career path for a third of the survey respondents and the time to stable employment differs between the two fields. Further, English has a greater representation of women, and the representation of women in a field has been shown to impact the labor market in that field (Reskin & Padavic, 1994).

First, we describe the basic career path in terms of the careers followed according to job titles and level of job satisfaction reported. Second, we summarize Ph.D. recipient evaluations of specific aspects of the curricula and professional development they experienced in their doctoral programs. These evaluations were done at the time of the survey, 10 to 14 years after students received their degrees. Since the retrospective accounts were made in light of the actual career paths Ph.D. recipients pursued, they are a particularly useful lens that faculty and administrators can use to assess their programs.

The Ph.D. Ten Years Later Study

The Ph.D.s Ten Years Later study was a national survey of nearly 6,000 Ph.D.s. It targets doctorates in six disciplines from five major fields of study: life sciences (biochemistry), engineering (computer science, electrical engineering), humanities (English), physical science (mathematics), and social science (political science). Three consecutive cohorts who received their doctorates from 61 U.S. doctoral-granting universities between July 1982 and June 1985 were surveyed. This group accounted for 57% of the total Ph.D.s awarded in the United States in these six fields during these three years. The response rate reflected 66% for domestic Ph.D.s and 52% for international Ph.D.s. The data generated by this survey are extensive, including information on career goals before starting and after completing the Ph.D., details about all postdoctoral appointments, experiences with initial (non-postdoc) job searches, detailed job history since Ph.D. completion, the importance of different aspects of first and current job, satisfaction with current job, doctoral program evaluation including instruction in teaching, advice and mentoring received from advisors and other faculty members, the usefulness of doctoral education in light of careers pursued, and the subjective value respondents placed on their doctoral education. We have not included a full analysis of all survey items. However, we have included the survey questions addressed in this chapter in Appendix A.

English and Mathematics: Similarities and Differences in the Career Paths

We begin with some general findings for the fields of English and mathematics. Overall, the survey includes 814 respondents in English (a 67% response rate) and 752 in mathematics (a 63% response rate). The gender breakdown within English was 46% men to 54% women, while mathematics was 82% male to 17% female. On average, time to degree was two years longer in English than mathematics with respondents in English reporting 8.3 years compared to 6.3 years for mathematics respondents. Mathematics, unlike English or any of the other four fields of the study, was unique in that its degrees can be relatively cleanly distinguished as either applied or theoretical. Fifty-five percent of the mathematics degrees awarded were for various purely theoretical mathematics fields, whereas 45% of the degrees awarded were for applied mathematics fields. Women respondents completed applied mathematics degrees in higher proportions than the men, 55% as compared with 43%. International Ph.D.s were more likely to enter the professoriate than domestic Ph.D.s. Theoretical mathematicians were more likely to enter the professoriate than applied mathematicians. Men in math were more likely to enter tenure-track academic jobs than were women in math. Analysis of qualitative data (responses to open-ended questions) suggests that more men than women go into the professoriate because of the difficulty for mathematics graduates in finding faculty positions for dual-career couples, and more women with Ph.D.s in math face this dilemma than their male counterparts.

For ease of analysis, the basic career paths for English and mathematics were divided into three general categories: Academic Ladder faculty (tenure-track and tenured faculty), BGN (business, government, or nonprofit job sectors), and Academic Other (administrative or nontenure-track faculty). Figure 4.1 shows that at the time of the survey—which ranges anywhere from 10 to 14 years after degree completion—survey respondents in English and mathematics look fairly similar in terms of academic placement. Ten to fourteen years after receiving their Ph.D.s, roughly 60% of the respondents were working in either tenured or tenure-track positions.

Notable differences between the two fields were in the proportions of respondents in BGN sectors and the Academic Other sector. About 30% of mathematics Ph.D. recipients were employed outside the academy in the BGN job sectors compared to only 19% of English respondents. Considerably more English doctorate holders than their mathematics counterparts were working in the academy not as Academic Ladder faculty (21% for English compared to 10% for mathematics; Nerad & Cerny 1999a).

Placement by Sector and Gender

Figure 4.2 illustrates Ph.D. placement by sector and gender for both fields. In general, the representation of women in Academic Ladder positions was lower in both fields, while their proportional representation was higher in the BGN and Academic Other sectors. Managers and executives in the BGN sector (a component of the BGN sector not illustrated) represented about 5% of all Ph.D.s regardless of field or gender.

Since women's disadvantage in any labor market—especially in a highly skilled professional labor market—accumulates with time (Martell, Lane, & Emrich, 1996; Ridgeway, 1991, 1997), examining the gendered nature of career paths several years after degree completion can be more illustrative than looking at placement at or immediately following degree completion. The data show that 10 to 14 years after degree completion, men were disproportionately likely to achieve tenure in either English or mathematics. In English, higher proportions of women had not yet achieved tenure or were in

FIGURE 4.1
Job sector at time of survey

FIGURE 4.2
Job sector by field and gender

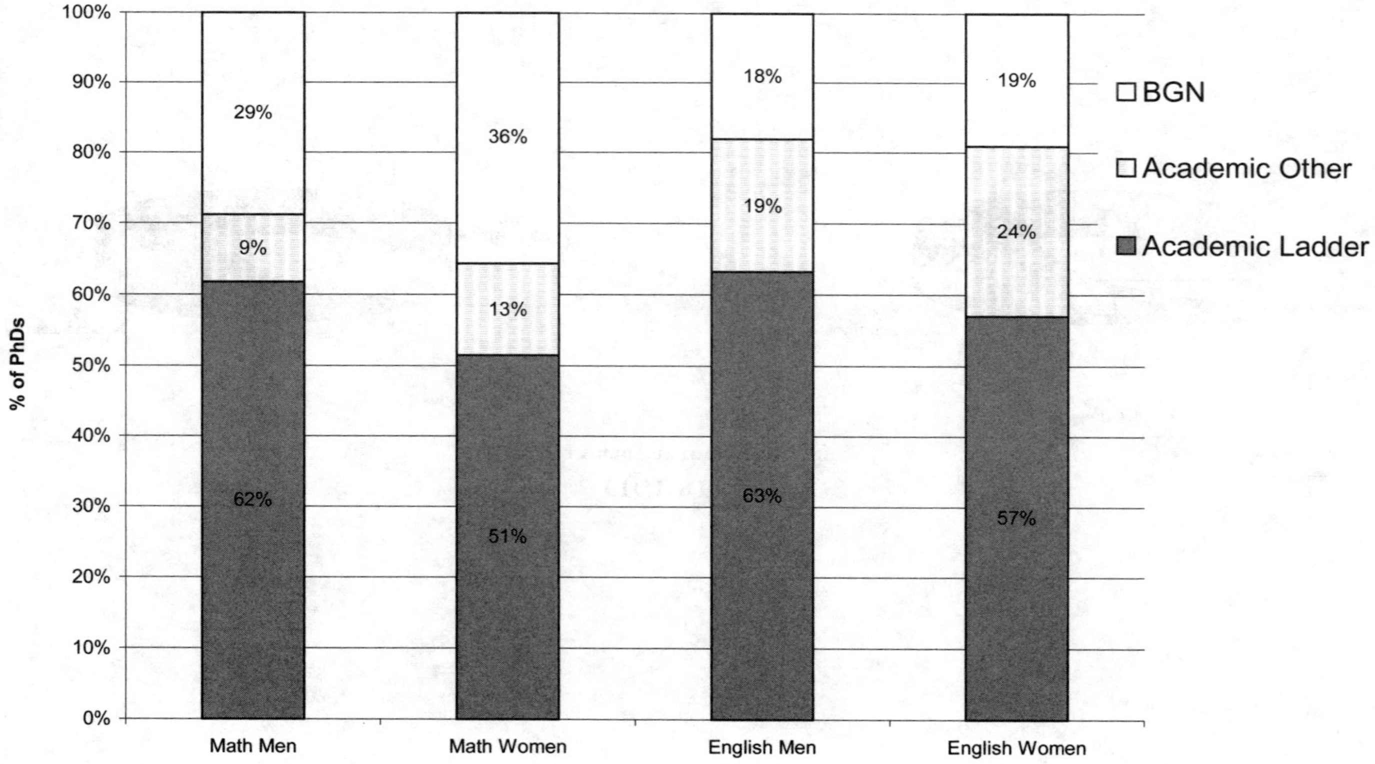

Academic Other positions. In mathematics, higher proportions of men (relative to women) were in the tenure-track but not-yet-tenured category. While the overall patterns are more apparent after 10 to 14 years, examining differences in initial placement, such as postdoctoral appointments, may help illustrate the overall disparate pattern of placement by gender 10 to 14 years later.

There is a relatively high representation of women mathematics graduates in the BGN sector (over one-third). This pattern is related to the unique role that a postdoctoral appointment plays in the career paths of mathematics graduates. Mathematics, unlike English, was more likely to have a postdoctoral appointment phase of the education process (31% and 8%, respectively). A postdoctoral fellowship provides an opportunity to gain additional knowledge and expertise in an area of research that differs in some way from the doctoral research. In can also be a means of developing one's research agenda beyond the dissertation. In general, more postdocs are available in the STEM (science, technology, engineering, and mathematics) fields than in the humanities or in the social sciences. These postdocs allow Ph.D. recipients to engage in cutting-edge research early in their careers and learn to teach independently. For example, the National Science Foundation awards prestigious postdoctoral fellowships for research as well as for teaching in math institutes and departments.[2] In general, completing a postdoctoral appointment was strongly associated with an academic career path: 15% of those graduates with a postdoc went on to hold a tenured faculty position at one of the top quartile research programs in 1995 versus 5% of graduates who did not spend any time in a postdoctoral position.

An important gender difference emerged with postdoctoral positions in mathematics based on the kind of postdoctoral appointment accepted. In general, postdoctoral appointments fall into two categories: portable or faculty-specific, with the former being far more prestigious and more highly associated with a faculty career path. Our analysis reveals that there were two predictors for having the less prestigious faculty-specific postdoc:

1. The age of the recipient at time of degree completion: Portable postdocs tended to be represented by younger Ph.D. holders.
2. The gender and marital status of the recipient: Married women who had a postdoc were far more likely to have a faculty-specific postdoc.

Women married at the time of receiving their degree took faculty-specific postdocs in proportions that far exceeded the proportion of married women in the population. The challenge that many women Ph.D. recipients faced in both fields, but particularly in mathematics, was the "two-body" problem. First, women in mathematics were more likely than their male peers to be married at degree completion, and those women were far more likely to be married to a man with a Ph.D. or a man working toward one. For married couples both in the job market, one possible way to manage the two-body problem is for institutions to bring more women into this faculty-specific postdoc. For women married to men completing their Ph.D. or also doing a postdoc at the same institution, the postdoc for women proved to be a common holding-pattern strategy. One respondent explained that she took the postdoc while waiting for her husband to complete his degree. We think this is not at all atypical. Because these faculty-specific postdocs are less prestigious, women may have a lesser chance of being hired into a faculty position. Moreover, women concentrated in applied mathematics, which is a subfield with fewer faculty positions. Whatever combination of factors was at play, many women left the academy following the postdoc.

In English the closest parallel to the faculty-specific postdoctoral appointment is the nontenure-track teaching position in which women are still disproportionately represented. According to our analysis, we found that in English women are still disproportionately represented in nontenure-track positions. In any given year, the odds that a woman will be in a nontenure-track teaching position will be two to three times greater than the odds for a man. Although a poor job market for English tenure-track jobs fueled the nontenure career path, many women with Ph.D.s in English reported taking these nontenured positions as a means not only to mediate a poor job market, but also to remain in the same location as their spouse.

Using Career Outcomes in Assessing Doctoral Programs

We want to highlight the assessment value of understanding the career path according to empirical rather than anecdotal data. The Ph.D. is a research degree that for many people is primarily needed for research careers and for producing the next generation of academic researchers (i.e., ladder faculty at most higher education institutions except two-year colleges). However, in light of the data from the Ph.D.s Ten Years Later survey, we know that the majority of Ph.D. recipients (more than 80%) did go on to careers in which their primary activities would likely include teaching, management, and industry- or government-based research. We argue that doctoral programs should track the career paths of their graduates—to understand the various kinds of jobs that Ph.D. recipients actually do obtain.

Figure 4.3 shows that of the survey respondents who were tenured at the time of the survey, about 15% of the Ph.D.s in mathematics and just under 10% of the Ph.D.s in English were tenured at Research 1 institutions. The majority were teaching in other doctoral, comprehensive, and liberal arts institutions. In both fields, fewer than 55% of respondents had tenure 10 to 13 years after completing their degree, in any type of academic institution. However, as Nerad, Aanerud, and Cerny (2004) make clear, controlling for the career goal of becoming a professor greatly increases the overall odds of getting tenure in English (60% of those who wanted to become a professor were tenured at the time of the survey), and 64% were tenured in mathematics.

By implication, not only did Ph.D.s take a variety of jobs outside the Academic Ladder route, but many of them knew when they completed their degree that it was not their intent to become a professor. Therefore, doctoral program evaluation should control for student career goals when assessing career outcomes. However, attempting to control for goals while students are still enrolled may prove unreliable since many people in the survey commented that it was not acceptable to express interest in any career other than becoming a professor while they were in their program. After all, most Ph.D. recipients in our study received their degree at a Research 1 university. They and their faculty often assume that this kind of institution is where they find employment.

At the heart of our discussion is this basic question: Should the ideal outcome of a doctoral education be placement in a ladder faculty position at a Research 1 university? Analysis of the data from the Ph.D.s Ten Years Later survey leads us to a resounding *no*. It is clear that doctoral education serves both individuals and society in many ways, some far removed from the traditional academic path. Given the evidence that the Ph.D. is a passport to multiple career destinations, we suggest that doctoral education assessment include an understanding of career paths, *how students feel about the jobs they actually take*, what they say about the *preparation* they experienced during the course of their doctoral education, and what they say about the *personal value* of the doctoral education.

Understanding the career paths of Ph.D. recipients through a study such as the Ph.D.s Ten Years Later provides important information for assessment

FIGURE 4.3

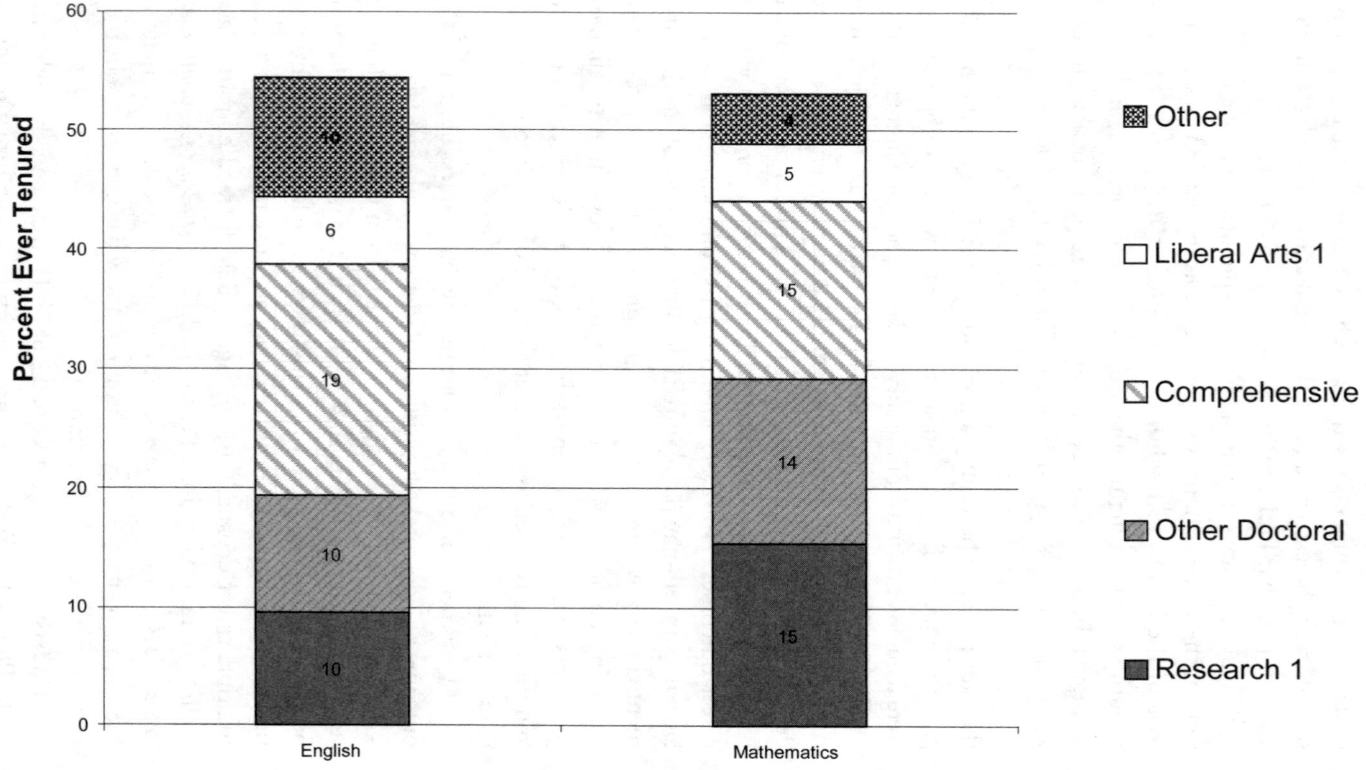

Percent ever tenured by Ph.D. field and Carnegie classification of placement

because it interrupts the anecdotal information that exists about doctoral programs. While it is certainly true that most Ph.D. recipients will not go on to tenure-track jobs at Research 1 universities, it is also not the case that they go into jobs where they are largely dissatisfied. To evaluate this claim, we looked at the Ph.D.s' job satisfaction ratings.

Ph.D. Recipients' Job Satisfaction

Respondents evaluated their satisfaction with 23 different aspects of their jobs, as well as assigning an overall satisfaction rating. The 23 individual items were factor analyzed, resulting in six dimensions of job satisfaction. These six dimensions and examples of each are illustrated in Table 4.1.

Figures 4.4 (English) and 4.5 (mathematics) compare the six job satisfaction dimensions plus the overall job satisfaction rating for those employed in the academic and BGN sectors. Because there is reason to expect job satisfaction to differ for groups that vary by occupational or organizational status (Brown, Gardner, Oswald, & Qian, 2005; Oshagbemi, 2003, 1999; Singh, 1994), job satisfaction was analyzed using four job sector categories:

1. Academic Ladder
2. Academic Other
3. BGN Manager/Executive
4. BGN Other

(To simplify our findings, job satisfaction is illustrated and discussed comparing all academic to all BGN in Figures 4.4 and 4.5; differences within these sectors are only discussed when statistically significant.)

Job satisfaction analysis revealed the following pattern: just under 25% of the Ph.D.s in the academic sector of both fields and about 33% in the BGN sector for both fields reported being "very satisfied" overall with their jobs. In both fields, Ph.D.s in the academic sector tended to be more highly satisfied with the "intrinsic rewards" of the job. This dimension of job satisfaction included use of doctoral education, content and autonomy of work, and satisfaction with opportunities to do research. Item-specific analyses indicated that Ph.D.s in the Academic Ladder and Academic Other sectors in both mathematics and English were more satisfied with the use of their doctoral education than were their counterparts in the BGN Other and BGN Manager and Executive sectors. Interestingly, in both fields the groups did

TABLE 4.1.
Dimensions of Job Satisfaction and Sample Items

Intrinsic Rewards
- Use of doctoral education
- Content of work
- Autonomy of work
- Opportunity to do research
- Opportunity to teach

Work Place Resources
- Equipment, lab space, or other physical resources
- Work environment

Tolerance
- Supportive environment for women
- Supportive environment for people of color

Quality of Life
- Level of stress at work
- Time for leisure, family, and my own interests

Compensation and Benefits
- Health and retirement benefits
- Salary level

Family/Geography
- Job opportunities for my spouse/partner in the area
- Geographic location
- Good location for raising children

Overall
- Overall level of satisfaction

not differ in their satisfaction with autonomy or content of work, nor with their opportunities to do research.

Ph.D.s working in the BGN sector in mathematics and English were more satisfied with the level of access to adequate workplace resources. Not surprisingly, English Ph.D.s in Academic Ladder and executive BGN positions were more satisfied with compensation and benefits than English Ph.D.s employed in the Academic Other positions or nonexecutive BGN sectors. Somewhat surprisingly, mathematics Ph.D.s did not differ across

FIGURE 4.4
Job satisfaction of English Ph.D.s by job sector

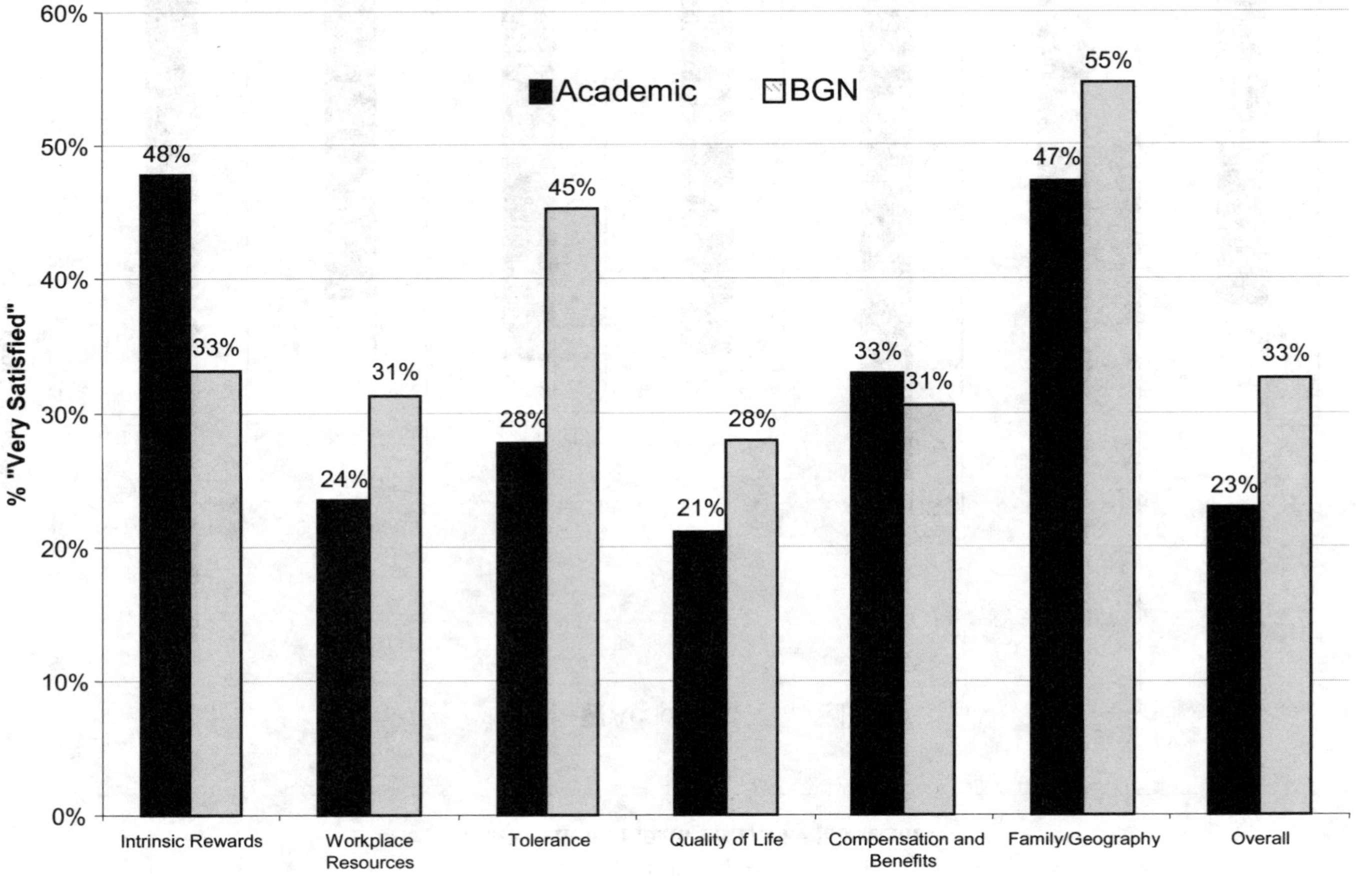

FIGURE 4.5
Job satisfaction of math Ph.D.s by job sector

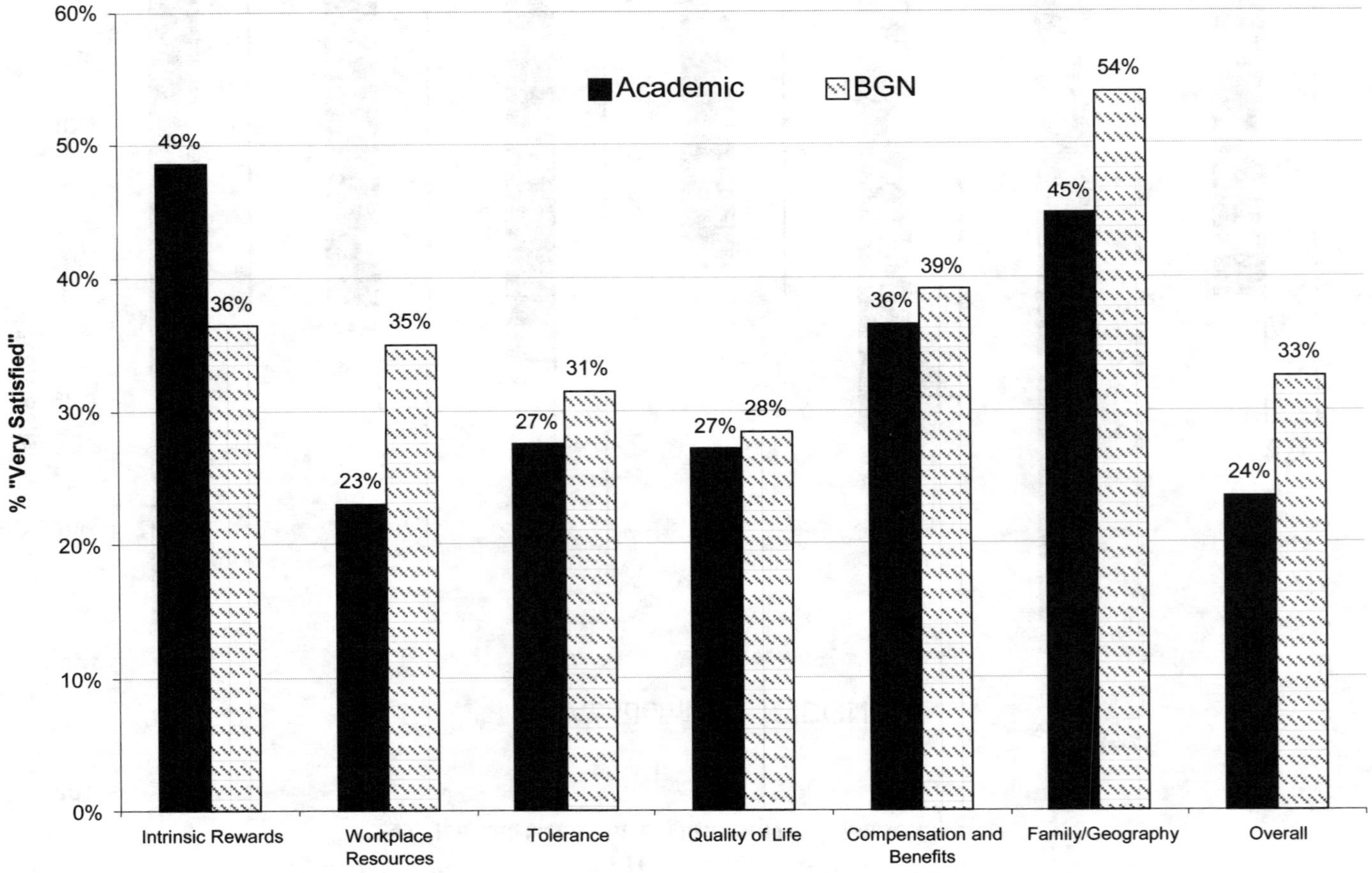

these job categories, or four sectors, in satisfaction with compensation and benefits. In fact, except for the two dimensions already mentioned (intrinsic rewards where Academic Ladder faculty were more satisfied, and workplace resources where those working in BGN were more satisfied), mathematics Ph.D.s did not differ statistically in satisfaction levels across all other dimensions and sectors.

English Ph.D. recipients working in the BGN sector were more satisfied with having a work environment that supports women and people of color and with the family/geography aspect of their jobs than their counterparts in the academic sector.

The overall patterns of difference in job satisfaction are similar in mathematics and English. In English, the more extreme differences and the somewhat larger sample size may both contribute to more statistically significant findings. While it is true that Ph.D. recipients in Academic Ladder positions reported greater satisfaction with their jobs in terms of how well the jobs made use of their education, when we looked more broadly at the job satisfaction of English and mathematics Ph.D. recipients across several dimensions and included those who were "fairly satisfied" as well as those who were "very satisfied," people with Ph.D.s, regardless of job sector, reported high levels of satisfaction with their jobs. From the standpoint of the Ph.D. recipients, most felt that they had fulfilling work that met many of their personal needs for family support, compensation, and intellectual stimulation, even though most did not find placement in Research 1 institutions, and many did not pursue academic careers at all.

Career path analysis that includes job satisfaction data makes an important contribution to the assessment activities of doctoral programs primarily in terms of mentoring and career development. Mentoring helps with completing the degree as well as preparing for a career. By understanding the overall level of job satisfaction enjoyed by Ph.D. holders, as well as the variations between and within different job sectors, doctoral programs are in a stronger position to mentor and advise students accordingly. For example, as one component of helping students work through various career options, graduate schools and faculty advisors might want to consider asking students to reflect on what dimensions of job satisfaction they expect to be most important to them, such as flexibility of work schedule, autonomy of work, workplace resources, prestige of the organization, time for leisure, compensation and benefits, career growth prospects, geographic location, job opportunities for the spouse, and so on.

Recommendations Based on Job Satisfaction

Because Ph.D. recipients do, in fact, enter careers in a range of job sectors, doctoral programs should be able to help their students determine the best career options for themselves and not limit career development and mentoring activities simply to preparation for Research 1 institutions. We argue that assessment of doctoral programs should include focusing on the programs' ability to help students make the transition to a post-Ph.D. career in a range of fields. Job satisfaction information based on empirical data, rather than assumptions (for example, the assumption that faculty jobs offer the most flexibility for raising families), provides another helpful tool for this transition. Next, we investigate students' perception of their doctoral programs in terms of the professional socialization they received and the skills they acquired in light of their current job.

Preparation for Careers: Professional Socialization

Faculty interaction with doctoral students is likely the most important aspect of the professional socialization that occurs in any doctoral program (Austin, 2002; Tierney, 1997; Weidman, Twale, & Stein, 2001). Socialization happens through transmitting both attitudes and professional skills. Students' perspectives on the socialization they experienced and the skills they acquired in their doctoral program *in light of their subsequent career paths* is valuable because it helps answer the question of whether the doctoral program prepared them for their jobs.

Despite the evidence that many Ph.D.s obtained employment outside the academy, survey respondents reported that faculty who expressed an opinion about career options tended to encourage academic careers. Table 4.2 summarizes students' perceptions of the career guidance and encouragement offered by the faculty in their respective graduate programs. Mathematicians were more likely to experience encouragement to pursue both academic and nonacademic careers (27%).

In both the English and mathematics fields, 19% of Ph.D. recipients said faculty did not have specific ideas about which career options graduate students should choose. Although this may be interpreted as merely a neutral stance, given that respondents could have selected the second option (faculty

TABLE 4.2.
Perceptions of Faculty Expectations with Regard to Students' Post-Ph.D. Careers

Faculty Expectations	English	Mathematics
Faculty mainly encouraged graduate students to pursue academic professions or jobs	73%	54%
Faculty encouraged both academic and nonacademic professions or jobs	8%	27%
Faculty mainly encouraged nonacademic professions or jobs	–	–
Faculty did not seem to have specific ideas about which professional options graduate students should choose	19%	19%

encouraged *both* academic and nonacademic professions), this seemed a likely indication of students' perceiving faculty as not being invested in students' careers.

Survey respondents were also asked to look back on six aspects of faculty mentoring (learning proposal writing, encouragement to publish, help in publishing, opportunities to present research, funding for national meetings, and interaction with nonacademic sectors) and to evaluate each statement according to whether each aspect of mentoring was "basically true" of their program or not. Figure 4.6 provides a summary illustration of English and mathematics Ph.D.s' perception of faculty mentoring. In both fields, the only aspect that these former students recalled being more true of their program than not was faculty encouragement to publish, while mathematics also included opportunities to present research. A great majority of English Ph.D.s (at least 75%) reported that they did not experience faculty mentoring in the following areas:

- learning how to write proposals
- getting assistance with publishing
- identifying opportunities to present research
- identifying sources of funding for national meetings
- identifying opportunities to interact with individuals from the nonacademic sector

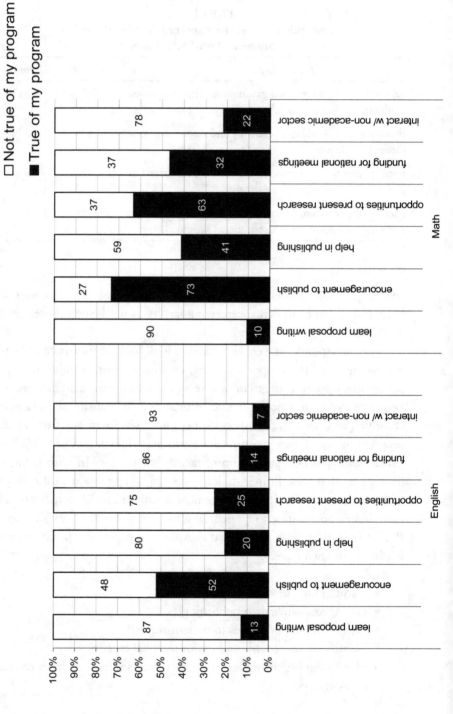

FIGURE 4.6
Mentoring received from faculty, by field

Similarly, a majority of mathematics Ph.D. recipients (59%) said they did not experience faculty mentoring in learning to how to write proposals, learning about publishing, obtaining funding for attending national meetings, and identifying opportunities to interact with individuals from the nonacademic sector.

Faculty assistance with publishing (e.g., *assisting* with the mechanics, etc., not to be confused with encouragement to publish) has been shown to predict future productivity in a faculty career path (Spalter-Roth, Kennelly, & Erskine, 2004). The data (only 20% of English Ph.D.s and 41% of mathematics Ph.D.s reported receiving help from faculty in publishing) are relevant for assessing how well various programs mentor their students in research skills critical for success in research positions, especially when compared with the greater proportions of Ph.D.s who reported being encouraged to pursue academic careers. Indeed, department chairs, graduate school administrators, and students who wish to pursue careers in research and publishing may be very interested in what previous students have said about the mentoring they received within a program, or even how it compared to national averages, as a method of assessing faculty socialization in this area specifically.

Multivariate regression analyses of faculty mentoring further indicates that Ph.D. recipients in English and mathematics as a group were less favorable about faculty mentoring they received than the comparison group of all other survey respondents (Ph.D. recipients in all of the other four fields surveyed), while Academic Ladder faculty in mathematics and English were generally more favorable across all the dimensions. These results indicate a rift between the retrospective perceptions of mentoring for Ph.D. recipients in mathematics and English in Academic Ladder positions and their counterparts in mathematics and English who were working in other sectors. Indeed, these results suggest that at some point during their doctoral program, students may have experienced disparate treatment with regard to faculty mentoring. Perhaps students that faculty deemed most worthy of investment received more/better mentoring in research skills. Since these results are retrospective, it may also be the case that students who ended up in the Academic Ladder track remembered their mentoring more favorably. Although this could be a valid alternative hypothesis, we do not currently have the data to test the relative validity of the competing hypotheses—the question of validity of retrospective analyses is an area for further inquiry. Based on the mentoring survey data we conclude that although academic careers were encouraged during their time as students, most respondents were not getting the research and publication mentoring critical for their success within academic (research) careers.

Preparation for Careers: Skills Development

Stereotypical ideas about the types of jobs Ph.D. recipients hold (Academic Ladder positions, for example) may not emphasize other skill dimensions, including broad interdisciplinary research skills or interpersonal skills such as collaboration, teamwork, and managerial techniques. Figure 4.7 illustrates the Ph.D. recipients' evaluation of the importance of these skills for doctoral education. A majority of Ph.D. recipients (employed in business, nonprofit, government, *and academic* sectors) said each of these skills was an important aspect of doctoral education, with one exception. In mathematics, only 48% of the respondents rated managerial skills as being either "very important" or "important," while another 34% of the mathematics Ph.D.s acknowledged management skills were "somewhat important" for doctoral education. For mathematics Ph.D. recipients, collaboration was most frequently seen as important (72% said it was "very important" or "important"). English Ph.D.s were most likely to say the ability to conduct interdisciplinary research was either "very important" or "important" (75%). Overall, interdisciplinary research skills, teamwork, collaboration, and managerial skills generally were seen by Ph.D. recipients as being important for doctoral education.

Survey respondents were also asked whether or not their own doctoral program included experience in or exposure to each of these four skill areas (interdisciplinary research, teamwork, collaboration, and managerial) and whether their current job involved using each of these four skills. Figure 4.8 illustrates the skills match between what the doctoral education included and what the jobs required for mathematics and English Ph.D. recipients.

A sizable proportion of English (40%) and mathematics (38%) Ph.D.s said their doctoral education did not include working in teams and neither did their current jobs. However, comparable and slightly larger proportions said working in teams was not an aspect of their doctoral education, and yet they did work in teams in their jobs (English 43%, mathematics 41%). Interdisciplinary research skills, the category rated most important by English Ph.D. recipients for doctoral education, was also the category most used by English Ph.D.s in their current jobs. Analogously, mathematicians

FIGURE 4.7

Importance of interdisciplinary research and interpersonal skills for doctoral education

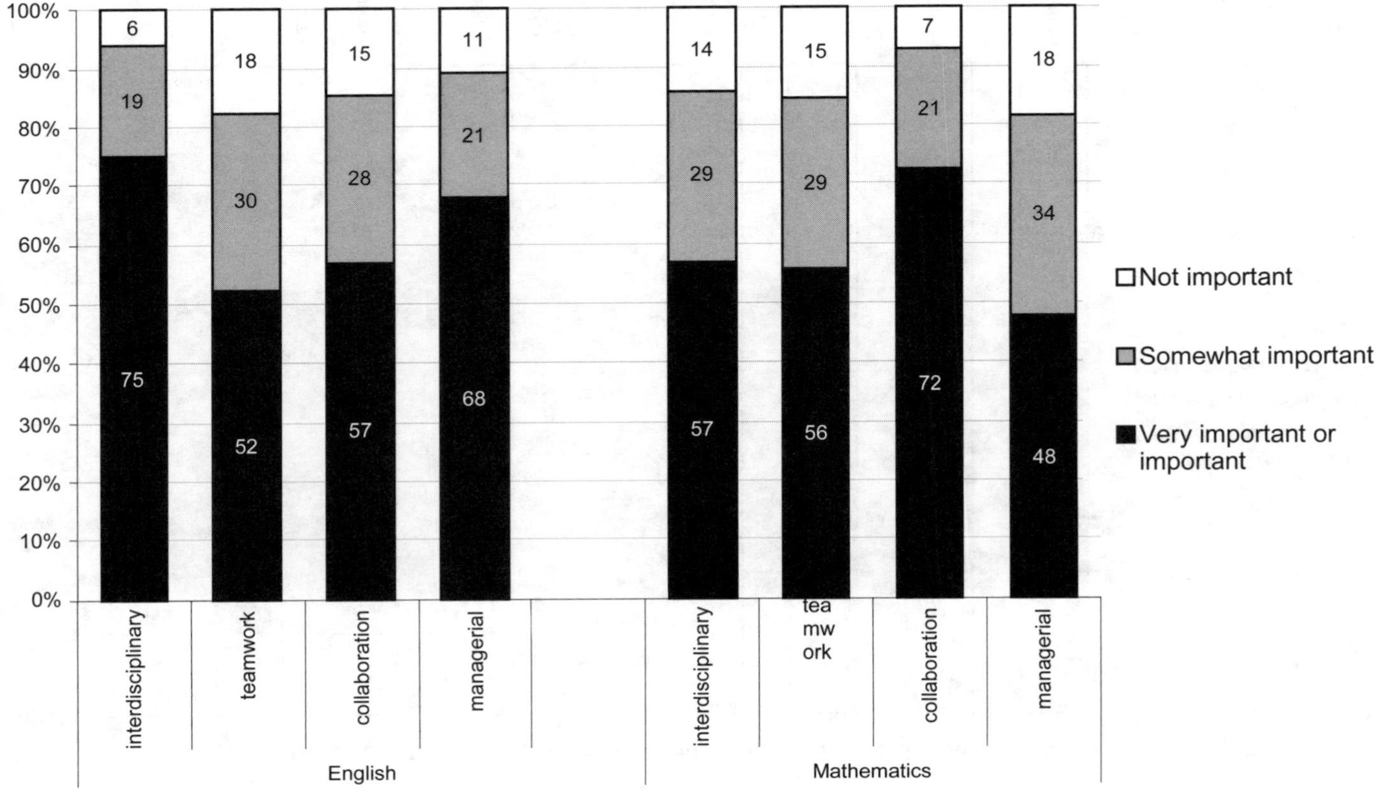

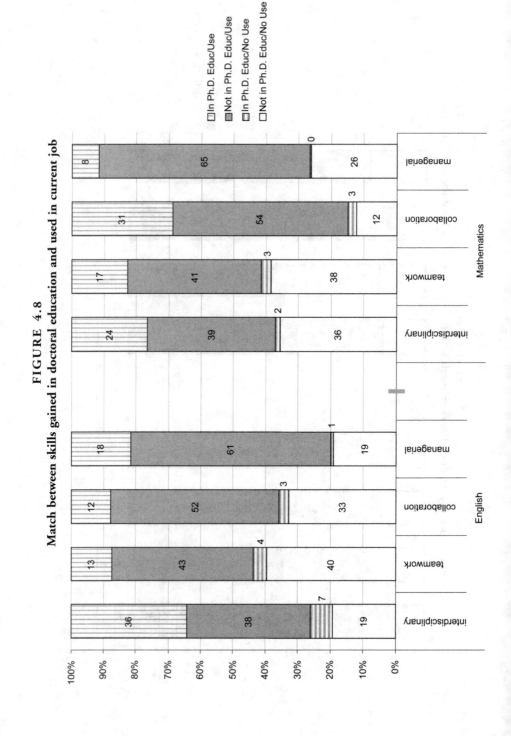

FIGURE 4.8
Match between skills gained in doctoral education and used in current job

were most likely to say collaboration was included in their doctoral education and was also the skill area that 85% of them reported using in their current jobs. Fifty-four percent said their doctoral education did not expose them to this skill, while a smaller 31% said their doctoral education did involve this skill.

Figure 4.9 illustrates the relationship between the skills gained in doctoral education and the current job within each employment sector (Academic Ladder, Academic Other, and BGN). For both English and mathematics, those working in the BGN sector were more likely to say the fit between the doctoral education and their current job was more loosely tied than in either of the academic sectors, with English Ph.D. recipients working in BGN reporting the "loosest" fit.

The information on the match between skills developed and those used on the job sheds further light on the question of whether doctoral education prepares students for the jobs they take, and the answer is an equivocal yes and no. Much of the time, the skills students developed while getting a Ph.D. were useful in later careers across a variety of settings, and yet there were skills even those in the Academic Ladder positions say they needed and didn't get in their education. While these data fail to give a single clear answer either critical or supportive of doctoral education generally, they are illustrative of the kinds of information that universities and departments may find useful in assessing doctoral programs. For example, a particular university or department may choose to amend its doctoral program if it finds that its students move into jobs that require a great deal of teamwork or collaboration or if it finds that former students report that they frequently use managerial skills in their jobs.

So far, we have examined the value of the doctoral education *in light of the jobs* the Ph.D. recipients acquired, and we have argued that this perspective is an important aspect of doctoral program assessment. However, many involved in education understand philosophically and intuitively that there is a value to education beyond the instrumental use of education (Strober, 2005). So, it also makes sense to include a less instrumental and more personal measure in doctoral program assessment methods.

Personal Value of the Doctoral Degree

When respondents were asked, "Was completing your Ph.D. worth it?" on average, over 90% said that it was (see Figure 4.10), although at 89%, English

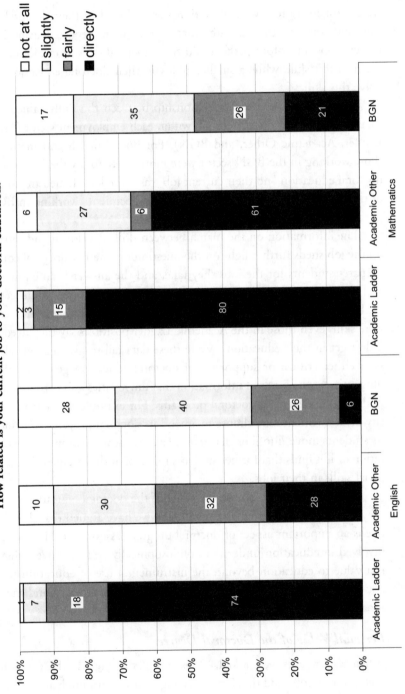

FIGURE 4.9

How related is your current job to your doctoral education?

FIGURE 4.10

Was completing your Ph.D. worth it?

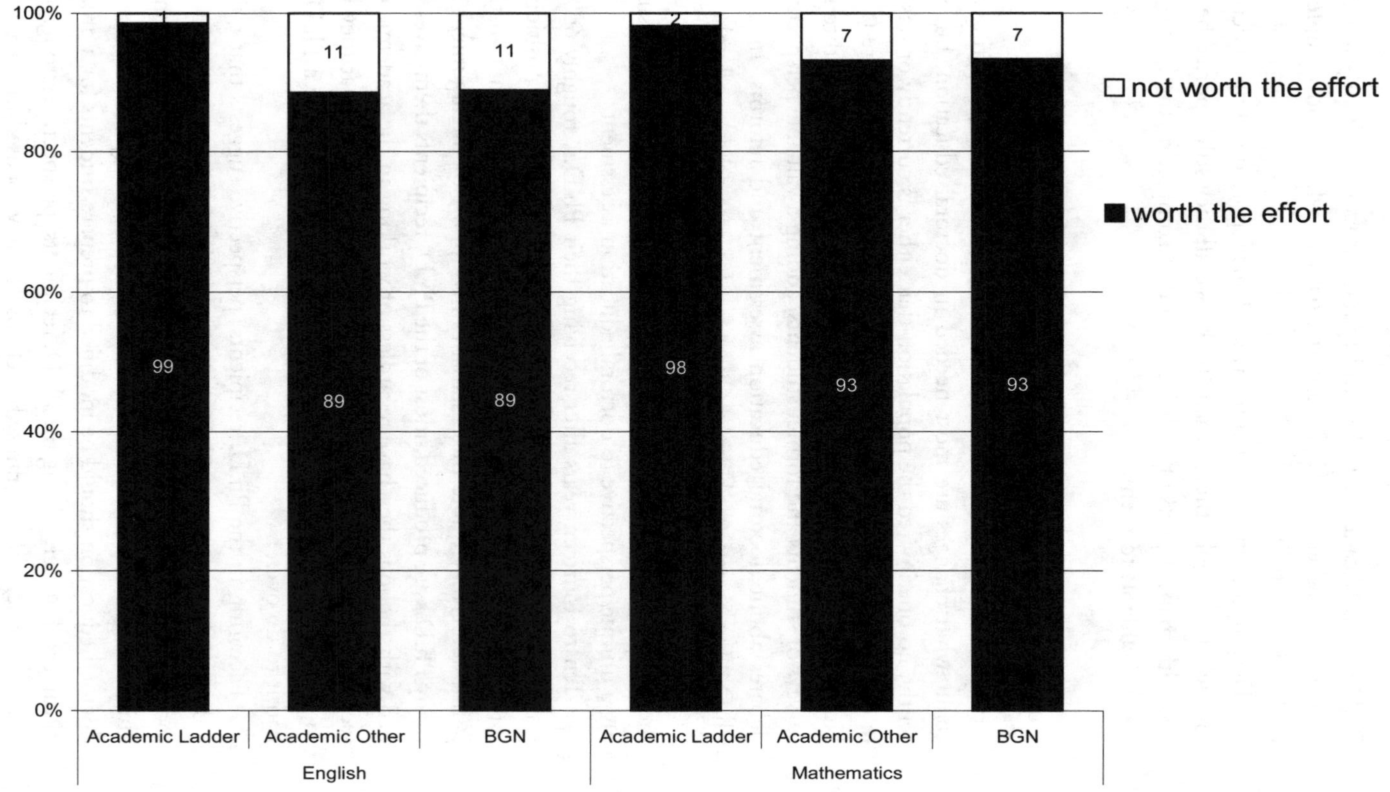

Ph.D.s in the Academic Other and BGN sectors were slightly less favorable than their mathematics counterparts, 93% of whom said completing the Ph.D. was worth it.

Despite the evidence that many students reported feeling underprepared for the kinds of jobs they actually took, overall they still reported being satisfied with many aspects of their jobs and that completing the Ph.D. was personally valuable to them.

Conclusions and Recommendations

Critics of doctoral education have varied and sometimes competing opinions about what changes are most needed in doctoral education, but until recently, no one invited the population that either is currently or was recently in doctoral education to join the conversation. Golde and Dore (2001) and Nerad and Cerny (1999a, 1999b) have remedied this oversight through their surveys of students and former students, adding a valuable perspective to the debates about doctoral education assessment and reforms. In particular, Ph.D.s Ten Years Later helps graduate faculty, researchers, and policy makers to understand Ph.D. recipients' reflections on the value and usefulness of their doctoral education *in light of* the careers the Ph.D.s have pursued, adding a unique perspective to doctoral education assessment.

Ten to fourteen years after receiving their Ph.D.s, roughly 60% of the respondents were working in either tenured or tenure-track positions, and a much smaller proportion (10% to 15%) were at Research 1 institutions. While some may quote these statistics in support of the argument that too many Ph.D.s are produced, most of the Ph.D. recipients themselves are satisfied with the jobs they have regardless of working in the academic or BGN sectors, and an even larger proportion say that knowing what they know 10 to 14 years after getting the degree, they would still pursue a Ph.D. if they had it to do over.

Factoring in the Ph.D. recipients' perspective suggests that rather than reducing the number of Ph.D.s produced, doctoral programs may want to focus on the kinds of skills developed during doctoral education and career guidance given to doctoral students. Overall, career path analyses indicate doctoral education should be modified to prepare students for a broad range of careers. Further, adding the Ph.D. recipients' perspective strongly suggests that even doctoral programs that choose to stay focused on preparing doctoral students for academic careers should consider what that preparation looks like in terms of mentoring, skills development, and career guidance.

Doctoral programs should broaden their socialization practices to introduce students to viable and valuable careers outside academia, regardless of students' initial career intentions. Socialization in doctoral programs should also include developing specific skills, such as working collaboratively or in teams, conducting interdisciplinary research, and managing people and projects.

Today, doctoral education is undergoing a number of changes, including a shift in the demographic makeup of doctoral students and the broadening career paths of Ph.D. recipients. In response to these changes the activity of doctoral program assessment must itself become more detailed and more comprehensive. Studies such as Ph.D.s Ten Years Later point the way to a more complex and nuanced approach to assessment by providing a national scope that eschews anecdotal "data" and by listening to the very people most affected by doctoral education—Ph.D. recipients themselves.

Notes

1. For an overview of criticism of U.S. doctoral education, see Nerad (2004). See also Committee on Science, Engineering, and Public Policy (1995); Nyquist, Woodford, & Rogers (2004); and Pruitt-Logan & Gaff (2004).

2. These findings are consistent with previous studies on career paths of Ph.D. recipients (see National Academy of Sciences, 1971; Ahern & Scott, 1981).

References

Ahern, N. C., & Scott, E. (1981). *Career outcomes in a matched sample of men and women Ph.D.s: An analytical report.* Washington, DC: National Academy Press.

Austin, A. E. (2002). Preparing the next generation of faculty: Graduate school as socialization to the academic career. *Journal of Higher Education, 73*(1), 94–122.

Brooks, R. L. (2005). Measuring university quality. *Review of Higher Education, 29*(1), 1–22.

Brown, G. D. A., Gardner, J., Oswald, A., & Qian, J. (2005). Does wage rank affect employees' wellbeing? (IZA Discussion Papers 1505). Bonn, Germany: Institute for the Study of Labor (IZA).

Committee on Science, Engineering, and Public Policy. (1995). *Reshaping the gradu-*

ate education of scientists and engineers. Washington, DC: American Academies Press.

Golde, C. M., & Dore, T. M. (2001). At cross purposes: What the experiences of doctoral students reveal about doctoral education. Philadelphia: The Pew Charitable Trusts. Retrieved from www.Ph.D.-survey.org

Goldman, C., & Massy, W. (2001). *The Ph.D. factory: Training and employment of science and engineering doctorates in the United States.* Bolton, MA: Anker.

Martell, R. F., Lane, D. M., & Emrich, C. G. (1996). Male-female differences: A computer simulation. *American Psychologist, 51*(2), 157–158.

National Academy of Sciences. (1971). Mobility of PhDs before and after the doctorate with associated economic and educational characteristics of states. (Career Patterns Report No. 3). Washington, DC: Author.

Nerad, M. (2004). The Ph.D. in the US: Criticisms, facts, and remedies. *Higher Education Policy, 17*, 183–199.

Nerad, M., Aanerud, R., & Cerny, J. (2004). So you want to become a professor! Lessons from the Ph.D.s Ten Years Later Study. In D. H. Wulff & A. E. Austin (Eds.), *Paths to the professoriate: Strategies for enriching the preparation of future faculty* (pp. 137–158). San Francisco: Jossey-Bass.

Nerad, M., & Cerny, J. (1999a). From rumors to facts: Career outcomes of English Ph.D.s. Results from the Ph.D.s Ten Years Later Study. *Communicator, 32*(7), 1–10.

Nerad, M., & Cerny, J. (1999b). Postdoctoral patterns, career advancement, and problems. *Science, 285*, 1533–1535.

Nyquist, J. D., Woodford, B. J., & Rogers, D. L. (2004). Re-envisioning the Ph.D.: A challenge for the twenty-first century. In D. H. Wulff & A. E. Austin (Eds.), *Paths to the professoriate: Strategies for enriching the preparation of future faculty* (pp. 194–216). San Francisco: Jossey-Bass.

Oshagbemi, T. (1999). Academics and their managers: A comparative study in job satisfaction. *Personnel Review, 28*(1–2), 108–124.

Oshagbemi, T. (2003). Personal correlates of job satisfaction: Empirical evidence from UK universities. *International Journal of Social Economics, 30*(12), 1210–1233.

Ostriker, J. P., & Kuh, C. V. (Eds.). (2003). *Assessing research doctorate programs: A methodology study.* Washington, DC: National Academies Press.

Pruitt-Logan, A. S., & Gaff, J. G. (2004). Preparing future faculty: Changing the culture of doctoral education. In D. H. Wulff & A. E. Austin (Eds.), *Paths to the professoriate: Strategies for enriching the preparation of future faculty.* San Francisco: Jossey-Bass.

Reskin, B., & Padavic, I. (1994). *Women and men at work.* Thousand Oaks, CA: Pine Forge Press.

Ridgeway, C. L. (1991). The social construction of status value: Gender and other nominal characteristics. *Social Forces, 70*(2), 367–386.

Ridgeway, C. L. (1997). Interaction and the conservation of gender inequality: Considering employment. *American Sociological Review, 62*(2), 218–235.

Singh, P. (1994). Perception and reactions to inequity as a function of social comparison referents and hierarchical levels. *Journal of Applied Social Psychology, 24*(6), 557–566.

Spalter-Roth, R., Kennelly, I., & Erskine, W. (2004). The best time to have a baby: Institutional resources and family strategies among early career sociologists. (ASA Research Brief). Retrieved from http://www.asanet.org/page.ww?section = Briefs + and + Articles&name = Briefs + and + Articles

Strober, M. H. (2005). Feminist economics: Implications for education. In M. A. Fineman & T. Dougherty (Eds.), *Feminism confronts homo economics: Gender, law, and society* (pp. 261–291). Ithaca, NY: Cornell University Press.

Tierney, W. (1997). Organizational socialization in higher education. *Journal of Higher Education, 68*(1), 1–16.

Weidman, J., Twale, D. J., & Stein, E. L. (2001). *Socialization of graduate and professional students in higher education: A perilous passage?* San Francisco: Jossey-Bass.

Appendix A

Questions from Survey Instrument Ph.D.s Ten Years Later

How satisfied are you with the following aspects of your current job at this time?

Please circle one answer for each item. If you are not currently employed please skip to question 12 at the top of page 10.

	Very Satisfied	Fairly Satisfied	Not Too Satisfied	Not Satisfied	Not Applicable
Salary level					
Career growth prospects					
Geographic location					
Use of my doctoral education					
Content of work					
Autonomy of work					

Job security					
Prestige of organization					
Staff support					
Equipment, lab space, or other physical resources					
Opportunity to do research					
Opportunity to teach					
Administrative responsibilities					
Level of intellectual stimulation from colleagues					
Work environment					
Supportive environment for people of color or differing nationalities					
Supportive environment for women					
Job opportunities for my spouse or partner in the area					
Location for raising children					
Flexible work situation (flex time, telecommuting, etc.)					
Health and retirement benefits					
Level of stress at work					
Time for leisure, family, and my own interests					

Did your doctoral experience involve the following? *Circle one answer for each item.*

	Yes	No
Working in a team (other graduate students, postdocs, etc.) in addition to your major advisor	1	2

	Yes	No
Collaborating with another person	I	2
Undertaking interdisciplinary research	I	2
Learning organizational or managerial skills	I	2

Was your doctoral experience with the following positive or negative?

	Positive	Negative	Not Applicable
Working in teams	I	2	3
Collaborating	I	2	3

Does your *current* job involve the following?

	Yes	No
Working in a team of three or more	I	2
Collaborating with another person	I	2
Undertaking interdisciplinary work	I	2
Organizational or managerial skills	I	2

How important do you think the following skills are to doctoral research/education in preparing people for future jobs?

	Very Important	Important	Somewhat Important	Not Important
Working in a team	I	2	3	4
Collaborating with another person	I	2	3	4
Undertaking interdisciplinary research/study	I	2	3	4
Learning organizational or managerial skills	I	2	3	4

Please evaluate you Ph.D. program in terms of the following:

	Excellent	Good	Fair	Poor
The overall advice and guidance your department gave you regarding your studies				
The curriculum of the Ph.D. program				
The quality of the graduate-level teaching by faculty in your department				
The quality of your research experience				
The financial support you got from your department or university				
The quality of training for teaching assistants (doesn't apply, I wasn't a teaching assistant)				
The quality of training in research methodology				
The quality of advice received from your faculty dissertation advisor(s) in developing your dissertation topic				
The quality of the guidance provided by your faculty dissertation advisor(s) to help you complete your Ph.D.				
Advice and assistance from your major advisor and/or department during your job search as you finished your Ph.D.				

Below are statements some doctoral students have made about their experiences. Please indicate basically true or basically false for each statement as it relates to your experience during your doctoral education, unless it does not apply.

	Basically True	Basically False	Does Not Apply to Me
During this period faculty provided me with opportunities to learn about proposal writing for support of research activities	1	2	3
Faculty generally encouraged me to try to publish my work	1	2	3

I got quite a bit of help from faculty in publishing my work	I	2	3
My department/faculty/graduate school provided funding to attend national professional meetings	I	2	3
During my doctoral education, my department provided opportunities for me to interact with people from the nonacademic sector	I	2	3

From the Ph.D.s Ten Years Later study by M. Nerad and J. Cerny, 1996. Available at the Center for Innovation and Research in Graduate Education, http://depts.washington.edu/coe/cirge/. Adapted with permission of the authors.

PART TWO

EMERGING CRITERIA AND
NEW MODELS FOR ASSESSING
STUDENT LEARNING
OUTCOMES

5

USING THE ASSESSMENT PROCESS TO IMPROVE DOCTORAL PROGRAMS

Kelly Funk and Karen L. Klomparens

G raduate education, especially doctoral education, is a system. In fact, graduate education is a complex system with multiple inputs, such as student and faculty characteristics; departmental, program, and national disciplinary cultures; financial and other resources; multiple processes, such as course work, comprehensive exams, theses and dissertations, and internships; and finally, multiple outcomes, such as degree completion, withdrawal, or dismissal from programs. Furthermore, "systems delays" such as stop-outs, program changes, or lapses in resources complicate our understanding of inputs, processes, and outcomes, and any intervention that we make to improve the desired outcomes. Efforts to determine the quality of graduate programs through avenues into the complexities of this educational system have traditionally relied upon inputs such as faculty and student characteristics; departmental, programmatic, and national disciplinary cultures; scholarly productivity; and financial and other resources.

While serving as a strong foundation to assess doctoral programs, this focus on input methodologies (such as evaluative national rankings) provides but one measure by which quality of programs can be determined. More attention needs to be paid to the educational practices and processes embedded within the graduate education systems themselves and the effects of such experiences as student course work, comprehensive exams, theses, dissertations, and internships on graduate student learning that, in fact, lead to students' degree completion and our final goal of preparing students to enter a productive career that contributes to the discipline and society—nationally and internationally. To date, much of the national discourse on assessing student achievement in higher education has been focused on the undergraduate level. Building on the assessment methods used in undergraduate education, doctoral programs can successfully adapt, apply, or create assessment methods that align with the intended learning outcomes of graduate programs and thereby provide another source of evidence about program quality.

This chapter aims to demonstrate to graduate deans and faculty that they can bridge or integrate traditional external doctoral program evaluation methods with an internal process of program assessment of student learning outcomes, providing graduate programs with a more comprehensive and robust picture of accomplishments and quality. To this end, this chapter has three foci:

1. an overview of the kinds of criteria used in external evaluation of doctoral programs—data collected and used for national rankings and assessment of doctoral programs, for example, the National Research Council (NCR) Assessment of doctoral programs and the standard practice of external department and program review processes
2. an overview of the process of conducting internal program-level assessment focused on student learning
3. a summary of ways in which graduate deans and the Council of Graduate Schools can support the integration of assessment of student learning with the data that exists from external program evaluation to provide more comprehensive information about our doctoral programs.

External Evaluation

The Role of Rankings

Rankings matter. The ability to hire excellent faculty and attract bright graduate students often depends on a national (and visible) ranking of a program. Some universities use rankings to determine additional financial investment and support of infrastructure based on the reported ranking or reputation of a program. And, rankings can have a positive (or negative) effect on assessment and the improvement of graduate programs depending on how rankings are used to make a variety of resource allocation decisions. For example, the National Research Council Assessment is a high-stakes, infrequent, and comprehensive attempt to provide evaluation of doctoral programs. *Assessing Research-Doctorate Programs: A Methodology Study* (Ostriker & Kuh, 2003) states the importance of assessing the quality of doctoral programs in order to ensure continued improvement.

Arguably, the NRC "ranking" of doctoral programs has a large impact on assessment of graduate programs by the nature of the questions it asks and the data that it is prepared to collect and share publicly. In the NRC analysis that was published in 1995 by Goldberger, Mayer, and Flattau, doctoral completion rates and student satisfaction surveys were not part of the data collection. In the NRC surveys scheduled for use in 2006–07, these topics, as well as student diversity, student support, quality of life, professional development opportunities, and placement, will be included along with the academic measures of quality. The importance of career placement of doctoral students was underscored by the work of Golde and Dore (2001). With the well-publicized inclusion of placement as an important assessment factor, NRC has effectively added a new indirect assessment tool to measure the outcomes of doctoral education nationally.

Other commercial rankings (e.g., *U.S.News & World Report* and Lombardi, 2003), as well as peer-group benchmarking (Association of American Universities, National Association of State Universities and Land Grant Colleges), provide comparative data of some aspects of graduate programs— numbers of degrees granted, research expenditures, endowment assets, faculty awards—and student characteristics, such as the average entering Graduate Record Examinations scores. It is important to remember that some rankings provide programs with valuable comparative data but still remain indirect measures of student learning because their focus is on perception and comparison rather than *direct* measures of what a student knows and is able to do or demonstrate as a result of that student's educational experiences. In addition, large-scale rankings often leave out the informative and necessary "footnotes" that should accompany all data to ensure accuracy. These comparative data, coupled with programmatic assessment of direct student learning, can provide a useful picture of a program's challenges, as well as its successes, but should be carefully, and perhaps skeptically, interpreted. In fact, Paul Boyer (2003) provides a compelling case for such skepticism regarding institutional rankings in his book *College Rankings Exposed*.

While not explicitly a "ranking" activity, federal funding agencies also play a role in setting goals for research and graduate education. One example of this is the review criteria for the National Science Foundation, a highly visible funder of graduate-level research. Included in these criteria are the expected assessment questions on intellectual merit, but there are also assessment questions on broadening participation of underrepresented groups and the societal benefits of the research. Indirectly, these criteria move some of our graduate programs to articulate new outcomes and ways to assess their efficacy and impact.

The Role of Accreditation

Disciplinary/professional accrediting bodies (such as nursing, medicine, engineering, education) have been moving *deliberately* toward student learning outcomes as a requirement for accreditation, in part as a means of providing public accountability. Professional accreditation focused on student learning also provides oversight of preparation for the work in the profession as well as a means of disciplinary recognition of programs that meet a certain standard of educational quality. Many professional associations, while perhaps not requiring assessment, are strongly advocating its use within disciplines. For example, the American Philosophical Association (2005) and the American Psychological Association (2005), moved toward explicitly supporting outcomes assessment.

In addition to the professional associations that accredit some programs, all institutions are subject to regional accreditation as a part of public accountability, and, more practically, because an institution's federal financial aid is linked to the accredited status. All six regional accrediting agencies developed requirements for assessment, and all public and private institutions have been required to engage in some form of assessment since 1990 (Ewell, 1993).

The Higher Learning Commission model is an excellent example of the serious incorporation of assessment (http://www.ncahigherlearningcommission.org/). The Commission Statement on Assessment of Student Learning states, in part, "An organization's commitment to and capacity for effective assessment of student learning will figure more prominently than ever in the accreditation relationship established between the Commission and that organization" (Higher Learning Commission, 2003, p. 3-4-2).

The Higher Learning Commission revised the criteria for accreditation, effective January 2005. The five criteria for accreditation and the related core components now have expectations of evidence embedded. While assessment has been an expectation of the commission for 14 years, the emphasis is now on both the evidence gathered from assessment of student learning and the ways that evidence is used to effect change in the teaching and learning environment at the undergraduate and graduate program levels. While these criteria and core components have just begun to be applied in accreditation self-studies, within a decade most of our institutions will have had experience using assessment methods to these ends.

The Role of External Program Review

Graduate programs at most universities undergo periodic external reviews. These are most often part of an overall departmental review that includes undergraduate education, research, outreach/engagement, and service. The Council of Graduate Schools (1990) provides an excellent summary of the components of academic graduate program review, although the concept of "evaluation" is more prevalent than a concept of the "assessment" of learning (see below for a description of both). The real value of external graduate program reviews is the process of the self-study, the evaluative exercise undertaken by faculty and students as they examine the challenges and opportunities in the discipline, as well as the data about who and what they have been, who and what they are, and who and what they will, or should, become.

Given this context of rankings, accreditation, and program review, what do faculty and administrators need to know to begin a serious consideration of assessment of graduate programs? What follows is a brief primer on key aspects of assessment that can be applied to graduate programs.

Internal Process of Program-Level Assessment

The terms "assessment" and "evaluation" are often used interchangeably when faculty and administrators talk about curricular and program improvement, yet it is important to differentiate between the two. Evaluation implies an external process, one that is developed by a set of standards explicitly prescribed by an outside entity. External evaluation of doctoral programs judges a doctoral program against a specific set of established criteria (Cross & Steadman, 1996; National Science Foundation, 1993). External evaluation carries with it a form of reward such as continued institutional or disciplinary accreditation, or a sanction such as a failing grade. In contrast, assessment implies an internal process, one that is developed, implemented, and used by faculty to learn about how well students are making progress toward and achieving commonly agreed-upon expectations for learning. More specifically, assessment is "the systematic collection, review, and use of information about educational programs undertaken for the purpose of improving student learning and development" (Palomba & Banta, 1999, p. 4). It is intimately tied to and should be reflective of the institutional, college, and departmental mission. The reason for engaging in assessment is not solely to satisfy standards imposed by outside constituencies, but rather to answer internal questions about what students learn in their academic programs and what they are able to do when they graduate. Because the assessment process is driven by institutional, college, and departmental learning goals, the expectations for learning, learning outcome statements, and the specific methods each department chooses to use to assess student achievement may differ. However, what departments share in common is the process of inquiry itself that involves collaboration among faculty, administrators, and even graduate students through the following steps:

- articulating department goals for doctoral programs
- operationalizing those goals into measurable learning outcome statements that describe what students should demonstrate, such as "students should be able to critique existing research from multiple perspectives"
- identifying multiple methods that best assess those learning outcome statements, and identifying criteria and standards of judgment for assessing student achievements
- closing the loop: analyzing results of the methods, interpreting those results, and using those interpretations to inform or change pedagogy, curricular design or sequencing, or advising, for example, to improve student learning

Articulating Department-Level Goals

Using assessment methods presumes that a department has established explicit goals and learning outcomes. While these department-level goals do exist in graduate education, they may be implicit (e.g., "everyone knows what those goals are") rather than explicitly stated in a program's literature or on its Web site. It is important to make the goals explicit for assessment results to have meaning.

In a set of preliminary discussions at Michigan State University with the University Graduate Council and the associate deans for graduate education, the following broad goals were identified for both master's and doctoral degree students in our programs:

- Acquire advanced knowledge and a deeper understanding of the skills and knowledge in their disciplines
- Develop a sense of responsibility to as well as an understanding of the ethical dimensions of the discipline
- Develop the competence, knowledge, and independence for the realization of leadership potential

In addition to these goals, the following goals have been identified for doctoral degree students:

- Master state-of-the-art disciplinary knowledge
- Develop an ability to synthesize existing knowledge with knowledge that does not yet exist, but may be generated by the students
- Generate new knowledge through research/scholarship and transmit that knowledge to others. Through this process, students critically evaluate the literature in the discipline, interpret that literature with respect to their own research/scholarship, and learn the necessary technical and intellectual skills to produce a written document that makes an original contribution to knowledge.
- Develop a deep understanding of scholarly conduct and the ethical dimensions of producing scholarship in the discipline

Operationalizing Goals into Measurable Learning Outcome Statements

How are these general goals of graduate education interpreted and fostered within individual doctoral departments? While most graduate programs would agree with these broad goals, in order to be effectively assessed, goals need to be operationalized into learning outcome statements within the context of the discipline and the department. These statements describe the attitudes, behaviors, skills, and ways of thinking students should develop during the course of doctoral-level study. What does "critically evaluate the litera-ture in the discipline" mean in the department of English, for example? If a student is successfully demonstrating this learning goal, what does it look like? What is it that a student should be able to do, to show, or to produce to indicate mastery of this learning goal?

The Department of Philosophy at Michigan State University expects that graduate students will read philosophical texts closely and accurately. The department operationalized this goal by stating that students should demonstrate a mastery of distinctive terminology and be able to recognize distinctive kinds of argumentation. The Department of Art and Art History operationalized the goal of building professional competence, in part as the ability to present aesthetic ideas in teaching.

Identifying Multiple Methods That Best Assess Learning Outcomes

Once a goal has been operationalized into a learning outcome statement, the next step in the assessment process is to determine how to assess the desired outcome. Because graduate program assessment is an internally defined and faculty-driven process, the types and levels of methods to assess learning out-come statements will vary across disciplines. Methods may include not only standardized instruments, such as tests or virtual simulations that rely on performance-level scores, but also student work, such as research projects or papers, for example, that provide another kind of evidence about how well students apply concepts or principles of student learning. A comprehensive exam may well provide one source of evidence of patterns of students' ability to apply a theoretical construct to solve a disciplinary problem. Gathering multiple examples of student work from the same examination allows a pat-tern of student learning to emerge that enables a department to pinpoint areas students are doing well in as well as areas where weaknesses might be present. For purposes of assessment, methods that provide evidence of stu-dent learning are either direct or indirect.

Direct methods of assessment capture evidence of students' learning based on various kinds of student performance (Palomba & Banta, 1999). Students demonstrate mastery of a faculty-determined set of outcomes through work or projects they have completed. Direct methods require students to show, in some fashion, what they can do and what they have learned (see Figure 5.1). For example, direct methods might include a written research proposal

FIGURE 5.1
Some Direct Methods to Assess Student Learning

Graduate programs already have traditional methods in place, such as the required literature review portion of the research proposal, that may well serve as evidence of student learning. The following methods may also serve as evidence of student learning and the means a department could use to assess learning outcomes:

Products from

- Courses—papers, projects, original work that provide evidence of students' level of achievement along the continuum of their studies, not solely at the end
- Comprehensive examinations
- Graduate Record Exam general test
- Graduate Record Exam subject test
- Certification examinations
- Licensure examinations
- Locally developed pretest or posttest for subject matter knowledge

Portfolios that provide chronological evidence of learning within the context of curricular design (see chapters 8 and 9 in this book)

Audio- or videotapings along the continuum of learning, as well as at the end of students' program of study

Theses/dissertations (see also chapters 6, 7, 8, and 9 in this book for new developments related to dissertations)

Peer-reviewed publications that demonstrate acceptance by other scholars

Disciplinary presentations that demonstrate openness to sharing research and commitment to scholarship

Funded grants and fellowships that require peer review

---

in which students synthesize the literature in the field and use appropriate research methodology, a comprehensive examination in which students demonstrate an acquisition of knowledge or the ability to critically examine the literature in the field, or internships or clinical settings that provide the opportunity for observers to assess students' skills.

Indirect methods of assessment capture students' self-reports on their learning, including the value of specific educational experiences, and may also capture others' reports on student performance (see Figure 5.2). For example,

FIGURE 5.2
Some Indirect Methods to Assess Student Learning

Comparison or benchmarking with peer institutions that provides comparative data in terms of graduate characteristics (upcoming National Research Council Assessment of doctoral program)

Career placement of graduates that provides supplemental and complementary data about student learning and its value as determined by faculty and the employer

Employer surveys that provide perception data about how well graduates are prepared for their career field

Advisory groups from professional/disciplinary societies and/or industrial or external university groups that help guide a department in curriculum development

Student graduation/retention rates that begin to define coherence of the curriculum, the program environment, successful socialization into disciplinary norms, and faculty commitment

Exit interviews with students graduating or leaving the program that help departments understand what students believe they learned and what concerns they have

Student satisfaction surveys that provide feedback to departments about the usefulness of processes and procedures

Focus group discussions
Alumni surveys
Alumni honors, awards, achievements
Analysis of grade distributions
Peer review of courses
Peer review of program

---

students might take part in exit surveys that ask them to reflect upon their learning experience and make suggestions for curricular improvement. Employer surveys might ask employers to share their perceptions of how well students are prepared for their careers.

Indirect methods also capture comparative data, such as are represented in departmental benchmarking reports or ranking reports or student and alumni satisfaction surveys. Comparison data are usually used in external program review and allow a department to see how "successful" it has been in relation to an established peer group. External ranking systems such as *U.S. News & World Report* or the National Research Council assessment/rankings of doctoral programs provide these types of data, although reputational rankings may lose sight of actual data and focus on perception. Perception data also allow a department to understand what students and alumni believe they have learned or gained from a program, or what their suggestions for improvement might be.

Indirect methods can also capture institutionally recorded data, such as placement data. Many graduate programs rely upon career placement as evidence of their graduates' success, which is demonstrated by the focus on placement in future National Research Council rankings and which was an important part of the Re-envisioning the Ph.D. project (2001). If students are offered and accept positions in the academic departments of doctoral-extensive institutions, departments then assume they have been successful in turning out scholars who are good researchers and teachers. They are using an *indirect* method of assessment as evidence of student learning. The difficulty with using career placement data as the sole evidence of student learning is that the department does not companion these data with evidence of student learning represented or demonstrated in students' actual work, another indicator of success. Instead, career placement data measure perception about learning, rather than actual learning, relying upon that perception as an indicator of success.

For example, if a department graduates four doctoral students and two take positions in industry and two take positions in baccalaureate institutions (instead of research-extensive entities outlined in its departmental goals as the indicator of success), is it accurate to say the department "failed" in its mission and that those four students did not learn research or teaching skills or meet any of the learning goals established by the department? That is, in essence, what the department is saying, even though a number of other factors (market forces, family obligations, a student's personal interest) influence student placement.

While indirect methods are very useful and important parts of the assessment process to demonstrate how outside constituencies might view a graduate program, they do not by themselves provide evidence of how well a student has met predetermined learning outcomes. Indirect methods provide very useful data that should be used in conjunction with direct methods in order to obtain a comprehensive understanding of student learning. Doctoral programs have the ability to conduct original research as an explicitly stated learning goal. If a department uses a direct method to assess research skills (for example, using the initial research proposal as a means of directly assessing students' ability to construct a sound research design), it is making the determination of student learning based upon something the student has produced and demonstrated to the department. It can be reasonably argued that the ability to conduct research is valued by doctoral-extensive universities and that through the hiring of a graduate as a faculty member with the expectation of conducting research, an institution is providing a piece of data about the graduate's ability to conduct the research. When used in this way, placement data become a complementary method of assessment that provides additional evidence of student learning of research skills.

Establishing and Closing a Feedback Loop

The key to effectively using assessment to improve graduate programs lies not only in the collection of evidence that is outlined in any assessment plan, but also in the active pursuit of closing the feedback loop in order to improve a program. Assessment evidence is only beneficial if it is used to improve student learning. To effectively close the feedback loop, answering the following two questions is essential in a well-executed assessment process:

- How/what did you change as a result of your assessment results?
- How did your changes, or will your changes, improve student learning?

The first question focuses on the usefulness of results in relation to students' demonstrated learning. A department using the dissertation proposal as a means of determining whether students are able to formulate a sound research design might answer this first question in the following way:

> An assessment of the initial dissertation proposals by individual faculty reveals a common weakness among students in their ability to choose the appropriate statistical procedures for data analysis. A review of the required curriculum reveals students are required to take a quantitative research design course, but not a series of statistics courses. The departmental faculty may decide to change curriculum requirements to include statistics courses, or they may decide to redesign the quantitative research design course to include an extended unit on statistical analysis, or they may choose to integrate a greater focus on quantitative research across the department's curriculum.

The second question addresses impact and can only be answered after a change has been implemented. The assessment feedback loop closes after a department or program has instituted a change and then measured student progress. Using the above example after a change has been implemented, a department would follow the same procedures of reviewing dissertation proposals of students who had participated in the new curriculum or a redesigned course to see if students improved their ability to choose appropriate statistical procedures for analysis.

To summarize, the iterative cycle of assessment begins with developing student learning goals that are operationalized into learning outcome statements that emerge from the set of educational practices (inputs) that support the achievement of those learning outcomes. Selecting both direct and indirect methods to assess how well students achieve those learning outcomes provides lenses to look at aggregate student learning. Data collection from the combination of assessment methods forms the basis of faculty and administrator interpretation about the level and patterns of student achievement. Interpreting these levels and patterns of achievement within the context of educational practices leads to discussions about possible changes to pedagogy, curricular design and sequencing, even advising, to improve student learning. Implementing agreed-upon changes closes the loop designed to ascertain how well these changes contribute to improving student learning and initiates yet a new cycle of assessment.

The Role of Graduate Deans and the Council of Graduate Schools

There are both administrative challenges and opportunities for the use of assessment in the improvement of graduate programs. Some of the challenges faced by graduate deans working with graduate-level department chairs include the following:

- Resistance by faculty who believe that U.S. graduate education is already the best in the world, and therefore, requires no changes
- Lack of integration of "the language of assessment" into the lexicon of doctoral programs. While assessment is often understood and used for the many professional programs that are accredited, it is not typi-

cally part of the culture in most doctoral or master's degree programs in the liberal arts and sciences.

- Already existing constraints on faculty time and a program's priorities that leave little time for what may be viewed as either "more work" or "unnecessary work"

There is an important role for graduate deans and their staff and for the Council of Graduate Schools in the use and practice of assessment of graduate programs. The Council of Graduate Schools has taken a major leadership role in working with the National Research Council to frame discussions over the past five or six years that relate to the assessment of doctoral programs. In fact, the 1995 NRC project (Goldberger et al.) was referred to as a "ranking," but the current terminology refers explicitly to this activity as an "assessment." Clearly changes are being made on a national level in both accreditation and in rankings/assessment. The focus now needs to shift to institutional and graduate program level. What can a graduate dean do to help his or her institution focus on assessment of student learning in graduate programs as part of program review? The following steps provide some ways that deans can support the integration of assessment to improve student learning:

Specific Steps to Support Assessment in the Improvement of Graduate Programs

- Share information with faculty, department chairs, and deans about the national context for accreditation and assessment. Most faculty understand their role in contributing to the general welfare of the institution and are willing to engage in assessment if they can see the value of the process. While some departments may begin the process by viewing assessment as an "unfunded mandate," engaging in thoughtful discussion about student learning outcomes, gathering evidence, making changes, and then seeing how effective those changes might be can serve as motivation to continue the process. In other words, faculty might begin conducting assessment because they have to, but they will likely continue it because they want to.
- Remind faculty members that assessment tools are already in place in most graduate programs in the form of, for example, comprehensive examinations, research proposals, internships, and dissertations. For

many programs, assessment is not a new idea. While requirements for disciplinary accreditation might differ from those required by regional accreditation, similarities do exist. Those existing practices should be used and evaluated before new ones are developed.

- Incorporate assessment of student learning into the program review process by asking programs to articulate their goals and learning outcomes statements, identify methods to assess those outcomes, establish criteria and standards of judgment to assess student work, and report on results and proposed changes in the structure or design of a doctoral program to improve student learning. For example, what do students learn and what skills do they possess upon graduation? Do those who employ your graduates agree with your assessment?

- Gather and present concrete evidence of what the department is doing now and might be able to do regarding assessment—how it is succeeding with its goals—in a time of tight budgets. These activities can demonstrate to a departmental faculty that assessment of goals and outcomes data may allow them to make a more compelling case to the graduate dean for receiving continued, or perhaps additional, funding for graduate fellowships. In this way, assessment can lead to increased rewards for the program and that, in turn, can encourage participation in assessment activities. Making public the assessment process and data, along with the rewards, will demonstrate institutional valuing of the activity.

- Build assessment into the administrative processes already in place within the institution. Michigan State University (2004) added a section on assessment to the official University Curriculum Committee Program Change form (http://www.reg.msu.edu/Read/UCC/assess info.pdf). Currently, those who request either a new graduate program or any changes in a current graduate program must provide a description of the programmatic learning outcomes and the intended assessment methodology. Any program going through a curriculum change process must have developed a means of program assessment that includes a focus on evidence of learning before approval is granted. Assistance by the MSU director of assessment is provided to the departments as they engaged in learning about assessment tools.

- Through workshops or during program meetings, introduce faculty to the assessment process with particular focus on effective uses and tools of assessment in relation to graduate program reviews. These workshops or meetings provide valuable information for members of a program and enable faculty to put in place the procedures they will need to engage in before an institutional accreditation review. Given regional accrediting agencies' focus on program-level assessment of student learning, many institutions now have either an individual or an office dedicated to assessment willing to assist faculty in the process.

- Provide evidence about how assessment can strengthen aspects of a doctoral program, such as in recruiting high quality graduate students, increasing completion rates, or shortening time to degree. Posting (positive) placement data on a graduate program's Web site can entice interested prospective graduate students to further explore opportunities with that program.

- Provide assessment of student learning in order to demonstrate to potential internship sites and/or employers the outcomes of student academic experiences. This information may increase opportunities for internships and encourage a variety of employers across multiple economic sectors to explore hiring doctoral students.

- Make use of other national initiatives, such as the Carnegie Initiative on the Doctorate (http://www.carnegiefoundation.org/CID/), to encourage faculty to engage in serious conversations about the structure, content, and requirements of doctoral education and the efficacy of educational practices, such as comprehensive examinations, in assessing student learning outcomes (Golde & Walker, 2005).

- Develop ways to provide feedback and comments to departments on their assessment efforts. Too often we ask or require faculty to participate in initiatives only to have them provide the data and do the work without ever providing recognition, assistance, or even acknowledgment of their efforts. If we are not asking departments about their assessment plans, commenting on what seems to be working well and what might be best looked at from another angle, then their plans will be developed but not implemented, or implemented but the results not used. We need to help faculty understand that if we ask them to engage in this process, it's because we believe it offers value to them as individual faculty members, to their departments, to their colleges, to the institution as a whole, and overall to doctoral students.

Conclusion and Recommendations

Graduate deans and the Council of Graduate Schools should be leaders in advancing assessment of student learning as part of graduate program review and in demonstrating how evidence of student learning can be integrated with data that programs currently collect or draw upon as part of external reporting demands. The upcoming NRC assessment of doctoral programs is a visible and prestigious focal point to begin with. The requirement by regional accrediting bodies of the assessment of student learning also provides a process to engage faculty. What we can and should do is move beyond simply collecting data for program reviews to using those data as a part of a thoughtful assessment plan.

Encouraging departments to discuss goals and learning outcome statements, methods of assessment, analysis and interpretation of direct and indirect assessment methods, and use of analysis and interpretation to improve teaching and learning through active feedback loops should become a regular part of program review. As the professional and disciplinary societies move toward a common expectation of engaging in assessment, and as graduate deans continue to demonstrate the effective use of assessment for improvement, we will begin to make assessment a part of the culture of graduate programs.

References

American Philosophical Association. (2005). APA statements on the profession: Outcomes assessment. Retrieved from http://www.apa.udel.edu/apa/governance/statements/outcomes.html

American Psychological Association. (2005). Outcome oriented evaluation focus. Retrieved from http://www.apa.org/ed/gp2000.html

Boyer, P. (2003). *College rankings exposed: The art of getting a quality education in the 21st century*. Lawrenceville, NJ: Thomson/Peterson's.

Council of Graduate Schools. (1990). *Academic review of graduate programs*. Washington, DC: Council of Graduate Schools Press.

Cross, K. P., & Steadman, M. H. (1996). *Classroom research: Implementing the scholarship of teaching*. San Francisco: Jossey-Bass.

Ewell, P. (1993). The role of states and accreditors in shaping assessment practice. In T. W. Banta & Associates, *Making a difference: Outcomes of a decade of assessment in higher education* (pp. 339–356). San Francisco: Jossey-Bass.

Goldberger, M. L., Mayer, B. A., & Flattau, P. E. (Eds.). (1995). *Research-doctorate programs in the United States: Continuity and change.* Washington, DC: National Academy Press.

Golde, C. M., & Dore, T. M. (2001). *At cross purposes: What the experiences of today's doctoral students reveal about doctoral education.* Philadelphia: The Pew Charitable Trusts. Retrieved from http://www.phd-survey.org

Golde, C. M., Walker, G. E., & Associates. (2005). *Envisioning the future of doctoral education: Preparing stewards of the discipline.* Carnegie essays on the doctorate. San Francisco: Jossey-Bass.

Higher Learning Commission. (2003). *Handbook of accreditation* (3rd ed.). Chicago: Author.

Lombardi, J. V., et al. (2003). The top American research universities. Gainesville: The Center, University of Florida. Retrieved from http://thecenter.ufl.edu/research2003.pdf

Michigan State University. (2004). Assessment in the curricular process. Retrieved from http://www.reg.msu.edu/Read/UCC/assessinfo.pdf

Frechtling, J. (2002). The 2002 user-friendly handbook for project evaluation (NSF publication 93-152). Arlington, VA: National Science Foundation.

Ostriker, J. P., & Kuh, C. V. (Eds.) (2003). *Assessing research-doctorate programs: A methodology study.* Washington, DC: National Academies Press.

Palomba, C., & Banta, T. W. (1999). *Assessment essentials: Planning, implementing, and improving assessment in higher education.* San Francisco: Jossey-Bass.

Re-envisioning the Ph.D. (2001). Retrieved from http://depts.washington.edu/envision/

6

MAKING THE
IMPLICIT EXPLICIT

Faculty's Performance Expectations for the Dissertation

Barbara E. Lovitts

The Ph.D. dissertation is the final product of years of study and independent research. Successful completion of the dissertation and award of the Ph.D. certifies that the degree recipient has the capabilities and preparation necessary for independent scholarly work (Isaac, Quinlan, & Walker, 1992; see also Association of American Universities, 1998; and Bargar & Duncan, 1982).[1] Yet, the standards by which the dissertation is evaluated are largely unexplicated and mysterious (Holbrook, 2002; Johnston, 1997). Graduate students are frequently exhorted to make an "original" or "significant contribution" to knowledge. Indeed, this is the most commonly, and often the only, explicitly stated criteria for the award of the Ph.D. (Tinkler & Jackson, 2000; Winter, Griffiths, & Green, 2000). But what "original" and "significant" mean does not appear ever to have been operationalized or objectively defined for graduate students.[2]

Dissertations reflect the education and training received, the technical skills, and the analytic and writing abilities developed in a doctoral program (Isaac et al., 1992). Thus, knowing the standards faculty use to judge dissertations could lead to the development of informed measures of learning outcomes. These measures would constitute powerful indicators of the success of research training (Holbrook & Bourke, 2002), provide evaluation standards for Ph.D. programs, and allow more objective comparison among them. Such standards would also make dissertation evaluation more valid and reliable across candidates in a department or field. In addition, having explicit standards would enhance faculty supervision and student research performance.

Evidence suggests that poor quality dissertations are often passed. In a study that looked at dissertation *abstracts*, Adams and White (1994) found that a significant number of dissertations that had passed had obvious and sometimes fatal flaws. Johnston (1997) and Mullins and Kiley (2002) found that external examiners of Australian dissertations were reluctant to fail poor quality dissertations. Thus the question arises on how faculty judge dissertations. What standards do they apply, and how do they discriminate among dissertations of different quality?

This chapter provides the results of a study in which faculty were asked to make explicit their implicit criteria for evaluating dissertations. The overarching goal of the study is for departments, disciplines, and universities to develop objective standards for the outcome of doctoral training—the dissertation—and to use these standards in a *formative* way to improve graduate education and training and make it more transparent to students.

Making the Implicit Explicit

During academic year 2003–04, 276 faculty in 74 departments across 10 disciplines (sciences: biology, electrical and computer engineering, physics and physics and astronomy, mathematics; social sciences: economics, psychology, sociology; humanities: English, history, philosophy) at 9 doctoral/research extensive universities[3] participated in focus groups in which they were asked to characterize dissertations and components of dissertations at four different quality levels—outstanding, very good, acceptable, and unacceptable. They were also asked:

1. what it meant to make an original and significant contribution in the discipline
2. what the purpose of the dissertation was (see Appendix A for the study's protocol)

Each university hired a facilitator to coordinate and conduct the focus groups, and some universities assigned an administrator to coordinate them. Faculty were selected and invited to participate in focus groups on the basis of their being high-Ph.D.-productive faculty; that is, they had advised many doctoral students and had served on many dissertation committees. It should be noted that Lovitts (2001) found that high producers have different attitudes and beliefs about graduate students and graduate education, and they interact with graduate students differently than their low-productive counterparts. Consequently, the comments made by the focus group faculty do not necessarily reflect the views, experiences, or expectations of all faculty.

Most focus groups had three or four participants; a few ran with only two, and one had eight. The faculty were asked to provide background data on the number of years they had been a professor and their experience with dissertations both as an advisor and as a committee member. Many faculty did not know exactly how many dissertations they had advised or how many dissertation committees they had served on, so they were asked to guesstimate. When the faculty provided a range (e.g., 25–30), the average of that range rounded to the nearest whole number was used. Table 6.1 provides background information on the 74 departments and the 272 focus group faculty who provided background data by discipline. Overall, these faculty had 6,129 years of experience, advised a guesstimated 3,470 dissertations, and sat on a guesstimated 9,890 dissertation committees. The average focus group participant had been a professor for 22 years, advised 13 dissertations, and served on 36 dissertation committees.

Each focus group session was tape-recorded, and the tapes were sent directly to a business services company for transcription. The transcripts were coded by protocol item and component cell (see Appendix A). The coded transcripts were entered by discipline for sorting into N6, a qualitative data analysis software program (QSR, 2002). After each node or item report was printed, each discipline's data were further reduced through a four-stage winnowing process:

1. In stage one, each node report was read and relevant information was highlighted. The highlighted information was then cut and pasted into an initial summary table by university.
2. In stage two, each initial summary table was read and the characteristics for that item were extracted and placed in a reduced summary table.
3. In stage three, the characteristics were synthesized across universities into discipline-based summary tables.

TABLE 6.1.
Background Information on Faculty Who Participated in the Focus Groups by Discipline

Department	Number of departments	Number of focus group participants	Total number of years as a professor	Average number of years as a professor	Total number of dissertations advised	Average number of dissertations advised	Total number of dissertation committees participated on	Average number of dissertation committees participated on
Biology	6	21	467	22	243	12	979	47
Mathematics	9	31	758[a]	25[a]	272[a]	9[a]	887[a]	30[a]
Physics	7	25	520	21	290	12	790	32
Engineering	6	24	450	19	350	15	1099	46
Economics	7	33	621	19	417	13	905	27
Psychology	7	28	690	25	454	16	1432	51
Sociology	7	25	567	23	336	13	1016	41
English	7	24	499	21	419	17	829	35
History	9	33	694[b]	22[b]	364[b]	12[b]	1045[b]	34[b]
Philosophy	9	32	863[c]	28[c]	325[c]	10[c]	908[c]	29[c]
Total/Ave	74	276	6129[d]	22[d]	3470[d]	13[d]	9890[d]	36[d]

Note: All averages were rounded to the nearest whole number.

[a] Totals and averages are based on the 30 focus group participants who provided data.

[b] Totals and averages are based on the 31 focus group participants who provided data.

[c] Totals and averages are based on the 31 focus group participants who provided data.

[d] Totals and averages are based on the 272 focus group participants who provided data.

4. Finally, in stage four, the characteristics that appeared in many of the discipline-based summary tables were extracted and synthesized into an overall summary for that item.

The summary tables for the main protocol items along with a summary of the faculty's ancillary discussion of each item are presented in the next section. Summary tables for the individual disciplines and the components of the dissertation, along with disciplinary-based discussions of those items can be found in Lovitts (in press).

It should be noted that the focus group protocol was initially developed as part of another study and was implemented exclusive of the matrix of components in seven departments (sciences: biology, electrical and computer engineering, physics and physics and astronomy; social sciences: economics, psychology; humanities: English, history) at each of two research universities.[4] Data from these focus groups are not included in the summary tables, though an occasional quotation from those focus groups is included in the text when it contributes something different from what was contributed by members of this study's focus groups. Those universities cannot be identified, but will be referred to in the text as Public or Private University, when one of their faculty members is quoted.

Characteristics of the Dissertation

Before presenting the results of the focus group discussion, a couple of caveats are in order. First, it needs to be made clear that faculty were not asked about their standards for the dissertation per se. Rather, they were asked about the characteristics of dissertations and components of dissertations at different quality levels. Consequently, it would not be correct to say that faculty hold students to the "standards" presented in the tables or even that they have standards for evaluating dissertations. Indeed, they asserted that they make holistic judgments about the quality of a dissertation after they have read it. In other words, they do not have a mental checklist of items used to assess a dissertation. However, the results below demonstrate that faculty do make quality judgments about dissertations and that they can (and did) make those judgments explicit.

Second, the items in the tables represent the different ways that dissertations are determined to be of a certain quality. However, no dissertation does or can do all of the individual things presented. Indeed, taken together, some of the items are self-contradictory.

The Purpose of a Dissertation

Despite the importance of the dissertation for obtaining the Ph.D., the mystique in which it is typically shrouded, and the weightiness of the task of completing one, the purpose of a dissertation in doctoral education is rarely made explicit to graduate students. Indeed, faculty in many focus groups initially had a hard time explaining the purpose. Yet, they ultimately identified many (see Table 6.2), and in the process they discussed the role the dissertation plays in students' doctoral education.

Overall, the faculty's discussion of the purpose of a dissertation indicates that they see it as both a process and a product. The faculty identified three basic processes. The first two are *to train* students to be professionals in the discipline and *to learn* the knowledge, skills, and thought processes necessary to engage in independent research. The third is *to demonstrate* that the student has mastered the discipline's knowledge base, acquired its professional skills and competencies, and is capable of doing independent research in the future. One goal of these processes is to produce a product that can be published. While the product serves as a union card or credential for admission

TABLE 6.2.
The Purpose of a Dissertation

- To train the student to be a professional in the discipline
- To ensure that the student learns how to and demonstrates the ability to:
  - ○ conduct independent, original, and significant research—identify/define problems and generate questions, review the literature, apply appropriate methods, analyze data/text, discuss findings, produce publishable results
  - ○ engage in a sustained piece of research or argument
  - ○ think and write critically and coherently
  - ○ be a professional in and contribute to the discipline
- To ensure that the student shows mastery of the field
- To help the student prepare for a career and get a job
- To provide a capstone on the graduate education and research experience, a rite of passage from student to professional, a union card or credential for admission to the profession

to the profession, participating faculty saw the dissertation as a first exercise or a first statement, the platform from which students would make subsequent, more important contributions. Indeed, an English professor said that he tells students that the first purpose of the dissertation is "to be done . . . to be written" and that the second purpose is "to get yourself a job."

One of the more interesting paradoxes of this study is that across focus groups and disciplines, participating faculty said that the purpose of the dissertation is to make an original and significant contribution. This purpose aligns well with most universities' stated criteria for the award of the Ph.D. Yet, in their discussion of what it means to make an original and a significant contribution (see the following section), the faculty often said that they did not expect graduate students to make such contributions. This is particularly striking because the questions about the meaning of an original and a significant contribution preceded the question about the purpose of a dissertation in the focus group discussions. One explanation for this apparent contradiction is that when discussing original and significant contributions the faculty may have been focusing more on their meaning with respect to the field/discipline than with respect to the dissertation, and the wording of the question may have contributed to it. Even so, in their later discussion of the unacceptable or failing dissertation, the faculty said that they will not accept a dissertation that does not make an original contribution.

Faculty in a number of fields noted that the dissertation is a rite of passage from student to professional/colleague. Faculty in mathematics and economics talked about the way the dissertation transforms people. They said those who complete it emerge with a new sense of who they are and with a new confidence in their ability to do original, independent research.

The Nature of an Original Contribution

The faculty in all disciplines defined "original contribution" with respect to its newness (see Table 6.3). The contribution can be made in almost any component of the dissertation—question, argument, theory, data, data source, method, analysis, results—by thinking, saying, or doing something that has not been thought, said, or done before. The novelty can originate wholly or in part from the student, or the student may borrow an existing contribution from another field or discipline and apply it to his or her field or discipline for the first time.

TABLE 6.3.
The Nature of an Original Contribution

- Something that has not been done, found, known, proved, said, or seen before that results from:
  - ○ Asking or identifying new questions, topics, or areas of exploration
  - ○ Applying new ideas, methods, approaches, or analyses to an old question, problem, issue, idea, source, thinker, or text
  - ○ Developing or applying new theories, theorems, theoretical descriptions, or theoretical frameworks
  - ○ Inventing, developing, or applying new methods, approaches, computations, techniques, or technologies
  - ○ Creating, finding, or using new data, data sets, archives, information, materials, or sources
  - ○ Applying old ideas, methods, approaches, or analyses to new data, material, or sources
  - ○ Developing or applying new analyses, analytical approaches, frameworks, techniques, models, or statistical procedures
  - ○ Coming up with new ideas, connections, inferences, insights, interpretations, observations, or perspectives
  - ○ Producing new conclusions, answers, findings, or proofs
  - ○ Combining or synthesizing things (experiments, facts, knowledge, models of inquiry, problems, sources, technologies, theoretical constructs) from other fields or disciplines
- Is publishable
- Adds to knowledge
- Changes the way people think
- Moves the field forward/advances the state of the art

There were some disciplinary differences about the nature of originality. Even though the English faculty were able to say what it meant to make an original contribution, most emphatically and categorically rejected the notion of originality. They noted that their discipline is recursive, not progressive, and asserted that people in their discipline did not make original contributions; rather, they join conversations. Although the philosophers did not reject the notion of originality, they noted that it was difficult to do something completely new and different in a field that has been around for 2,500 years. The mathematicians, by contrast, noted that there is a debate within their field over whether mathematics is discovered or invented/composed.

According to the faculty, the student's role in making an original contribution is more problematic in the experimental, teamwork-oriented disciplines where students tend to work on their advisor's funded research projects than in nonexperimental ones where students typically work on independently conceived research projects in their advisor's field of expertise broadly defined. Although asked by a psychologist, the following question could have come from faculty in any number of experimental disciplines:

> How many of us . . . allow students to do dissertations that are outside of the lines of research that are our own? If the answer is none, then the answer implies we don't produce any original dissertations.

In these disciplines and situations, the more the ideas originate with the student and the more the work diverges from the advisor's, the more original it is deemed. Faculty across the disciplines noted that there were levels or degrees of originality. The lowest level of originality typically involves applying old methods to new data, materials, sources, or the like, and results in a small, incremental addition to the knowledge base that is of little consequence. At the higher levels, making an original contribution typically involves asking new questions or applying new methods to old or new problems and achieving results that have consequence. That is, they are publishable, often in the highest-quality journals, and they advance the field. At the very highest level, the contribution has the potential to change the field. The faculty noted that it was rare for a graduate student to make a contribution at the highest level, and that doing so involved creativity.

The standards for originality are vague and vary across advisors. Students are often held to different standards based on their advisor's assessment of their capabilities. Indeed, the Ph.D. can be awarded for pure perseverance and technical accuracy rather than for originality (see "Acceptable," pp. 175, 177). An economics professor at Public University summed it up nicely:

> There are some students who have the ability to do very original research—to start with an idea that's original, important, interesting, and to carry it through. And for those students, we won't let them get away with the dissertation like the [lowest] kind [just mentioned], period, because we know that that they can do better. Then there are students that you realize somewhere along the way that . . . the standards you're going to hold them to are just going to be different. They're going to be lower. So, the amount

of originality in their dissertation may be far lower than another student's, and you're still willing to sign the dotted line at the end of the day.

Another participant at Public University made an interesting distinction between "original" and "contribution," suggesting that something could be original but not make a contribution. Given that original simply means new, it is not difficult to do something original; "it" just has not been said or done before. However, "contribution" is another matter. What is considered a contribution and the degree to which a dissertation makes a contribution is based on community judgment and shades into the next topic: what it means to make a significant contribution. The two concepts, as we shall see, are closely related.

The Nature of a Significant Contribution

The key distinguishing feature of a significant contribution is that it has consequence. The contribution has to be of interest and importance to the community and has to influence the field by changing the way people think (see Table 6.4). While judgments of significance are often highly subjective—"in the eye of the beholder"—significance is typically determined by community, not individual, judgment, and the judgment is often made retrospectively, sometimes many years after the fact.

The faculty's discussion of what it means to make a significant contribution demonstrates a close relationship between originality and significance.

TABLE 6.4.
The Nature of a Significant Contribution

A significant contribution
- Represents a nontrivial to very important original breakthrough at the empirical, conceptual, theoretical, or policy level
- Is useful and will have impact
- Is publishable in top-tier journals
- Is of interest to people inside and possibly outside the community and causes them to see things differently
- Influences the conversation and peoples' research and teaching
- Has implications for and advances the field, the discipline, other disciplines, and/ or society

They noted that something could be original without being significant, yet many questioned whether something could be significant without also being original. While they did not propose levels of significance, the faculty implied that in order for a contribution to be significant it had to be at the higher end of the original continuum discussed above. The timing of the contribution also appears to be important. Significant contributions seem easier to make in "hot" fields or trendy areas than in more stable or conservative ones. However, the most significant contributions are the ones that initiate a new trend or destabilize a conservative area, thus creating new questions and new research agendas.

Although significance is frequently stated as a requirement for the Ph.D., faculty do not expect graduate students to make significant contributions. Indeed, they noted that graduate students rarely make them. Instead, faculty look for evidence that the student has the ability to make a significant contribution in the future.

The Quality of the Dissertation

As the final product of doctoral education the dissertation embodies the performance goals and objectives of doctoral education. What those goals are and how well students achieve them are embodied in faculty's implicit standards for judging dissertations of different quality. To get at those goals and objectives, the focus group faculty were asked to think about dissertations they had read that were outstanding, very good, acceptable, and unacceptable. They were asked to describe what gave those dissertations a certain quality and what distinguished them from dissertations at the next higher quality level. Table 6.5 illustrates the quality distinctions or performance expectations for the dissertation as a whole that emerged from the focus group discussions.

Outstanding

When asked to characterize outstanding dissertations, the faculty often said that such work defied explication, that there was no single feature or set of defining features—"You know it when you see it." Even though outstanding dissertations are rare—they come along once or twice a decade, if that often—faculty liked talking about this quality more than any other, and provided a very consistent set of descriptors.

TABLE 6.5.
The Characteristics of Different Quality Dissertations

Quality	Characteristics
Outstanding	• Original and significant, and also ambitious, brilliant, clear, clever, coherent, compelling, concise, creative, elegant, engaging, exciting, interesting, insightful, persuasive, sophisticated, surprising, and thoughtful • Very well written and very well organized • Synthetic and interdisciplinary • Connects components seamlessly • Exhibits mature, independent thinking • Has a point of view and a strong, confident, independent, and authoritative voice • Asks new questions or addresses an important question or problem • Clearly states the problem and why it is important • Displays a deep understanding of a massive amount of complicated literature • Exhibits command and authority over the material • Argument is focused, logical, rigorous, and sustained • Is theoretically sophisticated and shows a deep understanding of theory • Has a brilliant research design • Uses or develops new tools, methods, approaches, or new types of analyses • Is thoroughly researched • Data are rich and come from multiple sources • Analysis is comprehensive, complete, sophisticated, and convincing • Results are significant • Conclusion ties the whole thing together • Is publishable in top-tier journals • Is of interest to a larger community and changes the way people think • Pushes the discipline's boundaries and opens new areas for research
Very Good	• Solid • Well written and well organized • Has some original ideas, insights, and observations, but is less original, significant, ambitious, interesting, and exciting than outstanding

	• Has a good question or problem that tends to be small and traditional • Is the next step in a research program (good normal science) • Shows understanding and mastery of the subject matter • Argument is strong, comprehensive, and coherent • Research is well executed • Demonstrates (technical) competence • Uses appropriate, standard theory, methods, and techniques • Obtains solid, expected results/answers • Misses opportunities to completely explore interesting issues and connections • Makes a modest contribution to the field but does not open it up
Acceptable	• Workmanlike • Demonstrates (technical) competence • Shows the ability to do research • Is not very original or significant • Is not interesting, exciting, or surprising • Displays little creativity, imagination, or insight • Writing is pedestrian and plodding • Structure and organization are weak • Project is narrow in scope • Question or problem is not exciting—is often highly derivative or an extension of advisor's work • Displays a narrow understanding of the field • Literature review is adequate—knows the literature but is not critical of it or does not discuss what is important • Can sustain an argument, but argument is not imaginative, complex, or convincing • Theory is understood at a simple level and is minimally to competently applied to the problem • Uses standard methods • Analysis is unsophisticated—does not explore all possibilities and misses connections • Results are predictable and not exciting • Makes a small contribution
Unacceptable	• Is poorly written • Has spelling and grammatical errors • Presentation is sloppy • Contains errors or mistakes • Plagiarizes or deliberately misreads or misuses sources

(continues)

TABLE 6.5.
Continued

Quality	Characteristics
	• Does not understand basic concepts, processes, or conventions of the discipline • Lacks careful thought • Question or problem is trivial, weak, unoriginal, or already solved • Does not understand or misses relevant literature • Argument is weak, inconsistent, self-contradictory, unconvincing, or invalid • Theory is missing, wrong, or not handled well • Methods are inappropriate or incorrect • Data are flawed, wrong, false, fudged, or misinterpreted • Analysis is wrong, inappropriate, incoherent, or confused • Results are obvious, already known, unexplained, or misinterpreted • Interpretation is unsupported or exaggerated • Does not make a contribution

According to the faculty, outstanding dissertations are characterized by originality, high quality writing, and compelling consequences. They display a richness of thought and insight, and make an important breakthrough. The writing is clear and persuasive, and provides a glimpse into the mind of the author—you can see how the student is thinking. Not only are outstanding dissertations a pleasure to read, they are "page turners." They surprise and edify the reader. When they read outstanding dissertations, faculty say, "Wow! Why didn't I think of that?" Everything is anticipated; all the reader's questions are answered. Faculty in sociology and the humanities noted that outstanding dissertations have a strong, independent, and authoritative voice. The body of work in an outstanding dissertation is deep and thorough. Each individual component of the dissertation is outstanding and the components are integrated seamlessly throughout. The results or conclusions push the discipline's boundaries and are publishable in the top-tier journals.

The faculty described students who produce outstanding dissertations as very creative and intellectually adventurous. They love, and are passionate about, what they are doing and display intense curiosity and drive. They are willing to leap into new territory and transfer ideas from place to place. Although they often have great advisors with whom they have rich and satisfying intellectual exchanges, outstanding students typically think and work independently of their advisor and of the educational process they have just been through. At the same time, an outstanding dissertation can also be a function of luck. The student may simply be in the right place at the right time.

Very Good

The faculty indicated that the majority of the dissertations they see are "very good," which is the level they expect of most graduate students. Because very good dissertations are the prototype against which all the other quality levels are compared, the faculty had less to say about very good dissertations than about the other quality levels.

Very good dissertations are solid and well written, but they are distinguished by being "less"—less original, less significant, less ambitious, less exciting, and less interesting than outstanding dissertations. They display mastery of the field, address the next question or problem in a research program, and are executed competently and confidently. One or more components of the dissertation may not be as strong as the others. The work expands rather than alters the thinking of a field and, thus, has less consequence than that of outstanding dissertations. Very good dissertations contain material for two or three papers publishable in good journals.

The faculty said students who produce very good dissertations show drive and ability. They have good technical skills, but may not be in control of all the elements of the dissertation. Sometimes, according to the faculty, what might have been an outstanding dissertation ends up being "only" very good because the student did not have or take the time to develop his or her ideas. The student may have run out of time or money, had a job waiting, or may simply have wanted to get on with life. In experimental disciplines, the dissertation may be very good rather than outstanding because the experiments did not work out as planned or the results were not as crisp and clear as expected.

Acceptable

In discussing the acceptable dissertation, faculty in many focus groups distinguished between acceptable dissertations and marginally acceptable ones, although their discussion of the two were often blurred. Acceptable dissertations meet the criteria for the award of the Ph.D., whereas marginally acceptable ones are just barely over the threshold of acceptability—they pass the "gag test."

The faculty agree that acceptable dissertations are rather pedestrian and are distinguished by being "not very"—not very original, significant, exciting, or interesting. They contain an acceptable amount of solid work that demonstrates that the student can do research. The work is often a highly derivative, small extension of someone else's work. The writing is good enough, but the dissertation is a "chore to read." In the humanities disciplines, where the dissertation is premised on an argument, the argument is weak and not convincing. The acceptable dissertation adds little to the field and lacks consequence. It may result in some conference papers, but has little in the way of publishable material, and what is publishable would get published in lower-tier journals.

Students who produce acceptable dissertations were described as functioning close to their capabilities. Although most are bright, they are missing "a certain quality of mind"—they lack intellectual power and the ability to think like a researcher. They also lack independence and initiative, and thus require a lot of coaching and hand-holding. Their advisors (or at least high-Ph.D.-productive advisors) often give them their topics or problems, feed them ideas, and spend a lot of time rewriting and copyediting their work.

Faculty do not expect these students to get—and the students often realize that they are not capable of getting—tenure-track jobs at research universities. However, they may feel that these students qualify for teaching jobs at state, liberal arts, and community colleges or for jobs in directed research at research institutions, government agencies, and the like. Sometimes acceptable dissertations are the function of circumstance or bad luck. In some cases, the students may not have been in residence and, consequently, may not have gotten the advice and guidance they needed to produce a better quality dissertation. More commonly, according to the faculty, the students rush their dissertations because they have accepted a job or a postdoctoral position, run out of funds, have a family to support, or have simply run out of steam. In experimental disciplines, otherwise good dissertations are considered acceptable when the experiment(s) does not work out and students get null or negative results.

The faculty said advisors and dissertation committees adjust their standards and expectations for students who produce acceptable and marginally acceptable dissertations. The primary consideration is that the student fulfilled the contract. That is, the student worked hard, did what he or she promised to do in the dissertation proposal, and demonstrated competence. The faculty also take into consideration such extraneous factors as their judgments about the person and the type of career the student is planning. Indeed, faculty in a few focus groups debated whether the Ph.D. should be awarded solely on the basis of the quality of the product (the dissertation) or whether their feelings about the person and their knowledge of the process the student had been through should play a role in their decision to award the degree. Ultimately, according to the faculty, the "hidden criteria" for the award of the Ph.D. is that the student will not embarrass or harm the reputation of the advisor, the committee members, the department, or the university.

Unacceptable

When asked about the unacceptable dissertation, the faculty balked. They asserted that they rarely, if ever, failed a dissertation, that dissertations of unacceptable quality were seldom allowed to come before a dissertation committee, that students who produced unacceptable dissertations would probably drop out of the program before advancing to a defense, and that it was the advisor's responsibility to prevent unacceptable dissertations from going forward. The faculty noted that when they did see an unacceptable dissertation, it was usually the advisor's fault; the student had not been given the opportunity to do well.

Very few of the focus group faculty had ever been on a committee that failed a dissertation. Those who had had the experience, with few exceptions, said that it had not happened in their department, but rather in another department where they were serving as the outside committee member. The faculty's characterization of the unacceptable dissertation is thus based primarily on their experience with unacceptable drafts.

Unacceptable dissertations are poorly written and full of errors and mistakes. They are distinguished by "not"—not original, not thoughtful, not well done. They do not have a good or clearly defined question or problem. They exhibit a poor grasp of the field and either do not use the proper methods or use them inappropriately. Unacceptable dissertations do not yield new or relevant results, and those they yield are often misinterpreted or oversold. In short, they are of no consequence and contain no publishable material.

The faculty said students produce unacceptable dissertations for a variety of reasons. Most, however, cannot master professional standards and do not have what it takes to be a researcher. Some should not have been admitted into the program in the first place or should have been stopped before advancing to candidacy. (This, of course, raises questions about why they were allowed to continue.) Others are not capable of handling a big project; they do not understand what needs to be done. Many cannot or will not take their advisor's advice or criticism into account, and, consequently, produce one bad revision after another. Yet others are capable of producing acceptable dissertations but fail to do so because they have taken jobs or otherwise left the university and have not kept up with the research in their area. The result is an unoriginal or out-of-date product. Some students fail because they push for their defense even though their advisors have told them they were not ready to defend.

Rather than proactively terminate students whose work is unacceptable, many advisors simply wait for students to get discouraged and leave. Some try to disassociate themselves from such students by sending signals or by telling them to find another advisor. Others use the dissertation defense to terminate the student. In rare instances when a student defends an unacceptable dissertation before the dissertation committee, the committee often seeks excuses to pass it. The committee members will take into consideration such things as their feelings about the person rather than the objective document. In the end, most defer to the advisor, hold their noses, and vote to pass.

Practical Implications and Important Caveats

The overarching goal of eliciting faculty's implicit standards for judging dissertations and codifying performance expectations for doctoral students is to help faculty, departments, disciplines, and universities identify the learning outcomes for doctoral education, improve the doctoral education process, and make it more transparent to students. This study was the first step in what I hope will be a multiyear project for graduate education. While I have compiled what can best be described as performance expectations for the dissertation and its component parts (see Lovitts, in press), faculty and administrators will want to develop performance expectations for their local circumstances and translate them into rubrics, or criteria, that identify expected levels of performance for various dimensions of a task, that can be used *formatively*, not summatively, as part of, not a substitute for, the advising process (see chapter 7, pp. 208–209). That is, they should be used to help doctoral students understand the goals of doctoral training, identify strengths and weaknesses, and identify what needs to be revised, why, and how, *while* the students are in the process of conducting their research and writing their dissertation so that students can improve their work along the way. The result of applying these rubrics to the doctoral training and dissertation writing process should be better quality research and dissertations, as well as better quality researchers, scholars, and skilled professionals, regardless of whether the students pursue an academic or nonacademic career.

I agree with Mullins and Kiley (2002) that these rubrics should *not* be used to rate dissertations or individual components of the dissertation, total the results and declare a dissertation passed or failed, or rate it of such and such a quality. A dissertation is an extended argument and should be viewed and judged as such. The purpose of establishing performance expectations for the dissertation and for the component parts of a dissertation is to clarify the learning goals of the enterprise and its individual components (e.g., literature review, theory, methods, analysis), thereby strengthening each piece of the whole while at the same time strengthening the whole.

Despite my call to create performance expectations and bring greater clarity and objectivity to the evaluation of the dissertation, many of the "standards" are indeterminate qualities that faculty can recognize but not articulate precisely (e.g., compelling, elegant, surprising) (see Delamont, Atkinson, & Parry, 2002; and Lovitts, in press). Indeed, it was not uncommon for faculty to respond to a protocol item by saying, "You know it when you see it," or "It's like pornography. You know it when you see it." Although these qualities may remain relatively undefined, faculty should at least be able to agree that they are or are not important outcomes of graduate training and are or are not found in the dissertation. These qualities are and should be conveyed to students through the process of professional socialization and through appropriate exemplars.

Another reason why the rubrics should not be used for summative assessment is because, as the faculty noted, there are many kinds of dissertations and they serve many different purposes. The focus group faculty were high-

Ph.D.-productive faculty, and like the high producers in my previous study (Lovitts, 2001), they commented that they, but not all their colleagues, held their students to different standards based on the students' needs and capabilities. Not all graduate students can produce outstanding dissertations nor should they be expected to. Indeed, the ability to produce an outstanding dissertation, one that says something totally new or opens up a new field, is often a function of the state of the field at the time the student is in graduate school. Some fields are ripe for analysis and criticism that will take them in new directions. Most are in a state of what Kuhn (1962) calls "normal science," where the bulk of the work is "mopping up operations" or expanding what is known within the dominant paradigm.

As the saying about dissertations goes, done is better than perfect. Graduate school is the beginning, not the end, of a career. Thus the goal should be to use a rubric in a formative way to help doctoral students understand the learning goals of their education; to help them to achieve the highest level possible given their needs, capabilities, and professional goals; and to help them make the transition out of graduate school and into their careers.

Research Implications

Further research designed to elicit faculty's implicit standards for evaluating dissertations can and should occur at several different levels—institutional, university, discipline, department. Each has different implications for graduate education. At the highest level, the institutional level, several focus groups could be conducted in each of many disciplines across a variety of universities and the results analyzed for universal themes in a manner similar to this study. A group of graduate school deans could be brought together to discuss the findings and then issue a statement of performance expectations for doctoral education writ large. The performance expectations contained in the statement would then provide an objective standard for educating and training doctoral students and for evaluating Ph.D. programs across disciplines and universities.

At the university level, the graduate school dean could require that all Ph.D.-granting departments convene focus groups and create clearly defined performance standards for their graduate students. The resulting standards could then be analyzed for cross-disciplinary themes, and the university could then compose its own performance standards, much the way universities currently have statements about the nature or purpose of the dissertation. The existence of such standards would allow universities to more easily arbitrate student claims that they are not receiving the education they came to the university to receive or that their dissertation had not been judged fairly. The existence of such standards would also facilitate the termination of students who cannot meet the standard, provide these students with objective reasons for their termination, and reduce the probability of (successful) litigation from disgruntled graduate students.

At the disciplinary level, professional organizations could convene one or more focus groups with leaders in the field to define the performance standards for the different types of dissertations in their discipline (e.g., theoretical versus empirical, quantitative versus qualitative, basic research versus applied research). The existence of such standards would allow for more consistent training and objective comparison across programs. They would also provide another measure for accreditation boards to use in determining whether departments are providing doctoral students with the expected level of education and training.

Finally, the creation of performance standards in individual departments would make the training process and its goals more transparent to faculty and students, thus enhancing faculty supervision and student research performance. (In the case study that follows this chapter, see one administrator's perspectives on how the University of Colorado at Boulder's participation in this Making the Implicit Explicit project is shaping doctoral practices.) Having codified standards should also lead to more valid and reliable judgments of quality across candidates in a department or field. Indeed, most of the focus group faculty found their discussion enlightening and beneficial. Some wanted to make their results available to their students.

The matrix (Table 6.6) contains the essential components of a dissertation and was designed to best match the structure or the intellectual tasks required of the dissertation in the different disciplines in this study. The essential components initially derived from my experiences as a doctoral student in three different disciplines (psychology, history of science, and sociology); my familiarity with the basic requirements of science and social science dissertations; and my sense that all dissertations had an introduction/problem statement, included some sort of literature review, were set within a theoretical context, had some sort of methodology for approaching and analyzing the data, and had a conclusion. Based on initial attempts to imple-

TABLE 6.6.

Matrix of Components of the Dissertation Used for Different Disciplines

Biology, Physics, Engineering, Economics, Psychology, Sociology	Introduction	Literature Review	Theory	Methods	Results/Data Analysis	Discussion and Conclusion
Mathematics	Introduction/ Problem Statement	Discussion of the Literature	Statement of Results/ Theorems	Approach to the Problem (techniques)	Proof of Results	Conclusion/ Future Directions
English	Introduction (of problem or concept)	Review of Sources	Approach to Analysis	Justification of Chosen Texts	Analysis of Texts	Conclusion
History	Introduction	Historiographic Review	Sources/ Methods	Exposition/ Analysis	Conclusion	
Philosophy	Introduction/ Statement and Clarification of the Problem	Demonstration of Knowledge of the Literature	Development/ Defense of the Thesis(es)	Recognition and Response to Possible Objections	Conclusion	
Outstanding						
Very Good						
Acceptable						
Unacceptable/ Failing						

ment the matrix at Public and Private Universities, it became clear that the original structure (introduction, literature review, theory, methods, analysis/ results, discussion/conclusion) would not work for mathematics and the humanities disciplines. Thus, the structure for the mathematics and humanities matrices was developed in consultation with the directors of graduate study or a high-Ph.D.-productive faculty member in those disciplines at two universities.

The study was already under way when one of the facilitators told me about a 1997 Council of Graduate Schools (CGS) publication, *The Role and Nature of the Doctoral Dissertation: A Policy Statement*, that describes a 1990 CGS study that was conducted in 50 universities in the United States and Canada on why universities require the dissertation and what it should be. The report recommends that the dissertation, regardless of the field, should do five things that correspond closely with the components of a dissertation identified for this study:

- reveal the student's ability to analyze, interpret and synthesize information;
- demonstrate the student's knowledge of the literature relating to the project or at least acknowledge prior scholarship on which the dissertation is built;
- describe the methods and procedures used;
- present results in a sequential and logical manner; and
- display the student's ability to discuss fully and coherently the meaning of the results. In the sciences the work must be described in sufficient detail to permit an independent investigator to replicate the results. (Council of Graduate Schools, 1997)

Notes

1. Despite all the new thinking on the purposes of the Ph.D., methods of training graduate students, and alternate careers for Ph.D.s, the Ph.D. is a research degree (Austin, 2002), one that signifies that the recipient has acquired the capacity to make independent contributions to knowledge through original research and scholarship (Association of American Universities, 1998). Indeed, according to the Council of Graduate Schools (as cited in Bargar & Duncan, 1982), the central purpose of doctoral education is "to prepare a student for a lifetime of intellectual inquiry that manifests itself in creative scholarship and research" (p. 1).

2. The nature of "original" and "significant" is addressed in a 1997 Council of Graduate Schools report. However, this report is rarely cited and does not seem to have had much influence on graduate education. The report mentions that Berelson (1960) addresses these concepts. Although Berelson is widely cited for his work on student attrition and retention, his work on "original" and "significant" are not included in contemporary discussions about graduate education.

3. Duke University, Michigan State University, Northwestern University, State University of New York at Stony Brook, Syracuse University, University of Colorado, University of Illinois, University of Kansas, and University of Southern California.

4. Overall, 55 faculty participated in focus groups at Public and Private University; 53 provided background data. These faculty had an average of 25 years of experience, advised an average of 15 dissertations, and sat on an average of 36 dissertation committees.

References

Adams, G. B., & White, J. D. (1994). Dissertation research in public administration and cognate fields. An assessment of methods and quality. *Public Administration Review*, *54*(6), 565–576.

Association of American Universities. (1998). *Committee on graduate education report and recommendations*. Washington, DC: Author.

Austin, A. (2002, November). Assessing doctoral students' progress along developmental dimensions. Paper presented at the annual meeting of the Association for the Study of Higher Education, Sacramento, CA. Retrieved from www.carnegie foundation.org/CID/ashe?austin.pdf.

Bargar, R. R., & Duncan, J. K. (1982). Cultivating creative endeavor in doctoral research. *Journal of Higher Education*, *52*(1), 1–31.

Berelson, B. (1960). *Graduate education in the United States*. New York: McGraw-Hill.

Council of Graduate Schools. (1997). *The role and nature of the doctoral dissertation: A policy statement*. Washington, DC: Author.

Delamont, S., Atkinson, P., & Parry, O. (2002). *The doctoral experience: Success and failure in graduate school*. London, UK: Falmer Press.

Holbrook, A. (2002, April). How examiners of doctoral theses utilize the written report. Paper presented at the American Education Research Association Conference, New Orleans, LA.

Holbrook, A., & Bourke, S. (2002, April). PhD assessment: Design of the study, qualities of examiner reports and candidature information. Paper presented at the American Education Research Association Conference, New Orleans, LA.

Isaac, P. D., Quinlan, S. V., & Walker, M. M. (1992). Faculty perceptions of the doctoral dissertation. *Journal of Higher Education, 63*(3), 241–268.

Johnston, S. (1997). Examining the examiners: An analysis of examiners' reports on doctoral theses. *Studies in Higher Education, 22*(3), 333–347.

Kuhn, T. S. (1962). *The structure of scientific revolutions.* Chicago: University of Chicago Press.

Lovitts, B. E. (2001). *Leaving the ivory tower: The causes and consequences of departure from doctoral study.* Lanham, MD: Rowman & Littlefield.

Lovitts, B. E. (in press). *Making the implicit explicit: Creating performance expectations for assessing the outcomes of doctoral education.* Sterling, VA: Stylus.

Mullins, G., & Kiley, M. (2002). "It's a PhD, not a Nobel Prize": How experienced examiners assess research theses. *Studies in Higher Education, 27*(4), 369–386.

QSR International Pty Ltd. (2002). N6 (Version 6 of NUD*IST) [computer software]. Doncaster, Victoria, Australia: Author.

Tinkler, P., & Jackson, C. (2000). Examining the doctorate: Institutional policy and the PhD examination process in Britain. *Studies in Higher Education, 25*(2), 167–180.

Winter, R., Griffiths., M., & Green, K. (2000). The "academic" qualities of practice: What are the criteria for a practiced-based PhD? *Studies in Higher Education, 25*(1), 25–37.

Case Study for Making the Implicit Explicit Research Project Conducted at the University of Colorado at Boulder

An Administrator's Experiences and Perspectives

Candice L. Miller

Implementation of the Making the Implicit Explicit Research Project at University of Colorado at Boulder

Participating in the Making the Implicit Explicit (MIE) Research Project provided the University of Colorado at Boulder (CU-Boulder) with a unique and enlightening opportunity for our faculty and senior administrators. Historically and traditionally, the process and content of the dissertation resided with the faculty advisory committee and the advisee only. This study allowed us to observe and investigate this privileged process from the perspectives of high-Ph.D.-producing faculty in 10 disciplines: ecology and evolutionary biology, economics, electrical and computer engineering, English, history, math, philosophy, physics, psychology, and sociology. As such, it provided a window of opportunity for us to hear and observe the deliberations related to the dissertation process as organized within the MIE study design.

Securing Participation

At CU-Boulder, our high level of administrative and faculty participation was attributable to several factors. This section will deal with retrospective observations of those factors. The first factor, administrative commitment, was signed off by our leadership, in this case our then dean of the Graduate School, Carol B. Lynch. She and I, director of research and information for the Graduate School and MIE study coordinator, felt that this doctoral-level topic was an important one. We were curious about the similarities and differences we might discover across the inner workings of the departments, and I was willing to expand my workload to do what was needed to complete our portion of the study. My overall time commitment on this six-month project amounted to about 100 hours, time well invested from my perspective, from the Graduate School's perspective (Dean Lynch and myself), and from participant feedback.

A second factor that contributed to a high level of faculty participation was the approach we designed to invite faculty to participate. Specifically, I made follow-up telephone calls after sending an initial letter from Dean Lynch to the graduate directors. As a previous fund-raiser, I knew that successful results are largely based upon the quality of the relationships developed. In this case, it was the relationships developed with potential faculty participants through brief but effective communications, not taking more of their time than necessary. Barbara Lovitts had provided us with several study design templates for every step of the process—from a copy for the graduate chairs' letters to the Human Research Committee (HRC) introductory letters and log sheets—that facilitated the flow of information from the graduate chairs to their high-Ph.D.-producing faculty. As such, we had a scaffold to work from, but we also had the freedom to describe each step appropriately to our academic setting and culture, and were not required to use any of the templates except the questions, categories, tape-recording introductions, and HRC informed consents for purposes of study reliability.

A third factor that enhanced participation and expedited the process for the graduate chairs was that I provided them with E-mail drafts for invitations they could send to their high-Ph.D.-producing faculty. (Sometimes I used a general idea that Lovitts had provided and then customized that for our campus culture.) The graduate chairs simply edited these E-mail drafts and forwarded them to faculty. This step provided both an opportunity for the graduate chairs to identify their department's high-Ph.D.-producing faculty and to compliment these potential faculty participants for their high levels of productivity. Again, I followed up the E-mail with a phone call within five working days.

Persistence must be considered a factor on its own merit and cannot be underestimated in terms of the results it can produce. In order to produce desired results, an administrator must carry both a sense of purpose and a sense or vision of a productive, complete, and successful project in order to counteract the continuous efforts required at times to make a project such as the MIE as important as 20 other items on a faculty member's plate.

In the context of faculty's heavy research and teaching loads at CU-Boulder, a major research institution, generating enthusiasm among high-performing faculty was key because this project demanded they carve out two hours of their valuable time during an academic year with no incentives other than coffee and cookies and a better understanding of their departmental dissertation-guiding processes. As participation was voluntary, to faculty's credit they decided that understanding more about their departmental process held value. Each participant was promised a copy of the results of the study, and Lovitts sent them a prepublication review of her findings, as well as a final report. Finally, collegial teamwork among Lovitts, CU-Boulder facilitator Thomas Cyr, and me proved critical to maintaining momentum, a positive state of mind, and the results themselves.

In summary, factors contributing to a high level of participation in the MIE project from an administrator's perspective included (a) leadership sign off (the dean's), (b) a high level of well-planned and brief communications, (c) graduate chairs' willingness to participate and sell their high-Ph.D.-producing faculty on the project idea, (d) well-organized study design templates—both letters to faculty and study protocols, (e) enthusiasm, (f) persistence, and (g) a collegial team.

The Gold We Mined

Gold serves as a useful metaphor, as it represents the significant value, purity, and clarity of results for our study. One gold nugget was the discovery that faculty had rarely, if ever, previously met together to discuss the consistency of expectations related to discipline-specific dissertation standards. Their level of engagement and comments indicated that the MIE discussions provided a valuable investment of their time.

Traditionally, evaluating the quality of dissertations has only occurred among faculty and behind closed doors. Discussing the process in a relatively open forum provided another gold nugget in this sense: such willingness to share time and expertise in order to clarify dissertation standards with the intent to improve dissertation quality represents a sincere effort to make a positive change in an institutional setting. Faculty willingness to do this as part of a study with an administrator and facilitator present broke tradition to a degree, but toward mutually beneficial ends. Although dissertation standards and expectations are not standardized across disciplines (the relativity of the process can be seen in the first part of this chapter by Lovitts), the discussions at CU-Boulder created a precedent for such discussions, and opened up possibilities, specifically, expressed interest in meeting more often to standardize expectations and communicate those more clearly to graduate students.

In several instances, Cyr and I shared discipline-specific distinctions with faculty from another discipline in the hopes that another perspective might provide discussion points. For example, in ecology and evolutionary biology, the dissertation is a compiled series of journal articles written by the student throughout the doctoral process. Each article can represent a different experiment, and can thus be discontinuous, unlike chapters in a humanities dissertation. We observed a pattern of the dissertation morphing into a custom form most suitable for the discipline and the culture of that discipline. As such, the MIE study provided the opportunity to update the Graduate School on diverging discipline-specific formats, and to update faculty in one discipline on how dissertations are organized in other disciplines.

This MIE study unearthed gold on our campus in surprising ways. Unexpectedly, this study forged bridges among discipline-specific faculty as well as between faculty and the Graduate School administration—yet another nugget. During the focus group discussions, it became clear that dialogue about expectations for a dissertation across disciplines held mutual interest for faculty and administration to pursue in the future.

As one who knows, having been both a faculty member (on another campus) and an administrator, I feel that finding these mutual interests, these "bridges," is not a minor achievement. In this regard, faculty members and administration members can share mutual interests: that doctoral students are valuable resources and any investment in their successful completion of their dissertation is worthy of attention, trying to find more transparent ways the dissertation can be qualitatively improved, having an interest in improving dissertation writing as a whole, and—overall—having the intent to improve the quality of dissertations. For example, the need to clarify and consistently share with students the disciplinary expectations for a dissertation was one need mutually agreed upon among faculty across the 10 disciplines.

While faculty seemed clear about their dissertation expectations and shared many of these expectations with us, it became evident time and again that these expectations had not always been shared with the doctoral students themselves. When we asked for descriptors of an outstanding or very good dissertation, faculty in several disciplines responded, "I know an outstanding or very good dissertation when I see it." While this observation may be useful for faculty, it does not provide guidance for a doctoral student. We then teased out specifics to share with doctoral students. The mutually agreed-upon need and desire to make these expectations more transparent to students was one of the noteworthy pieces of gold we mined, although we are still in the process of teasing out how best to make specifics most transparent and accessible to students.

Faculty unanimously voiced an interest in helping students improve the quality of their dissertation development and writing, but faculty also indicated that they did not have the administrative time to investigate how to do it. Given this opening and interest expressed by faculty, the Graduate School can now work collaboratively with the departments. One example could be to have the rubrics developed during the MIE project available for faculty, which faculty members could compare to their own dissertation expectations. The MIE project would then serve as an example of what some faculty expect, but other faculty could adapt or clarify these expectations based on their own department culture. As such, disseminating the MIE project findings could contribute to clarity, but not interfere with faculty's domains of curriculum, dissertation chairmanship, or advising a student on discipline-specific theory and practice.

Intentions to Use What We Learned

Nugget by nugget, we discovered that the MIE project generated helpful insights, such as the fact that very little has been done to standardize expectations within departments related to the dissertation style of that department. These expectations are now available, making it also possible for other departments across the university to review these results from the 10 participating disciplines and use what is most valuable for their own department.

One specific piece of feedback that will be implemented is to create a doctoral handbook model suitable for all departments because not all departments have one. Included in the handbook would be (a) rubrics and summaries from the MIE study, (b) chapters from this book, (c) Lovitts's MIE book (in press), and (d) organizational suggestions the departments' graduate directors might use. This booklet then would summarize guidance for all 10 disciplines, define what represents rigorous research and what does not, and summarize standards for dissertation writing and sources.

We also developed new relationships among faculty and between faculty and administrators that laid groundwork for any next steps. Finally, the MIE project allowed faculty and Graduate School administration to broaden and deepen our collective understanding of the status of standards and expectations for dissertations in 10 disciplines/departments. As CU-Boulder has 46 doctoral degree programs, other graduate departments could adapt successful practices developed in the 10 graduate departments that participated in this study. Overall, this study helped us to see that the traditional dissertation model was not student focused and assumed that students understood the conventions and norms of writing a dissertation. The goal now is to orient and support students through the process by articulating disciplinary expectations in order to provide more transparency for the dissertation process.

Through the MIE study, then, we determined that the following actions can improve the development and actual writing of the dissertation:

- Create discipline-specific booklets that reflect faculty expectations for dissertation writing.
- Make dissertation expectations as transparent as possible, perhaps using examples or case studies to facilitate students' understandings of what is expected.
- Include in the booklets the importance of communication going both ways: from faculty to student and from student to faculty. That is, faculty must make their expectations clear, and students must ask for clarification as needed.
- Include in the booklets an abbreviated version of the MIE rubric results so that the categories of outstanding to poor, by chapter, are expressed both in narrative and visual forms.

- Discuss with senior Graduate School administration the possibility of including in a department's program review process the following question: Could you please give specific examples of how your department provides graduate students with clear expectations for the development and writing of the dissertation?

An Administrator's Reflections

The Graduate School's participation in this project was partially because of an awareness that the study questions were timely and answers to them might provide a value-added component for doctoral education. Without persistence and continual communication among Barbara Lovitts and the coordinators, this study would not have been possible. In the end, I believe that the persistence and commitment that Barbara Lovitts and I share—a boon to this project—are grounded in our passion to address the national fact that, averaged across disciplines, a 50% doctoral noncompletion rate exists in this country (Bowen & Rudenstine, 1992; Council of Graduate Schools, 2004; Lovitts, 2001).

We believe that this noncompletion rate, a danger sign for higher education, is unacceptable. As well, a number of educators in this country have noted and discussed this issue at the 2003, 2004, and 2005 national meetings of the Council of Graduate Schools. As noted by the National Academy of Sciences report (1996), this issue must be addressed not just on a large scale but also on a local level, university by university, and discipline by discipline. To that end, CU-Boulder put forth its best efforts during this study to understand more thoroughly specific standards and expectations for dissertations as they are expressed and implemented in various disciplines, to contribute to improving both the dissertation development/ writing processes, and to increase completion rates among doctoral students.

One final gold nugget from this study was personally valuable. As an administrator and a doctoral student, my dissertation focus was inspired by the MIE study findings. That is, I will explore more deeply how the doctoral process works within three disciplines on our campus from both the faculty's and students' perspectives, and examine how all stages of discipline-specific doctoral work facilitate or hinder completion or noncompletion of the doctoral degree. In closing, I wish to thank Barbara Lovitts for her partnership and leadership. Because of Barbara's courageous stand to research issues of doctoral noncompletion (Lovitts, 2001) at a time when few have researched and published in this area, she is now cited frequently, and has given others new research opportunities.

References

Bowen, W., & Rudenstine, N. (1992). *In pursuit of the PhD.* Princeton, NJ: Princeton University.

Council of Graduate Schools. (2004). *PhD completion and attrition: Policy, number, leadership, and next steps.* Washington, DC: Author.

Lovitts, B. E. (2001). *Leaving the ivory tower: The causes and consequences of departure from doctoral study.* Lanham, MD: Rowman & Littlefield.

Lovitts, B. E. (in press). *Making the implicit explicit: Creating performance expectations for assessing the outcomes of doctoral education.* Sterling, VA: Stylus.

National Academy of Sciences. (1996). *The path to the PhD: Measuring graduate attrition in the sciences and the humanities.* Washington, DC: National Academy Press.

Appendix A

Protocol

Original and Significant Contribution

The most common and sometimes only requirement departments and universities have for the award of the Ph.D. is that the dissertation make an original and/or significant contribution.

1. Tell me what it means to make an original contribution in _____ (field)? What does it look like?
2. Tell me what is means to make a significant contribution in _____ (field)? What does it look like?

The Dissertation

Now I'd like to talk about the dissertation.

3. What is the purpose of the dissertation?
4. I'd like you to think about the most outstanding dissertation or dissertations you have read. Tell me what made those dissertations so outstanding. What are the characteristics of an outstanding dissertation?
5. Now think about a dissertation that was very good but not outstanding. What made it very good and what is the difference between a very good and an outstanding dissertation?
6. Now think about a dissertation that was acceptable but not very good. What made it acceptable and what is the difference between an acceptable and a very good dissertation?
7. Now think about a dissertation that was unacceptable or that you didn't pass. What made it unacceptable and what is the difference between an unacceptable and acceptable dissertation?

The Components of a Dissertation

8. Now I'd like to repeat this exercise focusing on the major components of a dissertation. I have a matrix that will help guide our discussion.

Pass out the matrix.

Go down each column: What are the characteristics of a _____ (quality) _____ (component)?

7

DOCTORAL STUDENTS' PERSPECTIVES ON THE DISSERTATION

Jeannie Brown Leonard

As the culminating product required to earn the Ph.D., the dissertation is a daunting, albeit exciting, rite of passage. Although talented at taking courses, doctoral students often struggle with the ill-defined nature of the doctoral dissertation (Biaggio, 2002; Lovitts, 2001). Very little research systematically explores doctoral student experiences with the dissertation. Brause (2001) acknowledged that many of the 250 doctoral students in her informal study were uninformed about what is required to complete a dissertation. Lovitts (2005) and others (e.g., Biaggio, 2002) have noted that doctoral students need different skills to complete a dissertation from those that helped them succeed with course work. Lovitts's research (2001) revealed that doctoral students who do not complete their degrees were derailed for a variety of reasons including problems related to the dissertation. Indeed, Lovitts's (2001) study of doctoral student attrition points to key factors outside individual student characteristics that constrain and impede students' progress on the dissertation. These factors include a lack of information and ineffective socialization to the graduate program and to the overall expectations in a field. In addition, the emergence of how-to books for dissertation writing implicitly acknowledges doctoral students' need for more guidance in completing strong dissertations (Becker, 1986; Bolker, 1998; Glatthorn & Joyner, 2005; Rudestam & Newton, 2001; Secrist & Wright, 1998).

The performance expectations for the dissertation developed by Lovitts and described in chapter 6 are intended to support students in the often mysterious task of conceptualizing and completing a dissertation. As a doctoral student working on the Making the Implicit Explicit (MIE) study, I read and coded transcripts of faculty focus groups. I can testify to the benefits of the descriptions faculty provided regarding overall quality markers and characteristics of the various components of the dissertation, reported on pages 173 to 180 in chapter 6. I learned about the dissertation, the different forms it takes, and the characteristics that shape very good and outstanding dissertations and distinguish them from those that are acceptable or unacceptable. Although the department in which I am pursuing a Ph.D. was not represented in the MIE study, I have been able to transfer many of the insights to my own field by asking my advisor clarifying questions. Using my subjective experience as a doctoral student as a base of questioning, Lovitts and I decided to explore more systematically student reactions to the first draft of the performance expectations described in the MIE study (outlined on pp. 174–176, chapter 6).

Context and Method

In this exploratory investigation at a large, research university, graduate departments corresponding to the disciplines represented in the MIE study (see chapter 6, p. 164) were asked in September 2004 to identify doctoral students who were at the dissertation stage of their academic program. Based on the nominations from either the department chair or the graduate study advisor, the researchers contacted students and invited them to participate in the study during fall semester 2004. Although focus groups of three or four students were the target size, scheduling challenges and a dearth of volunteers prevented this initial desired goal from being achieved. All focus groups had at least two confirmed participants, but in some cases only one student arrived at the appointed place and time. Rather than rescheduling the conversations, the protocol was implemented with one participant, creating more of an interview dynamic than a focus group experience. Table 7.1 provides a summary of the participants including the number of students taking part in each conversation, their gender, and their proximity to completing their degree.

TABLE 7.1.
Doctoral Student Participants

Department (represented in MIE study)	Number	Male	Female	Preproposal Stage	Engaged in Research	Expected to Complete by August 2005
Biology	1		1	0	0	1
Electrical Engineering	1	1		0	0	1
History	2		2	0	1	1
Mathematics	2	2		0	1	1
Philosophy	4	4		0	4	0
Physics	3	1	2	0	0	3
Psychology	1	1		0	1	0
Sociology	3	1	2	2	1	0
Total Participants	17	10	7	2	8	7

The focus group protocol (see Appendix A) probed three student-focused questions related to the dissertation:

1. Students' understanding of the dissertation in their field, including their understanding of what makes a dissertation original and significant
2. Students' concerns about their dissertation
3. Students' concerns about how their dissertation would be evaluated

Participants were then given copies of the tables from the MIE study detailing the performance criteria generated by faculty in their discipline and were invited to share their reactions. All focus groups were recorded on audiotape; a facilitator took notes. Transcripts based on the notes were created within 24 hours of each focus group meeting; the audiotapes were consulted as needed for accuracy and for confirmation for the material quoted in this chapter.

Results

Students' Understanding of the Dissertation

The student voices that emerged from the focus group conversations offer another perspective on the issue of assessing doctoral-level education. Only 4 of the students in this sample of 17 claimed to have much understanding of the dissertation and its scope when they started their doctoral programs. In each of those cases, the students had previous experience with extensive research through either an undergraduate honors thesis or a master's thesis.

The responses from the 13 uninformed students ranged from a matter-of-fact "I did not know anything about it. . . . Zero!" from a physics student to a philosophy student's vague notion of the dissertation being "a big mystical mountain" that was looming on the horizon. A biology student credited her perceptive powers in figuring out what was expected of her. The expectation to publish in good journals was never communicated to her directly. "[Eventually] my advisor said, 'so which articles are you going to send to *Nature*?'" Similar to the faculty responses in the MIE study (see chapter 6), some students emphasized the difference between the dissertation as a document and the research that undergirds it, making it clear that the research itself is more important than the bound volume submitted to the graduate school. A sociology student who had not yet defended her dissertation proposal added that, based on her experience with first-year graduate students, most were "terrified and mystified by the whole process [of writing the dissertation]."

Despite this relative lack of awareness at the beginning of their studies of what was expected of them to earn their degree, all focus group participants had navigated the curriculum successfully and were anticipating or actively engaged in their dissertation research. Not surprisingly, the students relied heavily on their faculty advisors for guidance in learning about the dissertation in their discipline. A mathematics student who participated in a research group credited those contacts, as well as his advisor, for helping him understand what his dissertation should look like in applied (versus pure) math. In cases where advisors were less helpful, students relied on peers for insights. This guidance came in the form of informal sharing and by reading completed dissertations. Departmental seminars showcasing the work of advanced doctoral students helped shape expectations as well. One physics student felt very much alone in the process of discovering what her dissertation needed to be. She used the search engine Google to find out what was expected for the dissertation in her field. Another student in psychology relied on "trial and error." He said he would write drafts and then use his advisor's comments and edits to learn what was expected.

Students' Concerns about the Dissertation

During the focus groups, the facilitator invited students to share their concerns about the dissertation. The responses differed according to where students were in the dissertation research and writing process. Those who had not yet proposed or were in the beginning stages of research expressed worries related to finding a good advisor, picking a meaningful and manageable topic, and finding enough participants. One sociology student commented:

> The people I want as my advisors are too busy this semester . . . to take on new students. . . . I'm worried that when I need that advice [in areas where I am less knowledgeable], how can I get it?

Another sociology student said, "I'm worried about the dissertation topic itself. . . . Will potential employers look at it as a credible and viable topic?" A psychology student noted, "The big concern I have . . . is finding participants. . . . It is getting all the data [that concerns me]."

Many of those engaged in research were concerned about completing their dissertation and about its importance. A physics student voiced her concern that "no one will care." A history student said she was worried about

> getting it done! . . . Just all the little details. I have so much paper . . . it overwhelms me. . . . [I'm worried about] losing my argument and getting lost in the details, and [not knowing] where to stop.

An engineering student recalled these earlier worries, but his proximity to completion allowed him to be optimistic and encouraging:

> [When I started] I was concerned I wouldn't be able to finish it [the dissertation]. . . . During the course of working on my dissertation I was concerned when I got stuck on the problem. . . . But if you stay with it and keep thinking about it and discuss it with your advisor, you can get through it.

Students' Concerns about Evaluation of the Dissertation

The students were asked to share any concerns they had about how their dissertation would be evaluated. Students who had strong relationships with their advisor and the other faculty on their dissertation committee, as well as those who had opportunities for positive feedback from peers and external audiences via publication, were more confident about the quality of their work. In mathematics, the advisors pushed students to produce an article for publication that would become a part of the dissertation. Success in publication was a great positive reinforcement. A math student said, "Once I got my first two articles published, that felt really good. I felt like, at least in my advisor's eyes, that this [work] is thesis material." Similarly, a physics student said, "All the chapters [of my dissertation] have been published or sent off to be published, so they have been scrutinized already." This student was not worried about how his work would be evaluated and anticipated an interesting conversation at his defense.

Most students found comfort in their dissertation committees. The following comments from sociology and math students are representative: "My committee is great. They get along well with each other. They are more colleagues rather than adversaries." A mathematics student said:

> No [I'm not worried]. I won't present until I am ready. . . . It's not aggressive; my committee is supportive. . . . I trust that my advisor wouldn't okay my thesis to present to the rest of the committee unless it was refined enough so it was appropriate to present it to them.

Consistent with the comments from faculty in the MIE study, students trusted their advisor to determine when they were ready to defend. Students who worked closely with an advisor felt that they received ample feedback and were able to gauge the quality of their work—at least whether it was acceptable and likely to pass through the committee. A physics student said, "I'm not really worried," because he had already received a lot of feedback from his advisor. Although most expected to have to make revisions based on the recommendations of the committee, they did not expect those revisions to interfere with earning the degree. According to a philosophy student:

> I don't have concerns about people judging my work . . . when I go into the defense, especially if I have a job, I think I'll pass and get the Ph.D.

Some of the stages I'm in now, I am concerned about what I'm doing and whether my ideas are any good, but I don't have concerns about getting the Ph.D. . . . I am concerned about my work being judged, but not worried about getting the Ph.D.

A history student emphasized the importance of clear communication with a faculty advisor:

I have a committee that's very diverse. Different people on the committee expect different things from the dissertation. . . . I have to think hard about what I'm going to do . . . I have to write the dissertation I want to write . . . knowing that it is good and my advisor is helping me.

A math student stated, "I'm not really concerned at this point about graduation. I believe my advisor when he says that I have enough to graduate, but I want to push it."

By contrast, anxiety about the quality of the dissertation is heightened when the advisor/advisee relationship is awkward or strained or when the advisor is a novice. A biology student responded as follows:

Things have not worked as well as I would have liked. . . . My advisor has a lot of grad students, so I have been on my own a lot for the last several years. . . . Whether or not I graduate depends one hundred percent on whether my advisor wants me to graduate. That's it. Period. It's why I'm a stress case. . . . I've never seen one of my advisor's graduate students finish.

A physics student reported on the uncertainty he felt about how his dissertation would be evaluated by various members of his committee:

I am my advisor's first student . . . in physics. I had one person say, "Can you give me drafts along the way?" and I have and he already told me he has no concerns with it [the dissertation]. . . . They [the committee] have heard me give talks based on it [my research], but have not been part of the process.

Another physics student expressed concern that her good relationship with her advisor was tempered by his inexperience: "I didn't get much feedback. . . . My advisor was a bit worried because I am his first physics student."

Weak relationships with committee members can be the source of anxiety, too. A philosophy student noted, "One of my committee members has not [provided feedback], so she is a wildcard." This unknown commodity in the form of a committee member can be devastating. Indeed, a physics student said, "I found out today that one member of my committee is not going to sign off on my dissertation. . . . I should find someone who finds this research worth doing." An engineering student differentiated between his advisor and others who will read his work:

> Yes, I do [have some concerns about how others will evaluate my dissertation]. But for my advisor, it might be different than others on the committee. Our relationship is very close and he knows the process I have gone through. He read my thesis and we exchange comments on my dissertation so I know where we stand. . . . I am more concerned about what others [besides my advisor] think. They may not think my work is important. I think it is important, but . . . it isn't a hot topic.

A history student was concerned about her work appealing to her diverse committee:

> My fear is that I'll get to the dissertation defense and they'll say, "Why didn't you do this?" or "Why didn't you do that?" I think that's what worries me the most. . . . My advisor says as long as we are working together and as long as we agree . . . that is all that matters.

Yet another history student said, "I have not thought about or worried about that [the evaluation] . . . Just getting it done is so overwhelming . . . that stage seems too far away. It is more important that I satisfy myself first. I have to trust that it will all work out."

Students' Perspectives on Performance Expectations

The performance expectations created by the MIE study (chapter 6, pp. 174–176; 184) outline the characteristics that distinguish an outstanding, very good, acceptable, and unacceptable overall dissertation and its component parts. Using the descriptions in the tables outlined in chapter 6, pages 174 through 176 and 184, students considered the reasonableness of the standards. Consistent with faculty perceptions, a history student surmised that most dissertations are in the "acceptable to very good range." Another math student stated, "I think most people in this department write very good dissertations and a few are acceptable. I can think of one that has been outstanding." A physics student found it difficult to distinguish between very good and outstanding quality levels. "It seems like the difference between very good and an outstanding one [dissertation] is did you get lucky? Did you happen to be at the right place at the right time?" Finally, a biology student reflected that it is likely "that a faculty member has one outstanding doctoral student in a lifetime. . . . Rarely does a person revolutionize the field with a doctoral thesis."

Most students used the quality criteria in the tables to judge their own work, thus affirming their face validity. A psychology student remarked:

> When I was reading through, I was trying to figure out where what I have done so far . . . fits and how I'd rate my own [work]. . . . It all seems very sensible, very consistent with what I would expect. . . . It [the tables] could be helpful.

Referring to the quality levels in the components, a math student said, "It puts things in perspective. I was able to use it [the tables] to assess my position. . . . Using this rubric . . . I am presently at the acceptable level . . . but aiming for the upper end of very good.

The engineering student who was worried about whether his work was important gave an example of how the tables made him less concerned with how his dissertation will be evaluated. In reference to the description of "significant" in the table he said, "It describes what I'm doing . . . so that's good." A math student found the tables "reinforcing." Another math student described how he had to adjust his expectations for himself once he became immersed in his research. "When I came here [to graduate school], I had very high expectations for myself and about what my dissertation would be like. . . . I really expected to do groundbreaking work. . . . After a while I realized that that's pretty rare, and that's okay." A biology student articulated a common interpretation of the quality levels equating the levels to grades where " 'outstanding' is the A and 'very good' is the B. Most of us were straight-A students. Looking at this [table], oh my god, I'm going to get a B! We're overachievers."

Students generally viewed the performance expectations as confirming what they had come to know about the dissertation process. "It's not surprising," according to a math student. A physics student responded:

I agree with the general gist of this [the tables]. . . . Even if you think you know what a good dissertation looks like, it is good to be reminded of some key points to keep in mind while writing it [the dissertation].

Another physics student affirmed, "It makes sense, most of it."

Yet, others clearly were hungry for the guidance the performance expectations provided. A psychology student described the usefulness of performance expectations in his discipline:

It's good to have a set of qualitative standards. . . . In my area . . . there are no clear criteria. Much of it is unspoken, things that you pick along the way . . . from your advisors and colleagues. Some set of guidelines, even if not exhaustive . . . would be helpful.

A history student was struck by the criteria: "Some of the things that they said [in the performance expectations] surprised me. It would have been interesting to know this earlier on." A history peer agreed, "It helps to know what the expectations are." A sociology student described the significance of performance expectations in helping students write their dissertations:

It's nice to have it laid out and see the differences [across levels]. It would be helpful to look at something like this as you're writing the dissertation and remind yourself [about what is important]. . . . It provides some sense of where you are headed.

Several students embraced the tables as tools that would help guide their dissertation research and writing. A history student said, "[It's helpful] . . . what is listed for the quality they are looking for is very helpful." Another history student concurred:

For me . . . the different components, the way you've broken them out, I think is helpful. . . . At times it is difficult to know what should be in the introduction . . . just what should be in each category is helpful. I've always had difficulty with the conclusion and what should be in the conclusion.

These history students and several others asked with some urgency for copies of the draft tables for their personal use. Similarly, the engineering student could see immediate applications of the tables to his work. "In the intro, I'm writing that [now] . . . I could be at a very good quality level right now, but maybe there is something that could be adjusted to make it outstanding. So that's only one thing. It offers a guide of what to include and what to strive for."

For students, the benefits of clear expectations include (1) improvement in the quality of their dissertation and (2) reduced anxiety about how their final product will be evaluated. Many students agreed that rubrics developed from the tables would clarify expectations and lead to a stronger overall product. From a physics perspective, "It [the tables] puts . . . concepts into words, and thereby clarifies them and allows you to implement them better . . . which might lead to improved quality." The engineering student affirmed that the tables were helpful and added, "The description of 'outstanding,' if I can get my dissertation to fall into this description, then it would be great. . . . The 'outstanding' description is very clear and it would help." The biology student said she would be less worried about her committee's judgment of her work if they gave a table or rubric to her: "That would definitely help, if everyone was on the same page."

Other students were less enthusiastic about the tables. A psychology student noted that the tables were helpful, but did not offer sufficient guidance. "I would find this helpful. I don't think you want to base how your dissertation is proposed or conducted based on these general criteria, but it provides an interesting way to think about the different components." Others observed that the tables were deficient in some way. A philosophy student said, "I can pick out where my dissertation lies . . . I don't see it [the tables] being helpful in the starting phase and I don't see it helping me now . . . [To be outstanding] I need to be 'groundbreaking' or 'smashingly interesting' or add more 'fire.'" Another philosophy student noted, "If my committee actually said, 'this is how we will judge your dissertation,' that would be helpful. But it's really too vague." A math student agreed that the tables would not help much: "I already know what I need to do to improve." A student in sociology was emphatic that the tables might actually harm the quality of the dissertation by making it too "formulaic":

> The distinctions . . . are common sense. . . . Part of the problem is that the way grad school is becoming, the dissertation becomes formulaic. . . . The graduate student gets the guide . . . and the more guides you have, . . . the less you're doing academic work and the more you're becoming an engineer.

For others, the tables were common sense, thus those students did not find them personally useful. Yet, even these students—who were all male—conceded that the tables and rubrics might be helpful for some students, particularly those at the beginning of their dissertation design and research. The following remarks come from philosophy students: "I've heard a lot of these things before." "Nothing shocking here. . . . It's nice to have something written down, . . . but I've picked it all up along the way." "It's not helpful, but I wouldn't refuse it. . . . what is listed under outstanding . . . is just good philosophy, which we already know." These comments could suggest that these students had strong relationships with their advisors who provided them with information offered in the tables.

The Role of the Advisor

The tables created by the MIE study are intended to complement the advisor/advisee relationship, not replace it. The tables can be developed into rubrics by department faculty and used to help advisors communicate expectations to their students. Students can benefit by learning up front and directly what a given department expects regarding the dissertation (Montgomery, 2002). The focus group students emphasized the importance of a good advisor. With a good advisor, a table or rubric may not be necessary. A math student asserted, "My advisor has shared this information with me in some form. If he hadn't, then these tables would have surprised me." This same math student noted that without a strong advisor, then a table or rubric "may provide a platform for discussion, . . . [a rubric] could help with communication." Thus, in the absence of strong support and guidance from an advisor, the performance criteria can provide the needed bridge for communication. A student in biology commented:

> Yes, definitely [the tables are helpful]. The way that it is broken out into the various sections so you could look at it when you're actually writing. . . . This could help students design their original research. I had to ask the right questions . . . I could tell by what my advisor said that this [the guidelines in the table] was exactly what they were looking for. I learned what was needed from my faculty, but only because I knew what questions to ask. . . . I would like to have something like this.

A math student explained:

> Generally, I don't think it would help as much as getting in contact with other students or with faculty. Going to conferences and seminars, you learn what is expected. . . . [The tables] are too general to help. You pick up this stuff as you learn math. . . . Maybe the tables could be among the many documents you get from the department. It could help an individual student in a personal way. There might be a phrase or an idea that someone could really latch on to and have that as a motto or goal for them.

Another math student recommended that "[the tables] would be good to have on a website with the department. It's not the end all and be all of success . . . it would be nice to have. . . . A good advisor is what's necessary." A history student echoed this comment about the role of the faculty advisor. She agreed that the tables would help make the dissertation better, "especially if it [the table] is used with the help of an advisor." This student insisted that a rubric based on the tables would have much more power "if you are working closely with the advisor and talking about it [a rubric]."

Yet, as previous sections of this chapter have noted, the advising experience of doctoral students is uneven. In some cases the advisor is helpful in articulating the scope and nature of the dissertation in his or her discipline. Advisors can mediate contentious committees and guide students through rough spots in the research. Good advisors also earn the trust of their advisees. Students in good advising relationships are more reassured that their advisor would not allow them to defend their dissertations until the product is strong enough to pass. With good advising, the performance criteria are less essential to students. In some cases, students perceive their advisors as being too busy or inexperienced to be helpful. A history student remarked:

> As an ideal, I would agree [that you should talk about the tables and rubrics with your advisor]. But, the reality here and at most large research universities, is that's not going to happen. It is still helpful to have the tables. If I can keep this, I'm not going to use it to talk with my advisor, but I'm going to look at it a lot.

Performance Criteria May Cause Anxiety

Several students remarked that seeing the quality criteria stated explicitly was a little intimidating—the "outstanding" category in particular. These students had high expectations of themselves, yet the criteria for outstanding are very high and demand a very polished product. A math student commented, "It [the tables] would be helpful, but also intimidating in the beginning." Similarly, a psychology student reflected that having the tables before writing his proposal would have helped, yet "in a sense, it [the tables] is a little bit anxiety-provoking, but . . . it can be nothing but helpful." Some individual quality markers prompted worries. "The emphasis [in the tables] is on the ability to write, but that is not taught in physics at all. You can even have an advisor who doesn't know how to write. It would give me an anxiety . . . about my writing style." The biology student summarized the concerns of many: "I think this [the tables] would make me more nervous. . . . The 'outstanding' category . . . is a great place to strive for, but you need to emphasize that there are other levels that are acceptable."

It is not too surprising that these concerns also lead to different opinions about when to share the performance criteria with students. Some students advocated for early dissemination. A history student agreed it would be great to have "early . . . as soon as you start writing your research paper . . . a lot of things apply to writing in general." Others thought a "just in time" approach would be better, that the tables should be distributed at the beginning of the writing process. A physics student explained, "I would want it [the tables] before I started to write, but not before I started the work. It [the tables] shouldn't be the first thing you see when you get to your lab." Similarly, an engineering student said, "The tables would be helpful before I started writing. . . . Even if your preliminary results are done, after reviewing the tables you could revise and improve your methods and results. It would also help me do a better job with the writing."

Study Limitations

Students' comments from the focus group conversations offer compelling support for the value of performance criteria details like those generated by the MIE study. Clearer expectations may help students produce higher quality dissertation proposals and final products. The reader is reminded, however, of some limitations of this exploratory study.

First, academic departments recommended most of the students who participated in this study. Although some departments offered the complete list of eligible students, others were selective and provided just a few names.

This recruitment method may have produced a biased sample if department personnel recommended their strongest students. Conversations with students who were struggling in their doctoral programs may have produced different perspectives. Weaker students may have responded differently to the performance criteria, either more favorably or with more anxiety.

Second, this study also included only students who were in the dissertation phase of their education. Several students recommended that the tables be shared with students earlier in their degree program. Perhaps students who are still engaged in course work are more anxious about the dissertation. If so, the guidance offered by tables might be comforting. In general, the results of this investigation might have been different if students were less talented, the academic programs less strong, or if student advising experiences had been less successful.

Conclusion

These doctoral student focus group conversations revealed a pattern of responses based on progress toward the degree and faculty advisor support. In general, the closer students were to completing their dissertation, the less enthusiastic they were about the need for performance criteria. They had already successfully negotiated the expectations and found the tables as stating the obvious. Even if the performance expectations were less relevant to them personally, some students recognized the value of tables and rubrics for others. Students earlier in the research and writing process were welcoming of the guidance offered by the performance criteria (see Table 7.1 for a summary of participants' degree progress).

The quality of faculty advising intersected with this pattern such that students with weak, inexperienced, or just adequate advisors enthusiastically embraced the performance criteria tables, even if they were close to completing their dissertation. The focus group participants across disciplines repeatedly mentioned that good advising was important. We know from Lovitts (2001) that doctoral students who succeed in completing their degrees are socialized into their departmental culture. Advisors contribute to this socialization in profound ways by providing support and information, taking an interest in students as people, providing academic planning, and, more generally, assisting students in their academic integration to the department. By actively engaging with their advisees, faculty members can help prevent the social and academic isolation that can interfere with degree completion.

The advising experiences of students in this study ranged from highly effective (e.g., engineering) to disappointing (e.g., biology) and included contact with novice faculty (e.g., physics) and inaccessible faculty (e.g., sociology). Many students described advising relationships that did not include clear guidance about the expectations for a strong dissertation. The quality guidelines provided by tables and rubrics, such as those presented in chapter 6, can offer an important supplement to these personal relationships. The focus group conversations indicate that by making implicit expectations explicit, performance criteria can demystify and clarify the demands of the dissertation for many. They can make doctoral students less anxious overall about how their work will be judged and may lead to stronger research and writing.

With clear performance expectations, students can aim for a dissertation of high quality. Many of the participants in this study espoused this goal. More explicit demands also could decrease the anxiety associated with vague or unknown expectations. With higher personal standards that are aligned with departmental expectations, it is plausible for students to produce stronger overall products and make more impressive and confident contributions to the literature of their discipline. As universities measure their success in part by the success of their graduates, embracing and sharing clear performance criteria with graduate students shows great promise for supporting apprentice scholars.

References

Becker, H. (1986). *Writing for social scientists: How to start and finish your thesis, book, or article*. Chicago: University of Chicago Press.

Biaggio, M. (2002, August). *Student perceptions of factors helping and hindering dissertation progress*. Poster session presented at the annual conference of the American Psychological Association, Chicago, IL.

Bolker, J. (1998). *Writing your dissertation in fifteen minutes a day: A guide to starting, revising, and finishing your doctoral thesis*. New York: Owl Books.

Brause, R. S. (2001, April). *Doctoral dissertations: What doctoral students know, how they know it, and what they need to know—a preliminary exploration*. Paper presented at the annual meeting of the American Educational Research Association, Seattle, WA.

Glatthorn, A. A., & Joyner, R. L. (2005). *Writing the winning thesis or dissertation: A step-by-step guide* (2nd ed.). Thousand Oaks, CA: Corwin Press.

Lovitts, B. E. (2001). *Leaving the ivory tower: The causes and consequences of departure from doctoral study.* Lanham, MD: Rowman & Littlefield.

Lovitts, B. E. (2005). Being a good course-taker is not enough: A theoretical perspective on the transition to independent research. *Studies in Higher Education, 30,* 137–154.

Montgomery, K. (2002). Authentic tasks and rubrics: Going beyond traditional assessment in college teaching. *College Teaching, 50,* 34–39.

Rudestam, K. E., & Newton, R. R. (2001). *Surviving your dissertation: A comprehensive guide to content and process.* Thousand Oaks, CA: Sage.

Secrist, J., & Wright, D. J. (1998). *Secrets for a successful dissertation.* Thousand Oaks, CA: Sage.

Appendix A

Focus Group Protocol

Introductions: name and current status in the doctoral program

Questions:

1. What did you know about the dissertation when you entered graduate school?

2. Do you know what the university's criterion is for the award of the Ph.D.?
   READ: "The ability to do independent research must be demonstrated by an original dissertation on a topic approved by the graduate program in which the student is earning a degree."
   2a. What do you think?
   2b. What is meant by "original?" How do you feel about it?

3. What concerns, if any, do you have about your dissertation?

4. What concerns, if any, do you have about how your dissertation will be judged or evaluated by your committee?

READ: "Barbara Lovitts has just completed a study in which faculty from 10 departments at 9 universities participated in focus groups where they were asked to make explicit their implicit standards or criteria for judging different quality dissertations and their components. The faculty were also asked about the purpose of the dissertation, and what it meant to make an original and significant contribution—the standard criteria for the award of the Ph.D. The faculty's responses have been compiled into tables of performance expectations. These performance expectations are intended to be used formatively with graduate students while they are researching and writing their dissertations, and not summatively to assign a 'score' to a dissertation when it is completed."

I'd like you to take a few minutes to read though the tables. Bear in mind that no dissertation is expected to do all the things in a single cell. Rather, the items in the cells represent the different things that different dissertations do at those quality levels. After you've finished reading the tables, I'd like to get your reactions to them.

Pass out tables and let students read through them.

Reactions?

Probes:

    a. Do you find them helpful? In what ways?
    b. Would you like to have something like this?
    c. Do you think having something like this would help you to make your dissertation better?
    d. Would having something like this make you less concerned about your dissertation?
    e. Would having something like this make you less concerned about how your committee will judge your dissertation?

8

PORTFOLIOS IN DOCTORAL EDUCATION

Thomas Cyr and Rodney Muth

M ost doctoral programs use the same traditional assessment approaches, such as course grades and comprehensive exams, to appraise the success of their doctoral students and, possibly, the success of their programs. An alternative to traditional assessment tools is the portfolio, a collection of student work produced along the continuum of students' studies. Used in K–16 for many years, portfolios also can add to or complement traditional tools used in doctoral education by providing a continuous and cumulative record of student progress and growth.

Discovering that limited research bears directly on the use of portfolios as assessment tools in doctoral programs, in this chapter we consolidate what we know about the overall types and purposes of portfolios, their benefits, common formats and structures, and one process for implementing portfolios in a doctoral program. Our goal is to provide a partial roadmap for others who wish to capitalize on the power of portfolios to engage students further in their learning, to build on faculty-student mentorships, and to measure evidence of learning against a doctoral program's learning outcome statements. Doing so allows faculty and students to identify patterns of strength and weakness within the context of what and how students learn. Finally, this chapter grows out of our personal experiences with portfolios in doctoral education: Tom, as a student in the Educational Leadership and Innovation (EDLI) Ph.D. Program at the University of Colorado at Denver Health Sciences Center, and Rod, as one of the founders of the program and a longtime portfolio advisor in doctoral and master's leadership education.

Traditional Methods of Assessment in Doctoral Programs

Attaining a doctorate is a long and difficult undertaking for students, expensive for them to pursue, labor intensive for their faculty, costly for universities, and none too successful if the measure is completion rates, which now hover around 50% across disciplines for all programs nationally (Lovitts, 2001; Smallwood, 2004). Perhaps because of their challenging complexity, or more likely simple traditions, practices in doctoral education have changed little in the United States over the years, suggesting that a few changes and innovations may be in order, both for faculty and for students (Nyquist & Woodford, 2000).

Now, a typical student enters a doctoral program after completing a baccalaureate or a master's degree. Often a master's is not required, or a student acquires one along the way as part of a doctoral program. New doctoral students take courses in their program areas, certifying their knowledge through focused papers, projects, exams, labs, and other assessments of knowledge and skill. Some programs have matriculation requirements that may include transition "exams," following a few courses or the first year to ensure that the student and the program are well matched. Many programs require comprehensive exams toward the end of the program to ensure that students have mastered the required knowledge and skill base before undertaking a dissertation. After successfully completing such exams, a student becomes a candidate for the degree and then is authorized to pursue a dissertation study. This authorization may require the approval of a prospectus or proposal by a doctoral committee and the permission of appropriate institutional research committees. Once approved, the study is undertaken, completed and defended, and the degree awarded.

Changes Challenging These Traditions

This series of assessments is traditional and long standing and was endured by most of us who now hold a doctorate. Nevertheless, current teaching-learning theories (Bransford, Brown, & Cocking, 1999; Pellegrino, Chudowsky, & Glaser, 2001), today's outcome-oriented and program-improvement-oriented accreditation policies (e.g., Accrediting Commission for Senior Colleges and Universities, 2005; Higher Learning Commission, 2003), and the need for more efficient and effective production of new scholars (Katz & Hartnett,

1976; National Research Council, 1996), especially in the sciences and engineering (Office of Technology Assessment, 1988), raise questions about traditional means of assessment. One specific question is whether traditional practices effectively support quality work and successful completion when compared to alternative methods, such as the use of assessment portfolios.

At the same time, universities and programs invest heavily in these traditional labor-intensive processes, suggesting, perhaps, that low completion rates are a proxy measure for rigor, albeit a seemingly poor indicator of program "success." A better alternative might be developing new measures that, in themselves, (a) support and facilitate program expectations about learning and competence, (b) help students self-assess as they progress, and (c) engage students more fundamentally in their own learning.

Many faculty in higher education have been seeking ways to ensure learning outcomes that are clearly related to program goals for content and skill expertise (Bilder & Clifton, 1996; Kolman, Gallagher, Hossler, & Catania, 1987; Nyquist & Woodford, 2000). Now, under pressure from various accrediting bodies, university faculty generally are creating or turning to methods of assessment that provide them "hard" data about how well their students are performing and whether such performance satisfies program knowledge and skill expectations. Such measures additionally should provide doctoral faculty with clear indicators of student performance at significant points in the program in order to facilitate counseling, redirection, modifications, and the like. We contend that assessment portfolios can facilitate these tasks well.

Types and Purposes of Portfolios

A portfolio is "a purposeful collection of student work that tells the story of the student's efforts, progress or achievement" and "must include student participation in selection of portfolio content; the guidelines for selection; the criteria for judging merit; and evidence of student self-reflection" (Arter & Spandel, 1992, p. 36). As an assessment tool, a portfolio provides a place (e.g., a Web page, a notebook, a CD) where a student can present current levels of accomplishment through artifacts, providing evidence that represents performance in prescribed areas and tasks. These artifacts can be viewed, reviewed, and rated by teachers, peers, and others, based on established or emerging criteria or well-developed rubrics (Gibson & Barrett,

2002). The reviewed and rated artifacts provide evidence and, perhaps, feedback on the quantity and quality of learning for both students and mentors. In fact, "the more relevant the evidence, the more useful it is for inferring a student's level of achievement in a learning area" (Forster & Masters, 1996, p. 2).

In different contexts, portfolios serve different purposes. In general, three basic types are favored (Hewitt, 2004):

1. A *documentation* portfolio shows growth relative to specified outcomes, serving as a diagnostic tool for assessing a student's mastery of required knowledge and skills.
2. A *process* portfolio verifies various phases of the learning process as a student progresses toward mastery, encouraging metacognitive awareness through written reflections about learning, the artifacts that represent it, and the challenges that the student faced or continues to face.
3. A *showcase* portfolio displays a student's best works and reflections on how these works were selected for the portfolio, what the selections represent, and what accomplishments and abilities the display supports.

Portfolios have at least two primary purposes: formative and summative assessment. Formative portfolios focus on development. They are especially useful for supporting teaching and learning processes and require considerable attention to validity (Klenowski, 2002): the evidence gathered in such portfolios should align with the "potential consequences of assessment use" (p. 61). As formative assessment tools, portfolios can show a student's growth over time by including goal-setting activities at the onset and then requiring periodic reflections on subsequent growth and progress toward those goals. Having both student and faculty contribute their reflections provides a multiperspective approach to effective assessment.

Summative portfolios, on the other hand, substantiate the attainment of learning outcomes for certification purposes. A summative portfolio "requires the specification of standards and contents" (Klenowski, 2002, p. 11) that support formal assessment. As high-stakes measures, summative portfolios can require critical attention to reliability of both content and process. However, they can be problematic in doctoral programs where available expertise and time are always in short supply. Further, summative assessments, despite concerns about reliability, can be used to document achievement at the course level or to demonstrate progress through a program toward established exit standards. Besides requiring clearly articulated and understood performance criteria, summative assessments also necessitate well-designed rating instruments that define for students how their work will be evaluated.

Benefits of Portfolios

Using portfolios for assessment in education is not new: art portfolios, writing portfolios, and education portfolios, for example, have been used in higher education for many years (Arter, Spandel, & Culham, 1995). Interest in portfolios has grown since the 1980s (Park, 2004), even though empirical evidence of their efficacy is limited (Carney, 2004), their use often conditional, their rigor unclear, and their use sometimes inconsistent (Heller, Sheingold, & Myford, 1998). Nevertheless, 90% of all teacher preparation programs in colleges of education in the United States use portfolios to certify teacher candidates (Salzman & Denner, 2002). Also, portfolios increasingly are being used in professional programs, including law (Dailey, 1997). Justifications for the use of portfolios in assessment are considerable (Carney, 2004):

a. They support the full inclusion of students in their own learning.
b. They support not only the apprenticeship model of instruction but also encourage collegiality and power sharing among students and their mentors.
c. They engage student and mentor in setting particular criteria for successful completion of a program through student-instructor collaborative design, based on programwide standards and performance expectations.
d. When appropriately designed, they align clearly with the principles of effective assessment by providing frequent and effective feedback to students, thus being educative as well as evaluative.

Each of these rationales advances ascending notions of constructivism and collaborative learning that now push faculty in higher education to use learning-outcome data to improve program practices. Most obvious among the curricular benefits of portfolios—as an instructional activity and assessment methodology—are that they promote student engagement, encourage faculty consensus on program and course purposes (e.g., goals and outcomes), facilitate the specification of assessment criteria, provide opportunities for addressing validity and reliability issues, and furnish tangible evidence of growth through both student and faculty reflections on products and processes.

Student Engagement

Including and engaging doctoral students in their own intellectual and skill development can be facilitated greatly through good assessment methodology (Klenowski, 2002; Pellegrino et al., 2001; Wiggins, 1998, 2004). Portfolios provide a means to accomplish this, both strengthening the mentor-mentee relationship and providing the student and the doctoral program with clear student-performance data, also a benefit for meeting accreditation requirements. Like other effective assessment tools, portfolios can be "educative" (Wiggins, 1998), both informing *and* improving student performance:

> If our aim is to improve student performance, not just measure it, we must ensure that students know the performances expected of them, the standards against which they will be judged, and have opportunities to learn from the assessment in future assessments. (Wiggins, 2004)

Program Goals and Learning Outcome Statements

Portfolios can be effective only if they represent the collective agreement of program faculty. Without agreement on program purposes, goals, and procedures (Muth, 2002), every student's program is idiosyncratic, and the existing requirements for program and university accreditation cannot be met. First, program faculty, through deliberate and often lengthy discussion, must agree on what graduates should know and be able to do when they complete their studies. These agreements can be formulated as learning-outcome statements. Faculty then can establish responsibilities for outcomes, including those that the program must address through the development and reinforcement of expectations and structures, those that faculty should undertake as mentors, and those that should fall chiefly to students, such as engagement, self-assessment, and learning.

Assessment Criteria

Once agreements are established and portfolios adopted as assessment tools, assessment principles need to be clarified so that everyone realizes performance and assessment expectations. Four common principles, drawn from California State University–Chico (University Assessment Committee, 1993; see also Alverno College Faculty, 1994), indicate that effective assessments must be

1. *Systematic*—a methodical and open process of acquiring evidence about abilities and achievement over time
2. *Cumulative*—a body of evidence collected over time that can be used in increasingly sophisticated ways to improve educational programs
3. *Multifaceted/multidimensional*—a selection of multiple dimensions using multiple methods and multiple sources to reflect the complexity of human and organizational behavior
4. *Pragmatic*—a collection and analysis of data useful to improving the educational environment, both for teaching and for learning

These and other criteria suggest that portfolios provide significant advantages over some traditional methods, if only because students and faculty engage in a known, interactive, developmental, standards- and outcome-based cumulative process that frames student learning and growth. To be effective, portfolios in any discipline need to be designed to fit the specific purposes, expectations, standards, and learning outcomes of those disciplines. Understanding and acting on common design principles of assessment (systematic, cumulative, multifaceted/multidimensional, and pragmatic) should help faculty clearly articulate their goals and expectations (e.g., University Assessment Committee, 1993). By facilitating the development of clear expectations, the uses of portfolios can help students and faculty work together by supporting what is known about how people learn, indicating how students should be assessed to support their learning most effectively, and requiring faculty to reach accord on standards and outcomes.

Validity and Reliability

Portfolios, like any other assessment system, require design and development work to establish validity and reliability as well as to maintain consistency. Validity issues pertain to having clear and accepted purposes for the portfo-

lio, guidelines for selecting materials for the portfolio, and relevant performance criteria for evaluating the quality of the artifacts. Specifying all of this
clearly and effectively requires coordination among those involved in the implementation of the system. Reliability means that portfolio evaluations are
consistent among raters yet manageable. As the Vermont Portfolio Assessment Program (Koretz, Stecher, & Deibert, 1992) shows, well-designed
inter-rater reliability can be time-consuming but necessary for high quality
assessments.

Validity and reliability principles that are transferable for practitioners in
higher education include the following:

1. The purpose, criteria for performance, and products included as evi-
    dence in a portfolio need to be very clear to both students and in-
    structors (Wiggins, 1998).
2. The important decisions about students' competence, promotion,
    and graduation should be based on collections of "convincing work"
    that represent students' knowledge and ability relative to "the most
    important intellectual performance genres" (Wiggins, 1998, p. 197).
3. Training for instructors is essential to the reliability of portfolio as-
    sessments (Mills, 1989).
4. Portfolio assessment can be effective for evaluating student growth if
    the portfolio process and assessment system are valid (Koretz et al.,
    1992; Krusekopf & Karr-Kidwell, 2003).
5. The work required as evidence must be meaningful to the students
    (Baker, Gearhart, Herman, Tierney, & Whittaker, 1991; Gearhart,
    Herman, Baker, & Whittaker, n.d.).
6. Well-structured opportunities for self-reflection need to be available
    (Wolf, 1989).

Promoting Learning, Reflection, and Growth

Portfolios are useful because they can represent growth in learning, showcase
student products and capabilities, and document student knowledge and
skills. Use of portfolios also encourages autonomous and reflective thinking,
both highly important to effective learning. In addition, portfolios can facilitate connections between theory and practice by requiring active intellectual
engagement with content as well as performance processes related to the content: "the engaged learner, one who records and interprets and evaluates his

or her own learning, is the best learner" (DiBiase, 2004). Further, portfolios can cater to individual learning styles, providing personal choice and control in their design and development. Finally, they encourage self-directed life-long learning and professional development (Snadden, Thomas, & Challis, 1999).

While portfolios are intuitively compelling to many, their uses and effects are not well documented. As a form of authentic assessment, portfolios align well with current learning and assessment theory relevant to doctoral education, including adult learning (Knowles, 1975); cognition, learning, and problem solving (Bransford et al., 1999); metacognition and learning (Flavell, 1976); and learner-centered instruction (McCombs & Whisler, 1997). Based in these and other perspectives on learning and assessment—teaching for expertise with novices (Caine & Caine, 1994), capitalizing on the variety of learning styles (Gardner, 1993), and using social interaction to heighten cognitive development (Vygotsky, 1978)—portfolios promote the development of important learning skills such as reflection, self-evaluation, critical analysis, and metacognition. They facilitate collegiality by encouraging faculty to explore with their students how pedagogy and learning are related (Maki, 2002b) as well as how students think and integrate knowledge and skills into "ways of knowing" characteristic of a field or discipline. Portfolios can support active self-directed learning, relevant knowledge, learner choice as well as control, and collaboration, all elements important to adult learners (Knowles, 1975; Paris, 1994; Wlodkowski, 1999). Portfolios also contribute to improved pedagogy by promoting structures and processes for reflecting on teaching practices (Laurillard, 1993; Lauvås & Handal, 1987; Schön, 1988) and by providing opportunities for teachers to reflect on the learning process as they align the curriculum, their pedagogy, and their assessment methods. Finally, portfolios facilitate grading schemes that emphasize individual student growth rather than competition with other students, although grading is not central to the effective use of portfolios.

Advances in understanding of cognitive processes have changed perspectives on effective teaching-learning strategies and outcomes (Caine & Caine, 1994; Gardner, 1993). Learning is seen no longer as the passive reception of bits of information (Duffy & Cunningham, 1996); rather, learners are viewed as constructors of their own meaning (Vygotsky, 1978), actively seeking and combining new information with prior knowledge, continuously constructing and reconstructing knowledge. These activities are observed better in the comprehensive collection and rating of artifacts in a portfolio, a process that encourages and facilitates the assessment of student performance and growth over time, than in traditional assessment schemes.

Examples of Portfolio Use in Higher Education

Following are several examples of portfolio use, first in undergraduate education, followed by graduate education. Each case provides insights about ways to think about and structure the use of portfolios.

Alverno College

At Alverno College (AC), a longtime leader in assessment in higher education, faculty and students use a Diagnostic Digital Portfolio (DDP), an electronic portfolio developed to enable students "to follow their learning progress throughout their years of study" (Alverno College, 2004). AC claims that the DDP "helps students process the feedback they receive from faculty, external assessors and peers." The DDP supports an assessment-as-learning model, producing "actual, accessible performance data from which graduates can create an electronic resume for potential employers or for graduate schools." Further, Alverno claims that their DDP enables their students "to look for patterns in their academic work so they can take more control of their own development and become more autonomous learners." Their studies also tell them that their "students are acquiring the knowledge and complex abilities that [their] faculty have identified and [that their] studies have verified to be keys to effective performance as workers and citizens" (Alverno College, 2004).

University of Minnesota

The eFolio, an electronic portfolio, has been developed by the University of Minnesota (UM; http://www.efoliomn.com/) for its students to provide a platform to "*showcase* [their] education, career, and personal achievements." In fact, all Minnesota residents have access to the eFolio for a fee. The university contends that the eFolio is an effective "interactive communications tool" that "provides feedback to students, as a tool to document and assess student learning, and to prepare students for their careers." For students, UM's eFolio appears to function as (a) a formal yet formative repository of student work, growth, and achievement and (b) a showcase of artifacts for students' future academic goals or future employers. UM also encourages faculty to use the eFolio as a teaching portfolio and includes several portfolio templates for faculty to help them with the teaching-learning process as they align the curriculum, their pedagogy, and their assessment methods.

Pennsylvania State University

Pennsylvania State University (PSU) sponsored an electronic portfolio initiative in 2002 and now maintains a Web service, e-Portfolio (DiBiase, 2004; Johnson & DiBiase, 2004), to support all portfolio users at the university. According to the Web site, portfolios are used in capstone courses as part of ongoing course activities. In using the e-Portfolio, PSU has realigned its curriculum to support "portfolio thinking, as well as the necessary technical skills" for developing and using portfolios. PSU also sponsors a Portfolio Information Fair to "promote the awareness of opportunities related to e-Portfolio activity for all students, faculty, and staff at Penn State." The university claims that its portfolio process encourages students' active engagement in learning because they are "involved in planning" and assume more responsibility for "their own educational goals." PSU also says that students benefit from opportunities to share "examples of their work with advisors, faculty, mentors or potential employers," while they develop important information technology skills and "skills and attributes gained beyond the classroom." Reflecting on knowledge and skills and articulating accomplishments are cited as important benefits of electronic portfolios.

University of Colorado at Denver and Health Sciences Center

At this newly merged urban research university, portfolios are used mostly to support capstone experiences at the undergraduate level. For example, an undergraduate archaeology instructor asks her senior students to respond to course activities by collecting their artifacts in an electronic portfolio. These artifacts are then evaluated according to established rubrics and rating criteria. In the pharmacy school, an instructor asks her pharmacy students to collect examples of their work, reflections on that work, and their experiences during their fourth-year clinical rotations. The students "paste them up" to an electronic portfolio, a recent replacement of bulky paper-based portfolios, where the instructor retrieves, reads, analyzes, and responds to them. Portfolios also are used as vehicles for assembling and critiquing writing assignments in humanities courses.

Florida State University

The Department of Computer Sciences in the College of Arts and Sciences at Florida State University (FSU) uses the portfolio as its principal means for monitoring a doctoral student's progress. Admission to candidacy is predicated on successful defense of the portfolio. Annual reviews are held, usually in spring, by the Portfolio Review Committee, prior to advancement to candidacy. The portfolio, then, provides the primary place in which students present their work and log feedback on their progress. The portfolio at FSU contains the following sections (Department of Computer Science, 2003):

1. Summary data, supplying personal information, doctoral committee members, test scores, core and elective courses taken, and exam areas
2. Curriculum vitae (CV), listing academic degrees, professional experience, honor and awards, publications, and service activities
3. Research publications and writing, including the list from the CV and a reprint or photocopy of one publication with a description of the student's role in its production; in lieu of a publication, a master's thesis or other research work can serve
4. Software engineering, providing at least one artifact that includes "design, engineering, and certification reports, software documentation, and actual code" (p. 6)
5. Dissertation research, including a one- to two-page abstract of research area
6. Support, summarizing all employment while in the department
7. Documentation, covering prior portfolio reviews, transcripts for courses, tests, and area exams

The program uses the following criteria to evaluate the portfolio: (a) general competency in computer science, (b) research aptitude, (c) software skills, and (d) communication skills. The overall strengths and weaknesses of each of these criteria are reviewed to determine if a student can "succeed and become a credit to the department" (p. 8).

The EDLI Program

Although the use of portfolios is still relatively new to doctoral education, models do exist, including one in the School of Education at the University of Colorado at Denver and Health Sciences Center. The Educational Leadership and Innovation PhD Program uses portfolios extensively to assess student knowledge and skills. While some students develop electronic forms, most stick with hard copies that support annual reviews and the comprehensive portfolio review before advancing to candidacy. Some faculty require their students to include a dissertation prospectus in the comprehensive portfolio to facilitate the transition from student to candidate to Ph.D. The program defines a portfolio as

> a selective collection of work and reflection gathered across diverse settings over time, framed by topic foci [concentrations], and refined by professorial and peer interaction. The purpose of the portfolio is to promote and represent the student's command of content, research, and leadership knowledge and skills leading toward independent scholarly work on complex problems of educational practice. (Educational Leadership and Innovation, 2004, p. 14)

First Annual Review

Portfolios are reviewed several times during doctoral students' studies, and for the initial portfolio students present a snapshot of their work during their first year of study to the three faculty members on their program review committee. This review occurs within the first four semesters following admission and is used to counsel students on their progress, including the development of their topic foci, and to determine whether the program and student are well matched.

The first annual review portfolio contains demonstrations of students' beginning expertise in four domains (Educational Leadership and Innovation, 2004): *core knowledge*, which includes at least three topic focus areas in which breadth and depth of knowledge are demonstrated; *interpretation and synthesis*, which shows the student's ability to "analyze, re-interpret, and synthesize issues, and frame problems in promising ways" (p. 16); *disciplined inquiry*, which provides evidence of clear lines of inquiry and mastery of research methods appropriate to such inquiry; and *professional and scholarly leadership*, which documents applications of knowledge to problems of practice and participation in scholarly venues. For this review, students only need to include:

a. a completed advising form that lists their advisor and the members of their program committee

b. a statement of their professional values and goals

c. a declaration of interest in three topic areas with an initial rationale and bibliography

d. a plan of study developed with the committee

e. transcripts of course work to date

f. a plan for developing the portfolio over time

g. at least two products that address one or more of the four domains

The purpose of this initial portfolio is not exhaustiveness but functions to anticipate possibilities; that is, student and faculty discuss progress to date, review plans for the student's program, and generally clarify focus areas and dissertation ideas. The baseline data in the initial portfolio provide all with an initial assessment of performance expectations.

Subsequent Annual Reviews

Each year in the program, students are expected to schedule and complete an annual review. This yearly assessment showcases the "authentic work products" that demonstrate "learning, development, and improvement of skills" through the "work done on the job and in labs, classes, and conferences" (Educational Leadership and Innovation, 2004, p. 5). The program committee reviews the portfolio's contents, meets with the student, discusses the student's progress, makes suggestions for changes in or refinements of topic focus areas, and provides direction about future course work, lab activities, other professional engagements, and dissertation development.

Comprehensive Review

The final or comprehensive portfolio review generally occurs from three to five years following admission, depending on a student's admission status (full- or part-time), yearly progress toward completing the domains and topic foci as assessed in annual reviews, and development of a dissertation prospectus or proposal.

Items suitable for inclusion in the comprehensive portfolio include published manuscripts, research reports, literature reviews, observation and rating scales, teaching evaluations, program or curriculum evaluations, referee comments on grants and manuscripts, letters of support from participants and service recipients, curriculum vitae, and review of products such as books, Web sites, and teaching materials (Educational Leadership and Innovation, 2004, p. 5).

This final portfolio in the EDLI Ph.D. program provides a comprehensive view of a student's program, growth, accomplishments, and readiness for undertaking a dissertation. The following sections are recommended (Educational Leadership and Innovation, 2004, pp. 25–26):

1. Introduction
2. Table of Contents
3. Professional Vitae
4. Transcript (reflecting all course work completed)
5. Executive Summary (using a chart or matrix to map domains to topic foci)
6. Statement of Goals and Philosophy and Reflections (including topic foci, annotated bibliographies, responses to previous feedback and reviews, etc.)
7. Required Forms and Plan of Study
8. Domain 1: Core Knowledge (including an introduction with reflections as well as reflections on each supporting product for each domain)
9. Domain 2: Interpretation and Synthesis
10. Domain 3: Disciplined Inquiry
11. Domain 4: Professional and Scholarly Leadership

This outline, thoroughly annotated in the EDLI handbook (2004), represents a set of consistent expectations for all students, except for the selection of topic foci that are particularized according to a student's intellectual and career interests. In addition, many committees expect a dissertation prospectus or proposal as part of the comprehensive portfolio. These similar expectations allow comparisons across students and doctoral areas in this schoolwide program, as well as provide a means for data collection for overall program improvements. (Chapter 9 provides yet another example of the use of portfolios—now a part of doctoral students' preliminary oral examination in the Department of Educational Leadership and Policy Studies at Iowa State University.)

The Portfolio Process

Before identifying the specific components of a portfolio for any doctoral program, faculty must first establish a foundation for its use by agreeing on program goals and student-learning outcomes. The recommended process for developing a portfolio for assessment is generally similar to that for developing any other assessment: a cycle of iterative events that successively and cumulatively establishes the learning, growth, and expertise of a student. The process described next is loosely based on Maki's (2002a) assessment guide and Freeman and Lewis's (1998) planning model.

First, faculty planners need to articulate clearly and fully the purposes and outcomes expected of a program and of the portfolio. Objectives and criteria need to be identified, clarified, determined, or developed: intended learning outcomes and their assessment, criteria and standards of performance, validity of assessment tools, and baseline of data. Because a portfolio is a repository of evidence that represents a student's knowledge and skills, the portfolio must include multiple means of assessment and not be left to a single instrument that might miss the complexities involved. The kinds of tools that can be used in assessments include paper and pencil tests, writing samples, case-based problem solving (individual and collaborative), rubrics for assessing skills, and simulations.

In developing the purpose and expectations for the portfolio, planners should use language free of ambiguity, respect the empirical nature of assessment, and point to observable and measurable evidence. A tool like a learning taxonomy (Bloom, 1956) can help novice assessors choose appropriate active verbs for effectively articulated outcomes. Standards of performance also should be developed for each of the various assessments included in the portfolio so that students are cognizant of the performance expectations. Because a portfolio should be able to show growth over time, an initial collection of data creates a baseline of evidence for appraising growth.

The second step in designing portfolio assessment processes is to set the timing and assign responsibilities for various assessment tasks, beginning with what is known about program scheduling. When are the seminars and courses scheduled? Which of those seminars, courses, or stages in the curriculum are the best points for collecting required evidence for the portfolio? Who analyzes and interprets the assessment results? How much time is needed (an important consideration when others are included in assess-

ments) to review and rate representative documents, observe live performances such as public presentations, or debrief field personnel on the adequacy
of clinical engagements? When is the evidence appropriate to become part
of the portfolio?

The third and last step in the design of a portfolio process is to determine how, how often, by whom, and to whom the results of the various
assessments will be interpreted and shared. The "who" may include instructors, peers, outside individuals, and the student. Including self-assessment
as part of the portfolio process provides the opportunity for reflection that
encourages individual development as a self-directed lifelong learner. The
outcome of this final step is reflecting on what worked and what needs improvement in the learning process. This outcome, combined with the outcomes of other individual portfolio reviews, provides a cumulative base of
opportunities to improve student learning and change processes to increase
overall program effectiveness.

Implications of Portfolios for Doctoral Education

Many believe that graduates of doctoral programs are unprepared for their
multiple responsibilities as future faculty (Nyquist & Woodford, 2000) or
for other professional endeavors (see also chapter 4, pp. 109–144). For example, in focusing on the responsibilities of future faculty, Nyquist and Woodford's "re-envisioning" report asserts that graduates generally are "inadequately"
prepared for the multiple aspects of faculty roles, concluding that doctoral
programs should prepare their graduates more broadly for their faculty
responsibilities: "teaching, collegial evaluation, collective and individual
curricular planning, and service to the college, university, and community"
(p. 5). Too often, however, the development and practice of such skills are
left to the student and chance, putting graduates at risk as they adapt to the
requirements of "being faculty" and strive to launch an independent research
and teaching career.

Two implications derive from the Nyquist and Woodford (2000) report:
(a) doctoral students, especially those aiming for faculty careers, are inadequately mentored, and (b) unclear program goals and expectations com-
pound the problem. Generally, mentoring in universities is based on an
apprenticeship model (Burnett, 1999), but even a casual reading of *Re-
envisioning* (Nyquist & Woodford, 2000) suggests that more conscious and

explicit mentoring procedures and supports are needed in doctoral programs if the preparation of students for faculty roles is going to be more than hit or miss.

While designing and developing portfolios for assessment in doctoral programs is challenging, well-structured portfolios can address some of the obstacles that affect degree completion, such as students' relations with their mentor or their lack of understanding of performance standards or criteria. The faculty-student collaboration required by a doctoral portfolio process encourages and supports such mentoring as a student becomes an "equal partner in every aspect of the design, implementation, interpretation, and resulting actions" (Guba & Lincoln, 1989, p. 11) of graduate training. In addition, a well-designed portfolio process specifies expectations for doctoral students that are transparent to them (Nyquist & Woodford, 2000), including selection criteria, progress expectations, and assessment methods as well as data on time to degree, completion rates, and placement success (Council of Graduate Schools, 2004; Denecke & Slimowitz, 2004).

Some Considerations

Using a portfolio for assessment provides frequent opportunities to attend to and reflect on a student's ability and performance, understanding, and attitudes and motivations. The reflective nature of portfolios provides both students and faculty with opportunities to work together, learn from one another, and collaboratively create a small learning community. In such ways, portfolios support the development of collegial relationships among teachers, students, and peers. The development and use of well-designed portfolios in doctoral programs also provide significant opportunities to socialize students to the explicit and implicit disciplinary norms, practices, and conventions inherent in each profession. During their quest for the doctorate, doctoral students can develop and reflect on the broad range of disciplinary or professional abilities, capabilities, ways of understanding, and dispositions that will prepare them for their entry into academic or professional communities.

Professionals in K–12 education have had considerable experience with portfolios, and their general concepts, principles, and precautions can usefully guide the development of portfolios in higher education. Regardless of educational level or specialty, portfolios "provide structure for involving students in developing and understanding criteria for good efforts, in coming to see the criteria as their own, and in applying the criteria to their own and other students' work" (Office of Education Research, 1993). Further, portfolios can serve as vehicles for enhancing student awareness of strategies for thinking about, producing, and completing tasks. The resulting products can be included in the portfolio as evidence of competence in doctoral-level disciplinary practices. As a positive alternative to traditional forms of assessment, particularly for doctoral students as adult learners, portfolios can enhance student satisfaction with learning and their overall program experiences. Intrinsic motivations are strengthened by the authenticity and relevance of the tasks, the opportunities for self-directed control, and the choices made available in the learning process (Knowles, 1975; Pintrich & Garcia, 1994; Wlodkowski, 1999). In addition, feedback about portfolio artifacts from peers and instructors helps develop positive professional and collegial performance outcomes (Keller, 1983) that also can increase student satisfaction. Further, the learner-centered nature of portfolios facilitates collaboration between teacher and learner in the design, development, and establishment of assessment strategies. Collaboration focuses attention on clear performance expectations and facilitates student connection to, responsibility for, and valuation of learning (McCombs, 2000), the center of any higher education program.

References

Accrediting Commission for Senior Colleges and Universities. (2005). *How to become accredited: Procedures manual for eligibility, candidacy, and initial accreditation.* Alameda, CA: Western Association for Schools and Colleges. Retrieved from http://www.wascsenior.org/wasc/Doc_Lib/HowtoBecomeAccred8.05.pdf

Alverno College. (2004). *The Diagnostic Digital Portfolio at Alverno College.* Retrieved from http://ddp.alverno.edu/

Alverno College Faculty. (1994). Student assessment-as-learning at Alverno College. Milwaukee, WI: Alverno College.

Arter, J. A., & Spandel, V. (1992). Using portfolios of student work in instruction and assessment. *Educational Measurement: Issues and Practice, 11*(1), 36–44.

Arter, J. A., Spandel, V., & Culham, R. (1995). Portfolios for assessment and instruction. *ERIC Digest.* Greensboro NC: ERIC Clearinghouse on Counseling and Student Services.

Baker, E. L., Gearhart, M., Herman, J. L., Tierney, R., & Whittaker, A. K. (1991).

Stevens Creek portfolio project: Writing assessment in the technology classroom. *Portfolio News*, *2*(3), 7–9.

Bilder, A. E. C., & Clifton F. (1996). Challenges in assessing outcomes in graduate and professional education. *New Directions for Institutional Research*, *92*, 5–15.

Bloom, B. (1956). *A taxonomy of learning*. New York: Longmans Green.

Bransford, J. D., Brown, A. L., & Cocking, R. R. (1999). *How people learn: Brain, mind, experience, and school*. Washington, DC: National Academy Press.

Burnett, P. C. (1999). The supervision of doctoral dissertations using a collaborative cohort model. *Counselor Education and Supervision*, *39*, 46–52.

Caine, R., & Caine, G. (1994). *Making connections: Teaching and the human brain*. Reading, MA: Addison-Wesley.

Carney, J. (2004, April). *Setting an agenda for electronic portfolio research: A framework for evaluating portfolio literature*. Paper presented at the annual meeting of the American Educational Research Association, Atlanta, GA.

Council of Graduate Schools. (2004). *PhD completion and attrition: Policy, number, leadership, and next steps*. Washington, DC: Author.

Dailey, S. R. (1997). Portfolios in law school: Creating a community of writers. In K. B. Yancey & I. Weiser (Eds.), *Situating portfolios: Four perspectives* (pp. 214–224). Logan: Utah State University Press.

Denecke, D., & Slimowitz, J. (2004). Ph.D. completion and attrition: Policy, number, leadership, and next steps. Washington, DC: Council of Graduate Schools.

Department of Computer Science. (2003, February 6). *PhD student portfolio guidelines*. Tallahassee: College of Arts and Sciences, Florida State University.

DiBiase, D. (2004). *ePortfolio rationale*. Pennsylvania State University. Retrieved from http://eportfolio.psu.edu/index.html and http://portfolio.psu.edu/about/e-Portfolio Rationale.pdf

Duffy, T. M., & Cunningham, D. J. (1996). Constructivism: Implications for the design and delivery of instruction. In D. H. Jonassen (Ed.), *Handbook of research for educational communications and technology* (pp. 170–198). New York: Macmillan.

Educational Leadership and Innovation PhD Program. (2004, September). *Educational leadership and innovation doctoral degree: Student handbook*. Denver: School of Education, University of Colorado at Denver and Health Sciences Center. Retrieved from http://www.cudenver.edu/NR/rdonlyres/etqgnpglgyaefplbelwk wurkimugq5biqkwqkwdvcquxklwfdgx33bj35bdfekpsrlo4neyucl7nrwafm4h554zt ptd/EDLIStudentHandbook202004-2005.pdf

Flavell, J. (1976). Metacognitive aspects of problem-solving. In L. Resnick (Ed.), *The nature of intelligence* (pp. 231–235). Hillsdale, NJ: Erlbaum.

Forster, M., & Masters, G. (1996). *Portfolios*. Victoria: Australian Council for Educational Research.

Freeman, R., & Lewis, R. (1998). *Planning and implementing assessment.* London, UK: Kogan Page.

Gardner, H. (1993). *Frames of mind: The theory of multiple intelligences.* New York: Basic Books.

Gearhart, M., Herman, J. L., Baker, E. L., & Whittaker, A. K. (n.d.). Writing portfolios at the elementary level: A study of methods for writing assessment. (Center for the Study of Evaluation Technical Report 337). Los Angeles: National Center for Research on Evaluation, Standards, and Student Testing (CRESST), Graduate School of Education and Information Studies, University of California, Los Angeles.

Gibson, D., & Barrett, H. (2002, November 30). Directions in electronic portfolio development. *IT Forum.* Retrieved from http://electronicportfolios.com/IT FORUM66.html

Guba, E. G., & Lincoln, Y. S. (1989). *Fourth generation evaluation.* Newbury Park, CA: Sage.

Heller, J. I., Sheingold, K., & Myford, C. M. (1998). Reasoning about evidence in portfolios: Cognitive foundations for valid and reliable assessment. *Educational Assessment, 5*(1), 5–40.

Hewett, S. M. (2004). Improving instructional practices. *TechTrends: Linking Research & Practice to Improve Learning, 48*(5), 26–30.

Higher Learning Commission. (2003). *Handbook of accreditation* (3rd ed.). Chicago: North Central Association of Colleges and Schools. Retrieved from http://www.ncahigherlearningcommission.org/download/Handbook03.pdf

Johnson, G., & DiBiase, D. (2004). Keeping the horse before the cart: Penn State's approach to e-Portfolio. *EDUCAUSE Quarterly, 27*(4), 18–26.

Katz, J., & Hartnett, R. T. (Eds.). (1976). *Scholars in the making: The development of graduate and professional students.* Cambridge, MA: Ballinger.

Keller, J. M. (1983). *Development and use of the ARCS model of motivational design* (Report No. IR 014 039). Enschede, Netherlands: Twente University of Technology. (ERIC Document Reproduction Service No. ED 313 001).

Klenowski, V. (2002). *Developing portfolios for learning and assessment: Processes and principles.* New York: Routledge Falmer.

Knowles, M. (1975). *Self-directed learning: A guide for learners and teachers.* Englewood Cliffs, NJ: Prentice-Hall.

Kolman, E. M., Gallagher, K. S., Hossler, D., & Catania, F. (1987). The outcomes of doctoral education: An institutional study. *Research in Higher Education, 27*(2), 107–118.

Koretz, D., Stecher, B., & Deibert, E. (1992). *The Vermont portfolio assessment program: Interim report on implementation and impact, 1991–92 school year* (Center for the Study of Evaluation Technical Report 350). Los Angeles: RAND Institute on Education and Training, National Center for Research on Evaluation, Standards, and Student Testing. Retrieved from http://www.cresst.org/Reports/TECH350.pdf

Krusekopf, F., & Karr-Kidwell, P. J. (2003). *Maximizing the impact of portfolio assessment through effective instructional leadership.* Retrieved from http://www.ericae.net/scripts/seget2.asp?db = ericft&want = http://www.ericae.net/ericdc/ED475367.htm

Laurillard, D. (1993). *Rethinking university teaching: A framework for the effective use of educational technology.* London, UK: Routledge.

Lauvås, P., & Handal, G. (1987). *Promoting reflective teaching.* Milton Keynes, UK: Open University Press.

Lovitts, B. E. (2001). *Leaving the ivory tower: The causes and consequences of departure from doctoral study.* Lanham, MD: Rowman & Littlefield.

Maki, P. (2002a). Developing an assessment plan to learn about student learning. *Journal of Academic Librarianship, 28*(1), 8–13.

Maki, P. (2002b). Moving from paperwork to pedagogy: Channeling intellectual curiosity into a commitment to assessment. *AAHE Bulletin, 54*(9), 3–5.

McCombs, B. L. (2000, July). *Learner-centered psychological principles: A framework for technology evaluation.* Invited paper presented at the U.S. Department of Education Regional Conferences on Evaluating Technology in Education, Atlanta, GA. Retrieved from http://www.pt3.org/VQ/html/mccombs.html

McCombs, B. L., & Whisler, J. S. (1997). *The learner-centered classroom and school: Strategies for increasing student motivation and achievement.* San Francisco: Jossey-Bass.

Mills, R. P. (1989, December). Portfolios capture a rich array of student performance. *School Administrator,* 8–11.

Muth, R. (2002). Scholar-practitioner goals, practices, and outcomes: What students and faculty need to know and be able to do. *Scholar-Practitioner Quarterly, 1*(1), 67–87.

National Research Council. (1996). *The path to the Ph.D.: Measuring graduate attrition in the sciences and humanities.* Washington, DC: National Academy Press.

Nyquist, J., & Woodford, B. (2000). *Re-envisioning the PhD: What concerns do we have?* Funded by the Pew Charitable Trusts. Seattle: Center for Instructional Development and Research, University of Washington.

Office of Education Research. (1993, November). *Student portfolios: Classroom uses.* (Consumer Guide No. 8). Retrieved from http://www.ed.gov/pubs/OR/ConsumerGuides/classuse.html

Office of Technology Assessment. (1988). *Educating scientists and engineers: Grade school to grad school.* Washington, DC: U.S. Government Printing Office.

Paris, S. (1994). Situated motivation. In P. R. Pintrich, D. R. Brown, & C. E. Weinstein (Eds.), *Student motivation, cognition, and learning: Essays in honor of Wilbert J. McKeachie* (pp. 213–237). Hillsdale, NJ: Erlbaum.

Park, T. (2004). An overview of portfolio-based writing assessment. *Teachers College, Columbia University Working Papers in TESOL and Applied Linguistics*, 4(2). Retrieved from http://www.tc.edu/tesolalwebjournal/Park.pdf

Pellegrino, J. W., Chudowsky, N., & Glaser, R. (Eds.). (2001). *Knowing what students know: The science and design of educational assessment*. Washington, DC: National Academy Press.

Pintrich, P. R., & Garcia, T. (1994). Self-regulated learning in college students: Knowledge, strategies, and motivation. In P. R. Pintrich, D. R. Brown, & C. E. Weinstein (Eds.), *Student motivation, cognition, and learning: Essays in honor of Wilbert J. McKeachie* (pp. 113–133). Hillsdale, NJ: Erlbaum.

Salzman, S., & Denner, P. R., et al. (2002). *Teacher education outcomes measures: Special study survey*. Washington, DC: American Association of Colleges of Teacher Education.

Schön, D. A. (1988). *Educating the reflective practitioner: Toward a new design for teaching and learning in the professions*. San Francisco: Jossey-Bass.

Smallwood, S. (2004, January 16). Doctor dropout. *Chronicle of Higher Education: The Faculty*. Retrieved from http://chronicle.com/free/v50/i19/19a01001.htm

Snadden, D., Thomas, M., & Challis, M. (1999). *Portfolio-based learning and assessment*. (AMEE Educational Guide No. 11). Dundee, Scotland: Association for Medical Education in Europe (AMEE) Secretariat Centre for Medical Education.

University Assessment Committee. (1993, Spring). *Guidelines for assessment*. California State University-Chico. Retrieved from http://www.csuchico.edu/community/assessment.html

Vygotsky, L. (1978). *Mind in society: The development of higher psychological processes*. Cambridge, MA: Harvard University Press.

Wiggins, G. (1998). *Educative assessment: Designing assessments to inform and improve student performance*. San Francisco: Jossey-Bass.

Wiggins, G. (2004). Assessment as feedback. *New Horizons for Learning Online Journal*, *10*(2). Retrieved from http://newhorizons.org/strategies/assess/wiggins.htm

Wlodkowski, R. (1999). *Adult motivation to learn: A comprehensive guide for teaching all adults*. San Francisco: Jossey-Bass.

Wolf, D. P. (1989, April). Portfolio assessment: Sampling student work. *Educational Leadership*, *46*(7), 4–10.

9

RECASTING DOCTORAL EDUCATION IN AN OUTCOMES-BASED FRAMEWORK

Mary Huba, John Schuh, and Mack Shelley

The faculty in the Department of Educational Leadership and Policy Studies at Iowa State University recently redesigned its doctoral program to focus on educational leadership, providing students in both educational administration and higher education with opportunities to understand and analyze the field of education from a K–16 perspective. The redesigned program is grounded in a set of intended learning outcomes in five areas: leadership, research, communication (written, oral, interpersonal, and intrapersonal), assessment and evaluation, and educational foundations. This chapter will explain how considerations related to assessing student learning prompted the faculty to broaden the scope of the program and how assessment data provide useful information for continued revision and fine-tuning of the program.

Our discussion addresses three broad topics. First, we discuss the process of programmatic change that has taken place in our doctoral program over an 11-year period, along with the successes and challenges the faculty have experienced in this endeavor. Second, we discuss the way the faculty recast the written preliminary examination, a lengthy and stressful test of content knowledge that formerly preceded the preliminary oral examination required by the Graduate College before commencing the dissertation. Third, we describe how the design of our program assessment provides us with ongoing data for continuous improvement.

Background, Rationale, and Processes for the Redesign of the Doctoral Program

For several years, the faculty in the formerly named Department of Professional Studies in Education supported several areas of doctoral emphasis (adult education; counselor education; educational administration; higher education; history, philosophy, and comparative education; and research and evaluation). In the 1990s, prompted by a board of regents study aimed at eliminating or reducing unnecessary duplication in the state, the department began to focus its efforts on educational administration and higher education alone.

As shown in Table 9.1, the process of doctoral program reform began in spring 1994, when outside consultants visited the department as part of an academic program review. These consultants urged the department to couple its downsizing with a forward-looking, integrated approach to doctoral education in which all education students would develop a K–16 perspective, whether their work centered on the elementary and secondary schools or on higher education. At the same time, the university was actively developing its outcomes assessment program, requiring that faculty in all programs develop statements of intended learning outcomes and gather assessment data to evaluate whether the desired outcomes are being achieved.

Thus, the professional studies faculty decided to follow best practice in the field of education and create an outcomes-based, learning-centered approach to graduate education. This approach was familiar to the faculty because it aligned with elements of best practice in education and it also reflected the findings of current research on how people learn. (For example, see National Research Council, 2000.)

Accordingly, in fall 1994, under the leadership of the department's Curriculum Committee, the faculty began a two-year process of identifying the central skills, abilities, and perspectives that they wished all students to possess upon graduation. The process culminated two years later in October 1996 when the faculty as a whole approved a Core of Common Learning in six key areas: leadership, research, communication, assessment and evaluation, educational foundations, and technology. This set of learning outcomes

TABLE 9.1.
Development of a Redesigned Outcomes-Based Doctoral Program

Key Event(s)	Time Frame	Party Providing Leadership
External program reviewers recommend forward-looking, integrated doctoral program	Spring 1994	
University initiates Student Outcomes Assessment	Spring 1994	
Faculty decide to develop a Core of Common Learning for doctoral program	Fall 1994	Curriculum Committee
Core of Common Learning approved by department faculty	October 16, 1996	
Department focus begins to change from professional studies to educational leadership	1996–1998	Curriculum Committee
Board of regents approves change of department name to Educational Leadership and Policy Studies	February 18, 1998	Curriculum Committee/ Department Faculty
Graduate College approves redesigned, cohort- and outcomes-based doctoral program	May 1998	Curriculum Committee
Development of rubrics	1997–2000	Ad Hoc Rubric Committee
Development of capstone project	1997–1999	Ad Hoc Prelim Revision Committee/Curriculum Committee
Rapid turnover of faculty	1997–1999	
Appointment of department assessment coordinator to provide leadership for assessment	Spring 1999	Department Chair
Affirmation of Core of Common Learning as "Intended Learning Outcomes" for doctoral program	August 17, 1999	Curriculum Committee/ Department Faculty
First cohort of doctoral students ($n = 19$) begins course work[a]	Fall 1999	
Development of doctoral portfolio	1999–2000	Ad Hoc Portfolio Committee
Annual surveys and/or focus groups with students	2000–2004	Ad Hoc Assessment Committee
Mapping of curriculum to learning outcomes	Fall 2001, 2003	Ad Hoc Assessment Committee
Review of completed portfolios ($n = 5$)	2001–2002	Ad Hoc Assessment Committee
Ad Hoc Assessment Committee becomes standing committee	2002–2003	Department Chair and Faculty
Review of completed capstone projects ($n = 8$)	2002–2003	Assessment Committee
Review of completed dissertations ($n = 25$)	2005–2006	Assessment Committee

[a] Subsequent cohorts of 20–25 students have been admitted annually.

provided the initial foundation to redesigning the doctoral program. During the next several years, through the work of both standing committees and ad hoc committees, the department developed an expanded framework for the program.

In the two years following approval of the learning outcomes (1996– 1998), the faculty accepted several recommendations from the Curriculum Committee regarding additional features of the proposed program. For example, while preserving the central role of the individual student's doctoral program advisory committee, the faculty decided to admit students in cohorts, require a set of common seminars for all students, and focus on the common theme of educational leadership across the department. The latter led to a decision to change the name of the entire department to Educational Leadership and Policy Studies, a modification that was approved by the board of regents in spring 1998 (see Table 9.1). Later that semester, the Graduate College approved the redesigned, cohort- and outcomes-based doctoral program in educational leadership.

During the same two-year time period (1996–1998), additional topics arose in faculty discussions that led to the creation of two ad hoc committees, the Ad Hoc Rubric Committee and the Ad Hoc Prelim Revision Committee. Because one feature of a learning-centered environment is having high expectations for students (Education Commission of the States, 1996), the Ad Hoc Rubric Committee's role was to create a set of public standards (i.e., rubrics) that describe the characteristics of excellent work in each of the learning outcome areas. Using these rubrics, students are able to monitor and shape their own learning and, in the process, develop self-awareness and lifelong learning skills (Huba & Freed, 2000).

The committee developed the rubrics over a 36-month period, and department faculty experimented with them in their courses and gave feedback for revision to the committee. Two examples, the rubric for leadership and the rubric for oral presentations, are shown in Appendixes B and C. As will be discussed subsequently, students use these rubrics to assess their own learning throughout the program, both in courses and in the process of developing their portfolios.

As understanding of and enthusiasm for a learning-centered approach to doctoral education grew within the department, the faculty began to examine the usefulness of existing assessments—the written preliminary examination, the preliminary oral examination, and the dissertation proposal and final dissertation document. In this initiative, the faculty were influenced by the newly emerging emphasis on authentic assessment, especially the work of Grant Wiggins who urged educators in the 1990s to develop "true tests" of students' knowledge and abilities (Wiggins, 1989). According to Wiggins, true tests *directly* evaluate the desired learning outcomes of a program, those difficult to assess but important abilities and dispositions that characterize educated citizens and admired professionals. Unlike traditional tests of facts and simple concepts, "true tests" require the performance of exemplary tasks, replicate the challenges and standards of performance faced by typical professionals in the field, and are responsive to individual students by asking for human judgment and dialogue.

The faculty felt that the preliminary oral examination met the criteria for authentic assessment in that it *directly* evaluates qualities that are needed in life beyond the doctorate, namely the abilities to:

1. Respond articulately to questions about issues in the profession that have no clear-cut correct answers
2. Think on one's feet and persist with confidence when there are no "right" answers
3. Identify trends and make informed speculations
4. Make judgments within a moral and ethical value structure

Similarly, the faculty viewed the dissertation as a direct and authentic assessment of students' ability to conduct research, as it requires that students competently investigate research questions worth investigating and defend their work to the faculty.

On the other hand, the faculty were concerned that the written preliminary examination was not an authentic measure of desired program outcomes. While the written exam did assess important knowledge such as command of subject matter and awareness of current issues in the field, it only *indirectly* assessed what the faculty actually desired, namely that students would be able *to use* this knowledge in a real-world professional context. Thus, an Ad Hoc Prelim Revision Committee was established to consider alternatives to the written exam; the committee's work took place between 1997 and 1999 (see Table 9.1). The issues associated with this process, along with the revised examination format, are discussed at length in the next section of this chapter.

As Table 9.1 illustrates, the redesign of the doctoral program took place over many years under the leadership of the department's standing Curriculum Committee, supplemented by the creative and diligent work of groups of faculty members who volunteered to serve on ad hoc committees that were established to achieve specific purposes. In addition to the committees already discussed, an Ad Hoc Portfolio Committee was established to develop a doctoral portfolio assessment process in 1999–2000. (See the next section on the revision of the preliminary exam for a detailed discussion of its work.) An Ad Hoc Assessment Committee, led by a faculty member who was appointed in by the department chair to be the department assessment coordinator, was created in 1999–2000 to gather feedback information to guide faculty decision making in the program. This ad hoc committee became a standing committee of the department in 2002–2003, and a description of its work concludes the chapter.

While a retrospective account makes the process of program redesign sound like a simple and straightforward process, it was not without challenges. For example, as shown in Table 9.1, between 1997 and 1999 a remarkable turnover of faculty occurred as individuals resigned or retired, taking with them a great deal of the institutional memory associated with the program redesign process. This turnover led to a new affirmation of the Core of Common Learning document developed by the faculty in August 1999 and to reframing the core as the program's Intended Learning Outcomes.

The faculty also faced other challenges in the process of redesigning the doctoral program. For example, they were faced with the simultaneous need to develop outcomes-based assessments in the department's master's programs. Another challenge was addressing occasional faculty resistance to the shared responsibility for doctoral education that the department was developing. A tradition in doctoral education is the autonomy of each student's program advisory committee, and the faculty were challenged to strike a delicate balance between the important role of this committee and shared decision making by the faculty as a whole. Finally, another challenge was to craft an integrated doctoral program while at the same time respecting the fundamentally different disciplinary contexts of faculty and students in the program—educational administration and higher education.

Despite these and other challenges, the faculty admitted the first cohort of students to the redesigned doctoral program in fall 1999, and additional cohorts have been admitted each year since then. We now turn to a more in-depth discussion of the redesign of the preliminary exam, followed by a discussion of how the department gathers ongoing assessment information to support data-based decision making to improve student learning.

Redesign of the Preliminary Examination

Iowa State University requires that all students pursuing the doctor of philosophy degree successfully complete a preliminary oral examination. The nature of the oral examination is determined by the academic program faculty in that they are permitted to determine the focus of the oral examination. Historically, in the department, the content of this examination was framed by a written examination, completed by the student in advance of the oral examination. Over a two- to three-day period, students wrote lengthy, closed-book essay exams on topics determined to be appropriate by their program advisory committees based on the courses they had taken. Content not included in the written examination also could be part of the oral examination. In effect, this type of prelim exam was designed to confer expert status on the student.

The written exam was a high-stakes, stressful experience for students. It emphasized recalling and applying information that already had been covered in the students' course work, and performance on the exam did not always align with the course grades that students had received. Further, the emphasis on attaining expert status sometimes created an atmosphere of "grilling" the student for knowledge at the oral examination.

After much discussion, the faculty decided to replace the written exam with authentic measures of two key abilities they see as central to life in education past receipt of the doctorate:

1. the ability to address real-world problems using disciplinary knowledge in a real-world context
2. the ability to gauge one's own level of expertise and the need for additional learning

Both of these abilities have been shown to be central in developing in-depth understanding in a discipline (National Research Council, 2000).

Thus, the faculty identified three goals for developing new student work products that would form the basis for a preliminary oral examination. First, they wanted students to be able to demonstrate that they could apply what they had learned in their course work and other experiences in a practical setting. This meant that a mechanism had to be devised to allow students to get into the field and address real-world, ill-defined problems. Second, the faculty wanted students to work with an organization or person who could use their assistance. The faculty hypothesized that this kind of relationship would serve students well in preparing them for leadership roles after completing their doctoral study. Third, the faculty desired to emphasize lifelong learning skills by providing students with opportunities to evaluate their learning over time (metacognitive ability).

With these objectives in mind, the faculty developed the capstone project and the learning portfolio as the student products that would be the focus of their preliminary oral examination. The faculty were guided by the outcomes they thought were appropriate for a contemporary Ph.D. degree in educational leadership and policy studies. Because the capstone project was designed to engage students in a consultative relationship with an educational agency such as a school district, college, university, or other educational organization, students would be able to demonstrate the application of their doctoral learning in a real-world situation.

In addition to the capstone project, the faculty designed a learning portfolio that students deliver to the advisory committee before the oral examination so that it can be discussed at the examination. The organization of the learning portfolio was framed by the learning outcomes for the doctoral program described above. Finally, both the capstone project and learning portfolio were designed to provide faculty with data they could use to make judgments not only about individual students' learning, but also about students' achievements collectively through program assessment activities. In short, the projects had the potential to establish a reciprocal learning and assessment relationship for both students and faculty.

The Capstone Project

As illustrated by the sample titles in Appendix D, the capstone project is designed to be a client-centered activity, in that the product should be of assistance in the resolution of a problem, issue, or concern to the client or the client's institution. The client is asked to work closely with the student in developing the consulting report and is invited to participate in the student's preliminary oral examination. When the client is unable to be physically present at the university to participate in the oral examination, arrangements are made for the client to join the examination by speaker telephone.

The capstone project is designed for students to develop competencies in the following areas:

1. A working knowledge of the field, including its research, its prominent individuals and their contributions, and its issues and trends
2. An ability to synthesize knowledge and demonstrate skills associated with the field in the five program domains: leadership, research, communication, assessment and evaluation, and educational foundations
3. An ability to write stylistically and intellectually at a level of sophistication commensurate with the dissertation
4. An ability to function effectively in face-to-face dialogue
5. An ability to create viable solutions to problems in the field (see http://www.elps.hs.iastate.edu/About/Assessment/assessment_capstone .pdf)

Preparation of the Capstone Proposal

Each student confers with the major professor in identifying a site for the capstone project. Typically, the student identifies the site, but in some situations the student's major professor provides assistance. After the site has been identified, the student prepares a proposal for the capstone project, which is reviewed by the student's doctoral advisory committee. The elements of the project are included in Appendix E.

The project often can be more complex and time-consuming than students anticipate. The following observation summarizes some of the challenges that students encounter in the course of their capstone project:

> The capstone took longer to complete than I had anticipated because of many factors outside my control. The institution I was working with was undergoing many changes, and so my initial client changed and the project evolved, too. I had to postpone my initial proposal meeting with my committee, and the final project turned out to be different from my initial proposal because of these factors. Thankfully, the committee seemed to anticipate this and was very flexible. In dealing with these issues, I kept in close contact with my major professor, and we made the appropriate changes. (Clayborne, 2004, p. 1)

Ethical Considerations

One of the issues that emerged from a faculty assessment of eight early capstone projects in 2002–2003 focused on how students should manage the ethical dimensions of their projects. This topic had not been clarified in initial descriptions of capstone project requirements. A number of questions to be clarified included the following:

> Who owns the data?
> Can the student present the project at a professional meeting?
> How will sensitive information be reported in the capstone report?
> May the manuscript be submitted for publication?

It was decided that students should resolve ethical issues such as these with their clients before their project begins. This decision led to our adding a specific section on ethics to the capstone proposal template. Of course, approval for dealing with human subjects must be secured from the university's Institutional Review Board; this approval process had been in place long before the concept of the capstone project was developed.

Presentation of the Capstone Report

The final presentation of the capstone project occurs during the preliminary oral examination. The format for the paper is included as Appendix F. As mentioned above, the client is invited to join the presentation and can answer questions and comment on the project. The student usually presents the paper for about 20 minutes and then answers questions for about 45 minutes. When the portion of the preliminary oral examination dealing with the capstone project has been completed, the student's advisory committee turns to discussion of the learning portfolio.

The Portfolio

The portfolio that students develop is centered on the learning outcomes for the doctoral program, identified above. Students are asked to assess their level of achievement in relation to these outcomes at three points in their doctoral study: upon entry into the doctoral program, at the midpoint of their course work, and as part of the process of assembling the portfolio. The portfolio includes both student reflections on their learning and sample artifacts representing their work.

A faculty assessment of a small number of early portfolios in 2001–2002 revealed that the portfolios were heavy on artifacts and light on reflection. As a result, the faculty revised the portfolio guidelines to emphasize metacognitive development rather than artifact collection. Now, the reflection papers are candid, thoughtful assessments by students concerning their development along the dimensions of each of the learning outcomes for the program, using the faculty-developed rubrics (http://www.elps.hs.iastate.edu/About/elpsrubrics.php) as a guide for their self-assessments. Students identify a limited number of artifacts to support each reflection paper. In preparing the final version of the portfolio, students write a narrative for the portfolio as a whole, orienting the reader to the content and organization of their work.

The portfolio is prepared for the committee's review and examination as part of the preliminary oral examination. The outline for the portfolio is included as Appendix G. When the department began the process, students made paper copies of their portfolios and presented them to their committee members at least two weeks in advance of the oral examination. Because the physical portfolios proved to be cumbersome, students moved to electronic means for developing their portfolios. Some students distributed their portfolios using a minimum of paper and a CD-Rom for their artifacts, whereas others developed a CD for their entire portfolio.

Now, a fully electronic Web-based format is available to all doctoral students, allowing them to concentrate on the content of their portfolios rather than having to create electronic formats. The new format provides an opportunity for someone other than the student to post commentaries and reactions to portfolio entries, and the student controls external access to his or her portfolio. Should students so desire, members of their doctoral advisory committees can respond online to students' portfolios prior to the preliminary oral exam.

Using Data to Guide Decision Making about Program Improvement

The department faculty have designed an approach to program assessment that provides continuous feedback information to facilitate data-driven decision making about the program. For the most part, data are collected annually and are presented to and discussed by the entire faculty each year at an August retreat.

As can be seen in Table 9.1, there are two components to the approach. The first consists of periodic reviews of program assessments by faculty committees. To date, the faculty have conducted one review of portfolios and one review of capstone projects, discussed above, and these reviews were largely exploratory and qualitative in nature. The reviews took place soon after the first portfolios ($n = 5$) and capstones ($n = 8$) were completed by students in the 1999 cohort. The findings from the review provided formative guidance about how to improve the *process* of preparing the capstone projects and portfolios, and they also provide insights about the level and type of *student learning* that result from these assessments. We have already mentioned that data from reviews of early portfolios guided the faculty in emphasizing student reflection in the portfolio process more than the collection of artifacts. The reviews of early capstone projects prompted the faculty to heighten students' awareness of the ethical aspects of their capstone projects.

In 2005–2006, the faculty plan to conduct the first review of the 25 doctoral dissertations that have been completed since the first cohort of students began their studies in fall 1999. The purpose is to develop a characterization of the type of research that our students pursue and to use this characterization in a collaborative discussion about how well the intended learning outcomes in areas such as research and written communication are being achieved. Appendix H describes the questions that will guide the review. Because individual students' program advisory committees traditionally have had sole oversight for student learning, this review and discussion of learning outcomes will be a new experience for the faculty. It will be important to focus the review on the *collective* learning of our students and to avoid any erroneous impression that the work of any individual major professor is being critiqued.

The second component of doctoral program assessment is input from students themselves about their experiences in the doctoral program, including the preliminary exam. At the request of the department faculty, this input is collected by the Research Institute for Studies in Education (RISE), whose mission is to provide services to Iowa State University's College of Human Sciences for contracts and grants, institutional research, and evaluation studies.[1]

Beginning in spring 2000, RISE staff members have annually conducted surveys on all aspects of the doctoral program with current doctoral students (see Table 9.1 and Appendix I) and conducted focus group sessions with selected students in each cohort (see Appendix J). RISE staff members prepare written reports of both the survey and focus groups results, and those reports are presented to the department faculty for consideration. Following faculty deliberation and appropriate student input, faculty use the results of the RISE studies to refine various aspects of the program, including the structure and operation of the preliminary examination process.

For example, in the early days of implementing the portfolios, the faculty learned from survey results that students were generally comfortable writing reflections about their progress as learners and that portfolios help students gain perspective about their academic careers. We also learned that some students were not sure what was expected for the portfolio, particularly how the portfolio should be organized and what should be included in it. From focus group results, we learned that students wanted good examples of acceptable portfolios, better technical support, and clearer communication about guidelines for portfolio preparation.

In terms of the capstone projects, the faculty learned from surveys that the students were confident of meeting the capstone's written paper requirements and that they felt that they had received adequate information about the capstone. From focus groups, we gained several additional insights: students perceived discrepancies among major professors in expectations regarding the capstone experience, they wanted more examples of possible capstone projects, they desired more continuity between capstone projects and dissertation research, and they wanted clearer explanations of expectations for the capstone.

The faculty have taken these and subsequent assessment results seriously in that we have used them to guide decisions we have made to improve our doctoral program. For example, we responded to students' concerns about the portfolio and capstone projects, providing them with better and clearer information to guide the development of their own portfolios and capstones. In addition, based on survey and focus group results from spring 2003, we referred two items to the Curriculum Committee for consideration. The first was students' perception of the need for greater cohesiveness in the required seminars, a topic that is still under consideration by the Curriculum Committee. The second was the need to address the curriculum related to technology outcomes. As a result of the latter referral, the faculty have dropped the technology learning outcomes of the program, considering technology to be a cross-cutting tool in all courses rather than an area of learning outcomes.

As these examples illustrate, the faculty in our doctoral program are increasingly relying on regularly collected qualitative and quantitative data to support department decision making. The program's assessment initiative has been implemented deliberately and persistently, although it should be pointed out that the Assessment Committee had originally planned to collect more data on an annual basis than has been achieved. For example, the committee had planned to review capstone projects, portfolios, and dissertations each year, but it has managed only one review of each form of assessment in the past four years. Because faculty at land-grant, research universities have research and outreach responsibilities as well as teaching responsibilities, the faculty have had to scale back to some degree the anticipated pace of assessment. This, however, has not diminished the faculty's commitment to assessment nor has it undermined the substantial benefits that have accrued.

Because of our assessment program, our department faculty are creating community among ourselves and with our students around the topics of teaching and learning. We are assuming collective responsibility for student learning while respecting traditional components of doctoral education, such as the role of the program advisory committee. Most important, we no longer have to *assume* that students who can regurgitate content knowledge on a written exam know how to use that knowledge effectively. Under the guidance of their major professors, all students complete capstone projects, portfolios, and dissertations that are evaluated for scholarly quality by their program advisory committees. This process assures us that our students are prepared for the professional challenges they will face in postdoctoral life.

Note

1. Evaluation work in our doctoral program has been conducted primarily by a series of RISE's postdoctoral research associates—Robert Reason, William Nelson, and Kevin Saunders.

References

Clayborne, H. (2004). *Capstone reflections.* Iowa State University Department of Educational Leadership and Policy Studies. Retrieved from http://www.elps.hs .iastate.edu/Academics/document/capstone_reflection.pdf

Education Commission of the States. (1996, April). What research says about improving undergraduate education. *AAHE Bulletin, 48,* 5–8.

Huba, M. E., & Freed, J. E. (2000). *Learner-centered assessment on college campuses: Shifting the focus from teaching to learning.* Needham Heights, MA: Allyn & Bacon.

National Research Council. (2000). *How people learn: Brain, mind, experience, and school.* Washington, DC: National Academy Press.

Wiggins, G. (1989, May). A true test: Toward more authentic and equitable assessment. *Phi Delta Kappan, 70*(9), 703–713.

Appendix A

Learning Outcomes for Doctoral Students in ELPS

Upon completion of the Educational Leadership and Policy Studies doctoral program, the student . . .

In the area of leadership:

- balances the forces of stability and change in order to maximize human and collective organizational performance
- applies techniques, technologies, and strategies that promote required or desired change
- uses periods of equilibrium for the organization to engage in reflexive periods of self-appraisal and reflection
- engages in rational leadership activities such as planning, evaluation, implementation, and assessment regarding results
- considers how and why organizations engage in change from simple adaptive changes with responses that are well within traditional boundary decisions to more radical alterations when the survival of the organization is at stake
- engages in both rational, technical change strategies and technologies, yet understands the impact of emotion and morale on organizational climate and performance
- understands that stability is a key to productivity
- balances the need for stability and the need for stimulation in the work environment
- creates parallelism between promoting human growth as well as organizational growth

In the area of research:

- comprehends the basic elements of research and inquiry
- conducts scholarly inquiry

In the area of communication:

- expresses ideas clearly, both orally and in writing
- articulates his or her philosophy of life
- acknowledges his or her own beliefs and values
- subscribes to lifelong learning
- exhibits ethical standards consistent with professional commitment
- understands issues and trends in a multicultural, nonsexist society
- demonstrates sensitive awareness and knowledge of one's own cultural background and that of others
- works effectively with individuals from diverse cultural backgrounds
- listens and responds in an exemplary manner

In the area of assessment and evaluation:

- demonstrates skills necessary for delineating, obtaining and providing information to assist in judging the worth and guiding the improvement of educational programs
- understands theoretical perspectives, evaluation and assessment models, professional standards, historical trends, and current issues in the fields of program evaluation and educational assessment

In the area of educational foundations:

- understands education as a social institution
- uses diverse analytical and interpretative approaches appropriate for the study of education for persons of all ages
- understands the historical, philosophical, social, and cultural contexts of education for persons of all ages
- understands diverse philosophical orientations
- articulates the orientations in thought that underlie democratic systems of government and their relationships to education
- uses a comprehensive knowledge base about adults as learners within the contexts of their work

Appendix B
Leadership Rubric

Leadership: The ability to balance the forces of stability and change in order to maximize human and collective organizational performance; knowing when and how to apply techniques, technologies, and strategies that promote required or desired change; using periods of equilibrium for the organization to engage in reflective periods of self-appraisal and reflection; knowledge of and ability to engage in rational leadership activities such as planning, evaluation, implementation, and assessment regarding results

Levels of Achievement:

Criteria	Exemplary	Proficient	Marginal	Unacceptable
Balance: fostering actions toward achievement of vision, mission, and goals	Analyzes a hypothetical situation in which the elements and interactions of vision, mission, and goals can be maximized and lead to an inclusive action plan or agenda that is clear, easily translated into work tasks, and evaluated when completed	Understands and, with minor difficulty, analyzes a hypothetical situation exhibiting the interrelatedness among vision, mission and goals, and plan development	Has some knowledge about the process of analysis and the interrelatedness of vision, mission, and goals. Is unable to translate this relationship into planning, work, and evaluative agenda	Is not able to analyze a hypothetical situation or exhibit an understanding of the interactive nature between vision, mission, and goals, or translate them into a coherent action plan or agenda

(continued)

Criteria	Exemplary	Proficient	Marginal	Unacceptable
Balance: facilitating group process	Leads and empowers group members towards consensual solutions that maximize members' commitment to and satisfaction with agreed-upon responses within a specified time limit, for example, 30 minutes	Is hesitant but able to lead and empower group members in consensual solutions resulting in group satisfaction with agreed-upon responses within a specific time, for example, 30 minutes	Requires significant assistance in leading and empowering group members in consensual solutions resulting in group satisfaction with agreed-upon responses after an extended time period	Is not able to lead or empower a group to develop a consensus that results in the members' commitment/satisfaction regarding their responses within a specified time limit, for example, 30 minutes, even if extended
Balance: using situational, contextual, and cultural aspects of organizations effectively	Is able to identify the situational, contextual, and cultural aspects of an organization that are necessary to attain balance and that will lead to improvement in productivity of the individuals and the sub-group and organization	Has some understanding of the situational, contextual, and cultural aspects of an organization relative to balance and improved productivity of individuals and organizations	Has difficulty understanding and identifying the situational, contextual, and cultural aspects of an organization relative to balance and improved productivity of individuals and organizations	Is not able to identify or relate any specific organizational context, culture, or situationally unique aspects of organizational balance in any setting. Is not able to identify the contrasting settings or conditions within settings involving stability between chaos and equilibrium

Change: understanding change models, processes, and impacts	Articulates and distinguishes the benefits and limitations of change models, processes, and impacts, and possesses the ability to stimulate potential benefits to enhance educational practice and outcomes	Articulates and distinguishes the benefits and limitations of change models, processes, and impacts. Has some difficulty in relating the potential benefits to educational practice and outcomes	Is limited in ability to articulate and distinguish the benefits and limitations of change models, processes, and impacts. Has limited understanding and inability to stimulate the potential benefits that enhance educational practice and outcomes	Is not able to interpret the benefits and limitations of change models, processes, and impacts
Change: understanding the impact of change	Is able to analyze and articulate the impact of change within and outside an organizational system	With limitations, is able to analyze and articulate the impact of change within and outside an organizational system	Has limited understanding and difficulty analyzing and explaining the impact of change within and outside an organizational system	Is not able to explain the impact of change, nor articulate the impact of change within and outside an organizational system
Change: understanding the dynamics of change and its impact on the human condition	Is able to make informed choices, and synthesize the potential gains and limitations of the dynamics of change and its impact on human conditions and performance	Is generally able to make informed choices and synthesize the potential gains and limitations of the dynamics of change and its impact on human conditions and performance	Has difficulty in making informed choices and synthesizing the potential gains and limits of the dynamics of change and its impact on human conditions and performance	Is not able to make informed choices, or compare and contrast the potential gains and limitations of the dynamics of change and its impact on human conditions and performances

(continued)

Criteria	Exemplary	Proficient	Marginal	Unacceptable
Stability: understanding the balance between chaos and equilibrium	Is able to distinguish work settings that are balanced between chaos and equilibrium from those that are not. Can write prescriptions or recommendations in which either chaotic or at-risk settings can be rebalanced, leading to improved human productivity and satisfaction	Is generally able to identify the concept of organizational balance in a work setting. Is able to analyze and identify the contrasting settings or conditions involving rebalancing and improved human productivity	Has little understanding and some difficulty demonstrating the concept of organizational balance in work settings. Has difficulty identifying the contrasting settings or conditions within settings involving stability between chaos and equilibrium	Is not able to demonstrate an understanding of the concept of organizational balance in work settings. Is not able to identify the contrasting settings or conditions within settings involving stability between chaos and equilibrium
Stability: applying traditional management practices	Is able to explain how the management of practices of planning, influencing, and organizing must be implemented and fused to attain the stated purposes of the organization via the goals, missions, and vision activities and statements to create and maintain organizational stability	Is generally able to explain the relationship of traditional management practices (planning, influencing, organizing, and implementation) to the achievement of stated purposes of the organization via the goals, mission, and vision activities of organizational stability	Has some understanding but exhibits significant difficulty in explaining how stipulated goals, missions, visions, and purposes can be developed and interrelated in the traditional management practices	Is not able to demonstrate verbally or visually how stipulated goals, missions, or visions and purposes can be developed and interrelated in the traditional management practice of planning, influencing, and organizing

Appendix C
Oral Presentation Rubric

Oral Communication: Expressing ideas clearly when communicating orally

Levels of Achievement:

Criteria	Exemplary	Proficient	Marginal	Unacceptable
Organization	Presentation is clear, logical, and sequential. Listener can follow line of reasoning.	Presentation is generally clear and well organized. A few minor points may be confusing.	Listener can follow presentation with effort. Some arguments are not clear. Organization seems haphazard.	Logic of arguments is not made clear. Listeners are confused.
Style	Level of presentation is appropriate for the audience. Presentation is a planned conversation, paced for audience understanding. It is *not* a reading of a paper. Speaker is clearly comfortable in front of the group and can be heard by all.	Level of presentation is generally appropriate. Pacing is sometimes too fast or slow. The presenter seems slightly uncomfortable at times, and the audience occasionally has trouble hearing him or her.	Aspects of presentation are too elementary or too sophisticated for audience. Presenter seems uncomfortable and can be heard only if listener is very attentive. Much of the information is read.	Presentation consistently is too elementary or too sophisticated for the audience. Information is read to audience. Presenter is obviously anxious and cannot be heard.

(continued)

Criteria	Exemplary	Proficient	Marginal	Unacceptable
Use of Communication Aids (e.g., Transparencies, Slides, Posters, Handouts, Computer-Generated Materials)	Communication aids enhance the presentation. They are prepared in a professional manner. Font on visuals is large enough to be seen by all. Information is organized to maximize audience understanding. Details are minimized so that main points stand out.	Communication aids contribute to the quality of the presentation. Font size is appropriate for reading. Appropriate information is included. Some material is not supported by visual aids.	Communication aids are poorly prepared or used inappropriately. Font is too small to be easily seen. Too much information is included. Unimportant material is highlighted. Listeners may be confused.	No communication aids are used, or they are so poorly prepared that they detract from the presentation.
Content: depth of content	Speaker provides an accurate and complete explanation of key concepts and theories, drawing upon relevant literature. Applications of theory are included to illuminate issues. Listeners gain insights.	For the most part, explanations of concepts and theories are accurate and complete. Some helpful applications are included.	Explanations of concepts and/or theories are inaccurate or incomplete. Little attempt is made to tie theory to practice. Listeners gain little from the presentation.	No reference is made to literature or theory. Listeners gain no new insights.

Content: accuracy of content	Information (names, facts, etc.) included in the presentation is consistently accurate.	No significant errors are made. Listeners recognize any errors to be the result of nervousness or oversight.	Enough errors are made to distract a knowledgeable listener, but some information is accurate. The presentation is useful if the listener can determine what information is reliable.	Information included is sufficiently inaccurate that the listener cannot depend on the presentation as a source of accurate information. Listeners may have been misled.
Use of Language: grammar and word choice	Sentences are complete and grammatical, and they flow together easily. Words are chosen for their precise meaning.	For the most part, sentences are complete and grammatical, and they flow together easily. With a few exceptions, words are chosen for their precise meaning.	Listeners can follow the presentation, but some grammatical errors and use of slang are evident. Some sentences are incomplete/halting, and/or vocabulary is somewhat limited or inappropriate.	Listeners are so distracted by the presenter's apparent difficulty with grammar and appropriate vocabulary that they cannot focus on the ideas presented.
Use of Language: freedom from bias (e.g., sexism, racism, ageism, heterosexism, etc.)	Both oral language and body language are free from bias.	Oral language and body language are free from bias with one or two minor exceptions.	Oral language and/or body language includes some significant bias. Listeners may be offended.	Oral language and/or body language frequently reflects bias. Some, if not all, listeners will probably be offended.
Personal Appearance	Personal appearance is completely appropriate for the occasion and the audience.	For the most part, personal appearance is appropriate for the occasion and the audience.	Personal appearance is somewhat inappropriate for the occasion and audience.	Personal appearance is inappropriate for the occasion and audience.

(continued)

(Oral Presentaion Rubric continued)

Criteria	Exemplary	Proficient	Marginal	Unacceptable
Responsiveness to Audience: verbal interaction	Highly responsive to audience comments and needs. Consistently clarifies, restates, and responds to questions. Summarizes when needed.	Generally responsive to audience comments and needs. Most of the time, clarifies, restates, responds to questions, and summarizes when needed. Misses some opportunities for interaction.	Reluctantly interacts with audience. Responds to questions inadequately.	Avoids or discourages active audience participation. Is not responsive to group.
Responsiveness to Audience: body language	Body language reflects confidence and ease when interacting with audience.	Body language reflects comfort when interacting with audience.	Body language reflects some discomfort when interacting with audience.	Body language reveals a reluctance to interact with audience.

Appendix D

Titles of Selected Capstone Projects and Their Authors

- *Ohio University Residential Learning Community Peer Mentor Evaluation Report,* by M. Benjamin
- *Academic Performance Policies at Iowa State University: A Policy Evaluation,* by S. Ellertson
- *Considerations for Tuition Fees at Humboldt University of Berlin,* by M. Feldmann
- *A Needs Assessment of a Faculty Fellows Program for University Housing Services at California State Polytechnic University, Pomona,* by J. Guardia
- *Program Evaluation of Grand View College's First Year Experience Program,* by K. A. Hensen
- *Formative Evaluation of Technology Integration in a Teacher Education Program,* by N. Johnson
- *An Institution in Transition: Adaptation at Humboldt University,* by K. Saunders
- *Educational Reform in the Federal Republic of Germany: Effects on School Leadership and the Implementation of Change,* by N. L. Shaw
- *Planning for the Future: A Strategic Plan for the Iowa Association for College Admission Counseling (IACAC),* by M. Wright

Appendix E

Capstone Proposal Format

The Capstone Proposal includes the following:

1. Names, postal addresses, telephone and fax numbers, and E-mail addresses (student and clients)
2. Name and responsibility of a person inside the organization with whom the student is working
3. A preliminary letter from an appropriate person in the host organization indicating that he or she is a willing participant in the experience
4. Approval signature of program of study (POS) chair
5. Overview of the project:
   a. Title
   b. Background of the problem

  c. Literature review (brief)
  d. The delineation of a clear line of inquiry supported by the preliminary literature review
  e. Statement of the problem including delimitations
  f. Objectives/methods of the study
  g. Timeline
  h. Budget
  i. Budgetary or logistical problems that may be part of or contribute to or detract from the proposed work (extenuating circumstances)
  j. Means of reporting results (i.e., report, presentation, product)
  k. Summary of deliverables to be completed by the end of the experience and presented to the POS committee for discussion at the preliminary oral
  l. Ethical considerations
  m. Definition of terms
  n. Human subjects approval (if appropriate)
  o. Bibliography

Source: http://www.educ.iastate.edu/elps/ELPSdoc.prog.2.htm

Appendix F

Elements of the Capstone Paper

  1. Title page
  2. Table of contents
  3. Executive summary (abstract)
  4. Introduction to problem (background and brief literature review)
  5. Methodology
  6. Data sources and methods
  7. The solution (maybe an invention, document, product)
  8. Ethical considerations
  9. Definition of terms
  10. Bibliography
  11. Appendix (include Human Subjects Approval form)

Source: http://www.elps.hs.iastate.edu/About/Assessment/assessment_capstone.pdf

Appendix G

Portfolio Outline

1. Table of contents
2. Student's program of study
3. Student's vitae or résumé
4. Reflective narrative on the portfolio as a whole
5. Materials for each learning domain
   a. Copy of ELPS rubric(s) for the domain
   b. Materials from entry self-assessment (self-assessment 1)
   c. Materials from midpoint self-assessment (self-assessment 2)
   d. Materials from final self-assessment (self-assessment 3)

Appendix H

Doctoral Dissertation Review Project (2005–2006)

Background

To date, 25 doctoral students (19 higher education, 6 educational administration) have completed dissertations in the current doctoral program. This year, an ad hoc committee of six faculty members will conduct a review of dissertations.

Purpose

The purpose is to conduct a systematic review of dissertations in order to develop insights about the research pursued by our doctoral students collectively. The review committee will provide a report to the ELPS faculty in order to promote reflection and discussion about the dissertation as a measure of student learning. The review will be organized around the following questions:

1. How frequently are students using the two formats available to them—the traditional five-chapter format versus the three-article format?
2. What types of research questions are students in the department addressing?
3. What types of theoretical/conceptual frameworks do our students use in their investigations?

4. What types of methods are employed in data collection?
5. What types of methods are employed in data analysis?
6. How do students approach the task of interpreting their findings?
7. As revealed in the dissertations, how well are learning outcomes being achieved in the areas of research, foundations, written communication, and evaluation and assessment (if relevant)?
8. How many presentations and publications have resulted from dissertation research in our department?

Appendix I

Doctoral Cohorts Survey

The purpose of this questionnaire is to give you an opportunity to assess the current configuration of the doctoral program in educational leadership. This survey is sponsored by the Department of Educational Leadership and Policy Studies with the assistance of the Research Institute for Studies in Education (RISE). Please answer each question as carefully as possible, and return your completed survey in the envelope, which will be delivered to RISE, in E005A Lagomarcino Hall.

Completing this survey is entirely voluntary. Your answers are anonymous and confidential. No identification code is used that could identify any person's individual responses. Aggregate response data will be analyzed by RISE staff, and results will be reported only in aggregate categories or through measures of central tendency and dispersion.

Thank you very much for taking the time to help your fellow students and yourself as we work to enhance the doctoral program to serve students' needs.

We'd like to start by asking for some basic information about yourself. Although at least some of this information probably is in departmental files, it will help to assess your needs in the doctoral program if you would please supply the following:

Demographic Information

1. Did you attend the doctoral program orientation?   Yes _____   No _____

2. Have you formed your program of study (POS) committee?   Yes _____   No _____

3. What is your area of emphasis?   Ed Admin _____   OLHRD _____   Higher Ed _____

4. My gender is   Female _____   Male _____

5. My current age is in the range of   less than 25   _____
                                   25–35   _____
                                   36–45   _____
                                   46–55   _____
                                   over 55   _____

6. I am enrolled this semester   full-time _____   part-time _____

7. I consider myself to be an on-campus student.   Yes _____   No _____

8. My current employment status is   _____ full-time   _____ part-time   _____ not currently employed.

9. I have a total of _____ years of professional employment experience. (If your answer is zero, please skip to question 11.)

10. **My last full-time professional experience was as** _____.

11. I live about _____ miles from campus.

12. I consider my race or ethnicity to be (please check all that apply)
     African American   _____
     Asian American   _____
     Hispanic   _____
     White (Caucasian)   _____
     American Indian   _____
     Other   _____
     Please specify _____

     Thanks very much. Next, we would like to find out what you think about several aspects of the educational leadership doctoral program.

13. Domains

     To what extent do you believe that each of the six components (domains) of the doctoral program is being addressed in your classes? Please circle the response below that best describes your opinion.

Domains	Not at all	Not very much	About average	Quite a lot	About as much as possible
a. educational leadership	1	2	3	4	5
b. educational research	1	2	3	4	5
c. communication	1	2	3	4	5
d. educational evaluation	1	2	3	4	5
e. educational foundations	1	2	3	4	5
f. educational technology	1	2	3	4	5

14. Rubrics

     The department has adopted rubrics to provide guidance to faculty and students regarding how courses should be structured and what material should be emphasized in the curriculum. Please respond to the questions below about these rubrics. Just circle the answer that best expresses your view.

	Disagree strongly	Disagree somewhat	Neither agree nor disagree	Agree somewhat	Agree strongly
a. The rubrics are being used in all of my courses.	1	2	3	4	5
b. The quality of the rubrics is high.	1	2	3	4	5
c. Faculty make good use of rubrics.	1	2	3	4	5
d. Students find rubrics to be helpful.	1	2	3	4	5
e. Rubrics are important.	1	2	3	4	5

15. Personal Considerations

A number of personal needs and interests are associated with student participation in the doctoral program. Some of these are presented below. Please let us know how you react to each of these matters.

	Disagree strongly	Disagree somewhat	Neither agree nor disagree	Agree somewhat	Agree strongly
a. The program is applicable to my job requirements or expectations.	1	2	3	4	5
b. I feel stimulated and challenged by the curriculum.	1	2	3	4	5
c. Family obligations clash with the demands of the program.	1	2	3	4	5
d. My work responsibilities get in the way of my studies.	1	2	3	4	5
e. The residency requirement makes the program more difficult to complete.	1	2	3	4	5
f. The time spent driving to campus is a problem.	1	2	3	4	5
g. Class scheduling needs to accommodate my needs better.	1	2	3	4	5
h. I have had no problems getting information from the department.	1	2	3	4	5
i. Faculty members often are not available when I need them.	1	2	3	4	5
j. Scheduling of research methods and statistics courses needs to be more flexible.	1	2	3	4	5
k. Classes provide a good opportunity to interact with students from different program areas.	1	2	3	4	5
l. Better use could be made of electronic communication.	1	2	3	4	5
m. Peer mentors would be helpful.	1	2	3	4	5
n. I really could benefit from class time explaining the challenges associated with attaining a doctoral degree.	1	2	3	4	5
o. I would like to see doctoral cohorts organized differently.	1	2	3	4	5
p. The purpose of new requirements needs to be made clearer.	1	2	3	4	5
q. A handbook would provide a useful single source of information.	1	2	3	4	5

Please let us know about any other personal considerations that the department should consider in implementing its doctoral program, or feel free to explain your answers above. _____

_____

_____

_____

_____

_____

_____

_____

16. Admissions

Please tell us what you think about the following aspects of the ELPS doctoral admissions process.

	Disagree strongly	Disagree somewhat	Neither agree nor disagree	Agree somewhat	Agree strongly
a. The admissions process is transparent.	1	2	3	4	5
b. Information about admissions was provided in a timely manner.	1	2	3	4	5
c. We have a good mix of students in the doctoral program.	1	2	3	4	5
d. Students should not be admitted if they can't support themselves financially.	1	2	3	4	5
e. Part-time and full-time students should have the same admission criteria.	1	2	3	4	5

Please let us know your perceptions of any other aspects of the doctoral admissions process and feel free to explain your answers above. _____

_____

_____

_____

17. One-credit seminars

The doctoral program features six one-credit thematic seminars: (1) Communication and Team Building; (2) Governance, Politics, and Policies; (3) Law, Equity, Equality; (4) Ethics, Justice, and Caring; (5) Problem Solving and Planning; and (6) Critical and Creative Thinking. Please let us know what you think about the following aspects of this program requirement.

	Disagree strongly	Disagree somewhat	Neither agree nor disagree	Agree somewhat	Agree strongly
a. The seminars are offered on good days of the week.	1	2	3	4	5
b. The seminars are offered at good times of the day.	1	2	3	4	5
c. The seminars cover the right topics.	1	2	3	4	5
d. I got out of the seminars what I had expected.	1	2	3	4	5
e. The level of rigor in the seminars was appropriate.	1	2	3	4	5
f. The assignments were appropriate.	1	2	3	4	5

Please tell us what else you think we should know about the one-credit seminars, or explain your answers above.

_____

_____

_____

_____

_____

_____

_____

_____

18. Committee Formation

Every graduate student must form a program of study (POS) committee. Please share your views on this aspect of the Educational Leadership PhD Program.

	Disagree strongly	Disagree somewhat	Neither agree nor disagree	Agree somewhat	Agree strongly
a. The procedures for setting up a committee are reasonable.	I	2	3	4	5
b. The student should take the lead in establishing a POS committee.	I	2	3	4	5
c. It is easy to put together a POS committee.	I	2	3	4	5
d. It is difficult to find an outside member for the POS committee.	I	2	3	4	5
e. Finding a major professor is not a problem.	I	2	3	4	5

Please tell us what else you want to say about POS committees. _____
_____
_____
_____

19. The Capstone Experience

The doctoral program requires a capstone community-building experience to provide students with exposure to and involvement in both public and private sector organizations.

	Disagree strongly	Disagree somewhat	Neither agree nor disagree	Agree somewhat	Agree strongly
a. The orientation was informative.	I	2	3	4	5
b. I have a clear understanding of what is expected from the capstone.	I	2	3	4	5
c. I have received adequate information about the capstone.	I	2	3	4	5
d. The role of the mentor is well defined.	I	2	3	4	5
e. I have a clear understanding of the role of the mentor.	I	2	3	4	5
f. The expectations for the written paper are clear.	I	2	3	4	5
g. The connection between the capstone and the preliminary examination needs to be clarified.	I	2	3	4	5
h. I am sure that I can meet the written paper requirements.	I	2	3	4	5

What else would you like to share about the capstone experience? _____
_____
_____
_____

20. Portfolio

A portfolio is required as part of the preliminary oral examination process. What do you think about this aspect of the program?

	Disagree strongly	Disagree somewhat	Neither agree nor disagree	Agree somewhat	Agree strongly
a. I have a good understanding of what is expected for my portfolio.	1	2	3	4	5
b. I need information about how the portfolio should be organized.	1	2	3	4	5
c. It would help if portfolios were worked on in seminars.	1	2	3	4	5
d. A portfolio helps students gain perspective on an academic career.	1	2	3	4	5
e. I don't know what should be included in my portfolio.	1	2	3	4	5
f. I'm not sure how my portfolio is going to be evaluated at my prelim oral.	1	2	3	4	5

What else would you like to say about the use of portfolios? _____

_____

_____

_____

_____

Suggestions and Comments

Thank you very much for completing this survey. Your valuable answers will be used in evaluating this program. Please let us know anything else that you believe would help to improve and strengthen the doctoral program. _____

_____

_____

_____

_____

_____

_____

_____

_____

_____

_____

Appendix J

Focus Group Protocol

1. We're interested in your general reactions to being a doctoral student in the ELPS department, so let's start with a relatively broad question: What has it been like to be a doctoral student this year?

2. We're also interested in your thoughts about the communication

flow between the department/faculty and you. Could you comment a bit on the communication flow this year?

   a. How might it be improved?

   b. When you have questions, how do you get them answered?

3. We would like to focus a bit on the one-credit-hour ELPS seminars you have been participating in. What do you think of them?

   a. How about having two each semester?

   b. How about their sequence?

4. We would like your reactions to the following aspects of the seminars:

   a. The format

   b. The scheduling

   c. How can the department improve the seminar?

5. We are especially interested in your learning this past semester. What factors or aspects of the program contribute to or detract from your learning?

   a. Contribute to

   b. Detract from

6. Are there other topics or issues that you would like to discuss related to your experiences as a doctoral student that we have not talked about today?

   a. Thoughts on understanding and preparing for the capstone

   b. Thoughts on understanding and preparing your professional portfolio

ABOUT THE AUTHORS

Rebecca Aanerud is the associate director of the Center for Innovation and Research in Graduate Education (CIRGE) at the University of Washington. CIRGE undertakes studies on various aspects of graduate education, with a particular emphasis on the career and family paths of Ph.D. recipients. She is also an affiliate assistant professor and lecturer in women's studies where she teaches classes on feminist theory and race theory. She has a number of publications in the field of critical race theory and whiteness studies.

Nancy A. Borkowski, Ed.D., most recently served as the program associate for The Responsive Ph.D. Initiative, a five-year national effort to improve doctoral education organized by the Woodrow Wilson National Fellowship Foundation. She served as primary researcher and coordinator for the Ph.D. Professional Development Assessment Project, an inquiry into innovative practices at 14 leading doctoral institutions.

Her background includes university positions in career services centers at the University of North Carolina Greensboro, Emory University, and Miami University (Ohio), and the Instructional Support and Development Office at the University of Georgia where she assisted graduate students and faculty with their career and teaching development. Borkowski received her Ed.D. from the University of Georgia in higher education with an emphasis in faculty development.

Andrea Conklin Bueschel's research spans all of higher education, from college readiness to doctoral education. She has held various administrative and research posts in colleges and universities, and has been managing director of an educational consulting firm. She currently serves as a research scholar at the Carnegie Foundation for the Advancement of Teaching, where she works on the Carnegie Initiative on the Doctorate and on the Foundation's project on community colleges. She is coauthor of a forthcoming volume on doctoral education and the Carnegie Initiative on the Doctorate.

Joseph Cerny is a professor of chemistry at the University of California at Berkeley. He received a B.S. in chemical engineering from the University of Mississippi in 1957, was a Fulbright Scholar at the University of Manchester, United Kingdom (1957–58), and received a Ph.D. in nuclear chemistry at Berkeley in 1961. Remaining at Berkeley, he was chair of the chemistry department (1975–79), associate director of the Lawrence Berkeley National Laboratory, head of the Nuclear Science Division (1979–1984), provost (1986–94), then vice chancellor (1994–2000) for research, and dean of the Graduate Division (1985–2000). Based on his 15 years as graduate dean, Cerny has developed a lasting interest in the evolving career patterns of recent Ph.D.s, both within academe and in business, government, and non-profit venues. Cerny and his colleague, Maresi Nerad, conducted a national survey called "Ph.D.s Ten Years Later" on the career outcomes of doctoral education for six disciplines, two of which are discussed in chapter 4, as well as a national study of the career patterns of art history Ph.D.s.

Thomas Cyr has an extensive background in education, including teaching and training in K–12 schools and in higher education. He has worked as a faculty development specialist at the U.S. Air Force Academy, the University of Colorado Health Sciences Center, and currently with the University of Colorado System office. As director of the University of Colorado's Cooperative Assessment Project, he provides faculty and administrators of all CU campuses with training and support regarding the design and development of classroom and program assessment. Two of his current projects involve the development of an Internet-based institutional portfolio used for self-study and accreditation purposes and the development of Internet-based tutorials on the process of creating rubrics. He also supports faculty in various academic disciplines in the design of student portfolios.

Kelly Funk is director of assessment at Michigan State University. She has a doctorate in educational policy and leadership from Ohio State University. Her interests are in the organizational structures of higher education, particularly organizational behavior and change. She serves as a peer reviewer for the Higher Learning Commission of the North Central Association of Colleges and Schools, as well as a mentor at the commission's workshops on assessment of student learning.

Chris M. Golde has researched and written on doctoral education for over a decade. Formerly a faculty member in educational administration at the University of Wisconsin–Madison, she was lead author of the 2001 report *At Cross Purposes: What the Experiences of Today's Doctoral Students Reveal about Doctoral Education*. She is currently a senior scholar at the Carnegie Foundation for the Advancement of Teaching where she is research director for the Carnegie Initiative on the Doctorate. She is coeditor of *Envisioning the Future of Doctoral Education: Preparing Stewards of the Discipline*, a compilation of essays commissioned for the Carnegie Initiative on the Doctorate (San Francisco: Jossey-Bass, 2006). She is coauthor of a forthcoming volume on doctoral education and the Carnegie Initiative on the Doctorate.

Lori Homer is survey director for the Center for Innovation and Research in Graduate Education (CIRGE). She is responsible for a national survey of Ph.D. recipients and their career transitions funded by the Ford Foundation. Before joining the center, Homer was a research consultant to Boeing Company's Leadership Center, where she worked on a number of research projects focused on leadership development, work group effectiveness, and organizational culture change. She is currently affiliated with Seattle University's "Leading with Dignity" executive leadership development program. She completed her Ph.D. at the University of Washington Business School in 2004. Her dissertation, *Status Characteristics and Institutional Legitimacy*, won a national dissertation award from Wharton, the University of Pennsylvania's business school. Her research interests include career paths and leadership development of professionals with a particular interest in women's career progression, the sociostructural perpetuation of gender stereotypes, and women's ability to gain and use power within organizations.

Mary Huba is a professor in the Department of Educational Leadership and Policy Studies at Iowa State University where she teaches graduate courses, advises graduate students, and pursues scholarly work in the areas of assessment and program evaluation. Huba has helped several colleges and universities refine their assessment plans and develop their assessment programs. She has served as a consultant-evaluator for the North Central Association's Commission on Higher Learning and as the chief evaluator on a number of projects funded by the National Science Foundation.

Laura Jones has taught anthropology, archaeology, and art history at Stanford University, serving as campus archaeologist and cultural resources planner since 1991. She is currently a senior scholar at the Carnegie Foundation for the Advancement of Teaching where she is director of the Carnegie Community Program. She is coauthor of a forthcoming volume on doctoral education and the Carnegie Initiative on the Doctorate.

Karen L. Klomparens serves as dean of the Graduate School and assistant provost for graduate education at Michigan State University. She is a professor of plant biology and is on leave as director of MSU's Center for Advanced Microscopy. Klomparens's passions as a graduate dean focus on completion issues for doctoral students, diversity of graduate students, interdisciplinary graduate education, and professional development opportunities for graduate students. Klomparens recently completed a two-year term as chair of the Big Ten (Committee on Institutional Cooperation) graduate deans group and is serving a three-year term on the Council of Graduate Schools' national board of directors.

Jeannie Brown Leonard is a Ph.D. candidate in college student personnel at the University of Maryland, College Park. Her research interests include assessment of undergraduate student learning, interdisciplinary and other forms of integrative learning, and the educational outcomes of living-learning programs. She anticipates a return to higher education administration where she can cultivate partnerships between academic and student affairs.

Barbara E. Lovitts is a senior program officer at the Center for the Advancement of Scholarship on Engineering Education at the National Academy of Engineering. She has worked as a research scientist at the University of Maryland, a senior research analyst at the American Institutes for Research, an associate program director at the National Science Foundation, and a program associate at the American Association for the Advancement of Science. She is author of *Leaving the Ivory Tower: The Causes and Consequences of Departure from Doctoral Study* and *Making the Implicit Explicit: Creating Performance Expectations for Assessing the Outcomes of Doctoral Study*. She holds a Ph.D. in sociology from the University of Maryland.

Peggy L. Maki, higher education consultant, specializes in assisting undergraduate and graduate programs, higher education boards, and disciplinary organizations to integrate assessment of student learning into educational practices, processes, and structures, including those in the cocurriculum. Her work also focuses on assessment within the context of accrediting agencies' expectations for institutional effectiveness. She previously served as assessment department editor for *About Campus* magazine where she now serves on the Board of Contributors, and serves as Stylus Publishing's assessment field editor.

She regularly serves as a consultant to colleges and universities across the United States and abroad as well as to consortia of colleges and universities that have received national or regional grants to support the integration of assessment into teaching and learning. Currently, under a multiyear project focused on integrating assessment across the state of Rhode Island's public higher education institutions, she serves as sole consultant to the Board of Governors of Rhode Island and its institutions. She teaches graduate-level seminars focused on assessment, annually teaches in the Association of American Colleges and Universities' Summer Institute on General Education and Assessment, and has served as a faculty member in the Carnegie Foundation's Integrated Learning Project.

Formerly senior scholar and director of assessment at the American Association for Higher Education (AAHE), she has served as associate director of the Commission on Institutions of Higher Education; New England Association of Schools and Colleges, which is New England's regional accrediting body; vice president, academic dean, dean of faculty, and professor of English at Bradford College, Massachusetts; and as chair of English, theatre arts, and communication, associate professor of English, and dean of continuing education at Arcadia University, Pennsylvania. She is a recipient of the national Lindback Award for Distinguished Teaching.

Maki has conducted or presented over 370 workshops and keynote addresses on assessment both in the United States and abroad, including New Zealand, Hong Kong, Mexico, Greece, Bulgaria, British Columbia, Mexico, and Malaysia. Her articles on assessing student learning have appeared in AAHE's *Bulletin,* AAHE's Inquiry and Action series, *About Campus, Assessment Update, Change Magazine, The Journal of Academic Librarianship, Leadership Exchange, NetResults,* and *Proceedings of the International Conference on Teaching and Learning* held at the National University of Singapore (where she gave the keynote address), and in books on assessment, most recently in *Revisiting Outcomes Assessment in Higher Education* edited by Peter Hernon,

Robert E. Dugan, and Candy Schwartz (Westport, CT: Libraries Unlimited, 2006). Her writing also includes articles, chapters in books, and a book on the teaching of writing. Additionally she conducts writing-across-the-curriculum workshops that develop and document student learning. Her handbook on assessment, *Assessing for Learning: Building a Sustainable Commitment Across the Institution*, was published in 2004 by Stylus Publishing.

Candice L. Miller is director of research and information for the Graduate School at the University of Colorado at Boulder. Miller served as Boulder's Making the Implicit Explicit Study coordinator, works in faculty development, writes and edits Graduate School publications, and serves on international education committees that grant students funds for international study. Previously she worked at the University of Colorado School of Medicine as an instructor, where she also served as assistant director for the campuswide Office of Education. In San Francisco, she served as a project manager with a global nonprofit organization on the book *Ending Hunger: An Idea Whose Time Has Come* (New York: Praeger, 1985), and in Boston Miller raised funds for the Boston Symphony Orchestra and Beth Israel Hospital. She is a fifth-generation Coloradan.

Rodney Muth is a professor of educational administration and policy. He coordinates the Administrative Leadership and Policy Studies (ALPS) Ph.D. Lab in the Educational Leadership and Innovation PhD Program at the University of Colorado at Denver and Health Sciences Center. The ALPS Lab has several research strands, including elementary and secondary administration and leadership; educational policy; school organization; leadership capacity building; higher educational administration, leadership, and policy; and postsecondary teaching and learning. Muth's research interests focus on the preparation of professional educators, particularly educational administrators; problem-based learning and the preparation of adult learners for professional roles in education; educational policy, governance, and decision processes; leadership theories and the measurement of leadership; and theories and uses of power.

Maresi Nerad is director of the national Center for Innovation and Research in Graduate Education (CIRGE), associate dean in the Graduate School, and associate professor of higher education in educational leadership and policy studies in the College of Education, all at the University of Washington in Seattle. She has completed extensive research and numerous publications on graduate and postdoctoral education across disciplines, including an edited volume on graduate education in the United States. Nerad spent the 2001 academic year as dean in residence at the Council of Graduate Schools. In 2005 she spent three months at the University of Melbourne, Australia, as a Miegunyah Fellow, and in September 2005, she organized the first CIRGE international conference on Forces and Forms of Doctoral Education Internationally. She received her doctorate in higher education from the University of California–Berkeley in 1988.

John Schuh is distinguished professor of educational leadership and policy studies at Iowa State University where he was department chair for seven years. Previously he held faculty and administrative assignments at Arizona State University, Indiana University, and Wichita State University. Schuh's scholarly work addresses the college student experience. He is particularly interested in measuring the effect of out-of-class programs, services, and experiences on student learning and growth.

Mack Shelley is professor of educational leadership and policy studies, and professor of statistics, at Iowa State University where he also serves as director of the Research Institute for Studies in Education. His research features the applications of advanced statistical methods to problems in higher education, as well as health and the environment, the "digital divide" in information technology, and other aspects of the social sciences. He has served as principal investigator, coprincipal investigator, statistical consultant, and evaluator on a wide range of grants and contracts from federal, state, and local agencies and from foundation sources.

George E. Walker is a theoretical physicist and former physics department chair, vice president for research, and dean of the Graduate School at Indiana University. He is currently a senior scholar at the Carnegie Foundation for the Advancement of Teaching where he is director of the Carnegie Initiative on the Doctorate. He is coeditor of *Envisioning the Future of Doctoral Education: Preparing Stewards of the Discipline*, a compilation of essays commissioned for the Carnegie Initiative on the Doctorate. He is coauthor of a forthcoming volume on doctoral education and the Carnegie Initiative on the Doctorate.

Donald H. Wulff is director of the Center for Instructional Development and Research, associate dean in the Graduate School, and affiliate graduate faculty in the Department of Communication at the University of Washington in Seattle. In these roles he leads a centralized campus program for instructional development in which he works closely with administrators, departments, faculty, and graduate teaching and research assistants. For the past 26 years, he has spent his time teaching, consulting, researching, and publishing about issues of teaching and learning in higher education, coediting or coauthoring five volumes on the preparation of graduate students as teaching scholars and two volumes on teaching and learning. In addition he has served in leadership roles in national educational organizations and on a variety of editorial review boards. Wulff received his undergraduate degree from Montana State University, his master's degree in interpersonal communication from the University of Montana, and a Ph.D. in communication from the University of Washington.

INDEX

AACU. *See* Association of American Colleges and Universities
AAHE. *See* American Association for Higher Education
Aanerud, Rebecca, 109–41
academic associations, assessment initiatives by, 25–26
acceptable dissertation, characteristics of, 175*t*, 177–79
accountability: academic community on, 21–26; faculty on, 26; push for, and assessment, 12–14; state initiatives on, 15; trends in, 39
accreditation, 17–18; and improvement, 148–49; resources on, 50–51
admissions data, at University of Pittsburgh, 75–77, 77*f*
advisors: role of, 208–9; students on, 202–4; at University of Pittsburgh, 79–80
alignment, definition of, 92
alignment model, 83–108; application of, 98–101; components of, 84–92; fitting together components of, 92, 93*f*; premises of, 92–98; sample questions, data sources, and procedures for, 102*t*–103*t*
Alverno College, portfolio use at, 224
American Association for Higher Education (AAHE), 25–26, 38–39
Andrew W. Mellon Foundation, 30–31
Angelo, Tom, 39
assessment: attitudes toward, as obstacles, 66–68; definition of, 3; learning outcomes for, 254; methods of, multiple, 152–56, 153*t*, 154*t*; term, 66–67, 149; Wiggins on, 243. *See also* doctoral program assessment; formative assessment
assessment criteria, portfolios and, 221
assessment movement, factors affecting: external, 14–21; internal, 21–26

assessment process, for doctoral program improvement, 145–62; supports for, 158–60
Association of American Colleges and Universities (AACU), 23, 26
Astin, Alexander, 25
Atlantic Philanthropies, 19
audience, formative assessment and, 96–98

benchmarking, peer-group, 147
Bologna Declaration, 32
Borkowski, Nancy A., 11–51
Boyer, Ernest, 21–22
Boyer, Paul, 147
Bueschel, Andrea Conklin, 53–82
Business-Higher Education Forum, 26–27

capstone projects, 246–48; elements of, 264; format for, 263–64; preparation of, 247–48; titles of, 263
career path analysis, 109–41; assessment value of, 116–17; recommendations for, 134–35
career preparation: professional socialization, 124–28; skills development, 128–31
Carnegie Foundation for the Advancement of Teaching, 31, 53
Carnegie Initiative on the Doctorate (CID), 38, 53–82, 160; purpose of, 59
Center for Innovation and Research in Graduate Education, 30
Cerny, Joseph, 109–41
CGS. *See* Council of Graduate Schools
Change magazine, 26
CID. *See* Carnegie Initiative on the Doctorate
Clarke, Eric, 75, 78–79
Cohen, Philip, 27
colleagues: junior, 86; in training, 86
Collegiate Learning Assessment project, 15